DI$RUPT

YOURSELF OR BE DISRUPTED

In life, nothing stays the same, and who would want it to anyway? We pivot, we evolve, we learn and we grow. This is truly the magic of personal disruption.

More Praise & Reviews for '*Disrupt Yourself Or Be Disrupted*'

'This book is a reality check in what is happening around us. It pulls no punches and encourages a disruptive approach in an effort to move away from traditional thinking of what the job landscape will look like in the future. The world is changing and this book is a practical guide to navigate through these changes. I found it inspiring and thought provoking.'

Dave Romero
Group CEO of CABAN Investments Limited
Cape Town, South Africa

'A very comprehensive overview on how technology is disrupting the world as we know it today. The picture created looks bleak (rightfully so) and there's an innate sense of urgency as to why we should disrupt ourselves.'

Cindy H. Adem
Founder at Village2Nation
Nairobi, Kenya

'This is an essential read for anyone (individual or policy-maker) who desires to make the paradigm shift in a world driven by AI, automation and other disruptive technologies. It offers a comprehensive roadmap for navigating the new economy.'

Austin Uzim
TedX Speaker| Founder of African Transporter Initiative
Abuja, Nigeria

'We always knew that digital was going to change everything, but we just didn't realize how close to home it would hit. This book is a must-have for anyone who wants to grow and scale their business because it shows that in every industry digital competitors are taking advantage of new platforms, tools and relationships to undercut competitors, get close to customers and disrupt the usual ways of doing business. The only way to compete is to evolve and Disrupt Yourself Or Be Disrupted.'

Carol Mhlauli
Founder and Group CEO of Masazie Holdings
Pretoria, South Africa

'This is a perfect study for young professionals who desire to go to the next level in this fast-changing marketplace.'

Javnyuy Joybert
Co-Founder & CEO COSDEF Group | AFA Designs Tech
Kumbo, Cameroon

'This book is an excellent tool for preparing Africa's youths to position themselves for the future. With great emphasis on why entrepreneurship and investing in your natural talents should be seen as a viable career paths not just last resorts to joblessness.'

Charles Anyomi
Author | Entrepreneur & Founder of Afripreneur Conference
Accra, Ghana

'Well written and skillfully explained in layman terms. I found it quite interesting and thought provoking to say the least. Nicky did a great job outlining and addressing how technology is shaping our world and different industries. It left me with a taste of hunger to really dig into and learn more about emerging technologies and how it's changing the world.'

Mckevin Ayaba
CEO Setup A Startup & Southern Africa Startup Awards
Johannesburg, South Africa

'As a business strategist, I can confidently say that Nicky Verd's perspective in this book is very relevant in today's economic landscape. It is the blueprint for success in personal and business development. This book will not only inspire you, but it will also disrupt your thinking patterns and force you to re-evaluate your way of doing things. Terrific book! I highly recommend!'

Oscar Emetuei
Author | CEO Billion House Consulting | Cape Town, South Africa

'Here finally comes a book that addresses Africa's next course of action. I wish I had come across such a book ten years ago in my early 20's. This is a masterpiece and I can guarantee whoever reads and understands it will be transformed forever.'

Mugumya Paul
CEO and Founder April Logistics Ltd | Kampala, Uganda

First published in 2019 by
Porcupine Press
PO Box 2756
Pinegowrie, 2123
South Africa
admin@porcupinepress.co.za
www.porcupinepress.co.za

ISBN: 978-0-620-81782-0
e-ISBN: 978-0-620-81783-7

Published and produced by Porcupine Press
Cover design by Julmon Empire
Editing: David Robbins
Proofread by Olivia Wong and Frances Perryer
Image Credit: Gallery.com
Text layout: wim@wimrheeder.co.za
Set in 11 point on 15 point, Adobe Caslon Pro
Printed and bound by Digital Action, Cape Town

Ordering Information:
Special discounts are available on bulk purchases by
Universities, Corporations, Libraries, NGOs, Schools,
Associations and Individuals.
For details, visit the website below or send an email to
nickyverdz@gmail.com

For more info:
www.nickyverd.africa

DI$RUPT
YOURSELF OR BE DISRUPTED

Escape Conformity, Reinvent Your Thinking and Thrive in an Era of Emerging Technologies and Economic Anxiety

NICKY VERD

Includes
25 Innovative Business Ideas & Business Nuggets for You to Create your Own Economy

Powered by
DI$RUPT YOURSELF OR BE DISRUPTED PODCAST

PORCUPINE PRESS
Johannesburg

Dedication

Dedicated to forward thinkers, non-conformists, game-changers, pathfinders, history-makers, difference-makers, rule-breakers, life-changers, thought-leaders, visionaries aka dreamers, entrepreneurs aka risk-takers, creatives, innovators, tech enthusiasts, and pioneers of Africa's future.

Contents

Foreword

I started out by pursuing a degree in medicine then four years later, I realised medicine wasn't for me. I then moved to marketing management, later became a change agent and a defender of democracy. I've worked in diverse corporate structures and today I am the CEO of Business Leadership South Africa (BLSA). My point is, we live in a world where the only thing that is constant is change. The ability to disrupt yourself has many forks and can take you on many incredible journeys. And with the rise in cutting-edge technologies, it is increasingly difficult to know the final destination of these journeys.

The era where massive corporations took care of everyone coming out of college is over. The world is changing. Markets are crashing. Old industries are being wiped out and new ones are emerging right before our eyes. The job market is shrinking. Machines are employable. Everything we cling to for 'security' seems to be fading. Unemployment remains stubbornly high. Retrenchment is on the rise. Middlemen are slowly being pushed out of the picture by digitalisation. In South Africa, we have more people on government welfare than jobs. No longer is someone coming to save you. It's on you to make the most important decision of your life and that is to 'Disrupt Yourself Or Be Disrupted.'

What I like about Nicky Verd and her book is that you can tell she comes from a roller coaster of struggle. She understands this journey of personal disruption. After being retrenched, she felt dejected and hopeless, yet she chose her own path to success without knowing the outcome. She boldly took a leap into the unknown and today you can read a mind-transforming book that came as a result of her own personal disruption. Each page will encourage you to leave behind what you're familiar with and to look at the world through a fresh lens, one that turns assumptions and conventions upside down.

New opportunities and tools have emerged to make it possible for individuals to recreate themselves, create art and change the world. There may not be as many jobs as there used to be; but there are many opportunities arising out of the ashes of the broken system to generate meaningful success. As Nicky mentions in her book, 'There are no longer gate-keepers blocking your way to success. Technology has broken barriers and made things easy for everyone. The internet is an equal opportunity for everyone and smart people are using it to create a spotlight for themselves. The number of digital start-ups, online courses and internet celebrities has exploded in recent years. Many people are becoming rich and influential through their creative outlets thanks to the power of the internet.'

Through dozens of captivating and inspiring stories written in this book, you'll understand that the economy and nature of work has shifted and so should your mindset. In this era, only those who dare to disrupt, explore, express, experiment and execute will emerge as winners. *Disrupt Yourself Or Be Disrupted* will ignite you to build a brand new world out of the wreckage of the old. The key is to be unconventional, bold and disruptive. Don't fight change; don't fight technology: embrace them and become part of the revolution.

Mr Bonang Mohale
CEO of Business Leadership South Africa (BLSA)

Preface

Retrenchment was one of the worst experiences I've ever had. My identity, my plans and my children's future were all wrapped up in my job and it was all stripped away in an instant. But I learned to thrive in spite of this major upheaval. It is not in spite of daunting circumstances that we grow but because of them. And so, this book isn't about what the corporate world, the government or anyone else can do for you but about what YOU can do for yourself to effect the changes necessary to your specific circumstances.

Let others leave their future at the mercy of someone else, but not you. Let others depend on government, parents and luck, but not you. Let others complain, blame and argue, but not you. The few who take matters into their own hands are usually the envy of the many who only complain and watch. As Deepak Chopra, author and public speaker, said, 'All great changes are preceded by chaos.'

We are the architects of our own development, and the time for transformation is now! You have the power at your fingertips to obtain whatever outcome you want for your life. I strongly believe that personal transformation and Africa's hopeful transformation lies in innovation, changing our mindsets and viewing entrepreneurship as a viable career path, not only as a last resort for joblessness.

Do something about your plight. Confront hard and uncomfortable issues head-on. Overturn conventions, beliefs and mind-sets that hold you back. Take the gloves off, be real, be awkward, and then you'll take your dreams, businesses, job, community and even the entire continent to greater heights, and thus find freedom to make yourself and the continent great.

In his book, *The 4-Hour Work Week*, Tim Ferris said, 'A person's success in life is measured by the number of uncomfortable conversations they are willing to have.' My message in this book is uncomfortable, edgy, provocative, informative, educational and transformational. It is meant to give you a fresh perspective on technology, life, chaos, uncertainty and a confidence that your destiny is not set in stone. Change is possible! Change is in your hands!

Nicky Verd, Johannesburg

Acknowledgements

Like parenting, writing takes a village, and I never could've done it without my tribe. I'll really want to acknowledge the special people in my life who made this all possible.

To my FAMILY and FRIENDS, thank you for your constant loving encouragement and your constant loving interruption, respectively. Thank you for standing by me through thick and thin. If I had to choose again, I'd still choose to be with you. You supported me even when you didn't understand what I was doing or where I was going with my crazy writings.

I'm eternally grateful to my elder brother, Bongdzeem Eugene Kumela, who played the role of a father in my life when he himself needed a father. I truly have no idea where I'd be if he hadn't stepped up to become the father figure I desperately needed when Mom passed away.

To Mary Wamey Wong, who took a chance on a desolate teenager and took in an extra mouth to feed when she didn't have to. You taught me discipline, unconditional love, forgiveness, respect, and so much more that has helped shape the woman I am today. Mamz (as we fondly call you), thank you for allowing me to be a part of your life. You are a universe of womanhood and motherhood. You are the best mom anyone could ever ask for.

And to my amazing kids, Ronnie and Rinah, two extra hearts that God hung outside my body; you both are my biggest motivation. You were the ones who had to put up with me during the writing process. I love you guys more than I can actually express in words.

Special thanks to Mr Bonang Mohale, CEO of Business Leadership South Africa. Thank you Sir for going above and beyond my expectations to make this dream a reality. I contacted you for a foreword and you gave more than words to me. For more than two years, I was chasing this dream of being a published author and met with all sorts of obstacles imaginable but in an instant you changed everything for me Sir. You became the sole sponsor of this book! I am deeply touched that you gave me the resources I needed and took time out of your busy schedule to listen to me and help me succeed. Mr

Mohale, the world is a better place thanks to people like you.

Another special thanks to my mentor, Dr Strive Masiyiwa, Founder and Chairman of global telecommunications group Econet Wireless. Your words carry enormous weight and have undeniably impacted my journey. I am deeply indebted to you for life-changing wisdom and your relentless effort in ensuring that I and million other African's don't become failures in life. Thank you Sir for being such an extraordinary leader.

And to my amazing and legendary sister, Olivia Wong. Thank you for all your support and for proofreading the first draft of the manuscript. You epitomise sisterhood and could take over the world if you wanted.

To my online family. Your engagement with my write-ups, blog posts, comments, sharing and giving constructive feedback, played a huge role in putting together this book. Thank you.

To my publisher, *Porcupine Press*, thank you for the impressive work you've done in turning a simple manuscript into an amazing book. Thank you for believing in this project enough to start working on the book even when I didn't know how the cost will be covered. This helped me to work extra hard in getting the funding we desperately needed.

My biggest acknowledgement and appreciation goes to my Creator, the Almighty God, for giving me the talents and the privilege to impact people and serve humanity.

Introduction

We live in a world where change has changed. Change used to be gradual but change is now rapid and exponential. Cutting-edge technologies are eliminating millions of jobs and entire industries are being wiped out. Companies that don't di$rupt themselves become outpaced; the same goes for individuals who don't evolve and grow. Every single business and industry is being disrupted by emerging technologies such as Artificial Intelligence, Drones, 3D Printing, Virtual Reality, Blockchain, Internet of Things, Augmented Reality, Big Data, and much more.

It seems science fiction is now becoming science fact. Automation is no longer a prediction but a reality. Businesses across the globe are doing more with fewer employees. You have to design a multi-faceted agenda to transform yourself to win in these turbulent times of relentless change, ferocious competition and unstoppable innovation. You can't afford to fiddle at the margins, you can't sit back and wait for government or someone else to hand you your future. It is either you di$rupt yourself or you will be disrupted. Either you drive disruption or you will get outpaced by it.

This is the time to rethink ideologies passed down to us about the way life, work and success should be. *Glassdoor*, one of the world's largest job and recruiting sites says, 'Global conglomerates like *IBM, Google, Microsoft* and *Apple* are no longer considering academic qualifications on their hiring processes.' We need to rethink the very fundamental principle from which personal success is built. Generation after generation has been told to go to school, get a certificate, and get a job. But machines don't go to school, yet machines are replacing humans in the workforce. This is the power of the 4th Industrial Revolution. You need new ways of thinking and new philosophies – in short, a personal revolution, a shift in mind-set, to cope with the external changes. If thousands of processes in factories and offices are going to shift from humans to machines, then the human talents that managed these processes in the past must be willing to di$rupt themselves so that they don't become obsolete. Think of new ways to foster your own disruption and position yourself for new opportunities in a world that's ferociously changing.

Jay Samit, author and digital media innovator, predicts that '3D printing will eliminate 320 million manufacturing jobs globally while self-driving vehicles will displace tens of millions more and office automation will cut corporate jobs in half.'

If these predictions are halfway correct, the social effects, retrenchments and unemployment will be huge in the not so distant future. We are already seeing massive retrenchment across all industries. We're at the dawn of the Fourth Industrial Revolution and the early adjusters will thrive in the new era.

> In life, nothing stays the same, and who would want it to anyway? We pivot, we evolve, we learn and we grow. This is truly the magic of personal disruption.

Standard Bank South Africa, recently announced plans to cut around 1,200 jobs and close a total of 91 branches as part of their strategy to digitise its retail and business bank. The bank said that the vast majority of these branches will be closed by June 2019. Absa bank is also investing in digital banking, restructuring its South Africa retail and business unit and jobs are on the line. The new implemented national minimum wage in South Africa is also a huge threat to jobs.

The world is wildly different now than it was ten years ago. The job market is facing turbulence and retrenchment is on the rise. Whether by circumstances or by deliberate choice, your life will be disrupted. To survive and grow your opportunity margins you need to drive an agenda where innovative thinking is embraced and personal disruption is viewed as inevitable. Indeed, this combination is really the only sustainable strategy for creating long-term value and success for yourself. As an anonymous writer once said, 'It is not the strongest of the species that survives, nor the most intelligent, but the one that is most adaptable to change.'

However, there is no reason for you to panic. Sometimes the greatest chapter of your life begins only when you are thrown out of the ordinary and what you're familiar with. Being forced to question the status quo or dealing with seemingly insurmountable challenges can sometimes turn out to be the best thing that ever happened to you. In life, nothing stays the same, and who would want it to anyway? We pivot, we evolve, we learn and we grow. This is truly the magic of personal disruption.

In a world of fractured certainties, battered economies and robotic invasion, you have to be clear as crystal about your own mandate and what matters most to you.

Be brave enough to confront yourself with these uncomfortable questions:

- Is what I am doing now really my greatest calling in life?
- Am I tired, bored and uncomfortable with what I do?
- Am I living life or just paying bills?
- Is there a soul-deep purpose or dreams buried deep within me longing for an escape?
- Is there a bolder, braver, smarter way I need to take to fulfil my purpose?
- Am I stuck or am I pushing my own limits?

This book offers bold, edgy, provocative, informative, educational and transformational content designed to shift mind-sets. Do you have the attitude needed to drive change? The book provides practical insights, innovative solutions and tactics to show you how to disrupt yourself before someone else does. The audacious tone of what I have to say is meant to educate, empower, uplift, ignite human potential, and provoke an entrepreneurial revolution that will liberate people, especially the youth, from hopelessness, poverty, dependency, and inspire them to create their own futures.

Di$rupt Yourself Or Be Disrupted is a wakeup call for everyone. The message is unequivocal: exponential change is here as employment continues to diminish due to automation and the turbulent economic climate. Companies in Africa and across the world are on a severe diet to lose weight. Understanding the threats and opportunities now will ensure you are well-prepared for the bleak jobs market. You can either succumb to the prospect of early obsolescence or step into the world of business, follow your passion, learn new skills and turn your dreams and ideas and academic qualifications into a thriving venture. It's up to you to di$rupt yourself.

As US President John F Kennedy said in his 1962 State of the Union address, 'The time to repair the roof is when the sun is shining.' Knowledge of the future can reshape and redefine your present priorities. Analyse all the pieces that come together to form your identity. If you are going to find opportunities to make things work, you are going to have to change your approach.

> You cannot stop the Fourth Industrial Revolution but you can influence its direction and impact in your life. Don't focus on the threats, focus on the opportunities.

Three in One

This book is divided into three parts:

- **One:** Takes a look at how cutting-edge technologies and self-service automated systems are reshaping the world of work, as well as the impact of these automated systems on employment.
- **Two:** Offers the blueprint for how you can shape your own future, discover your unique talents, take hold of opportunities and the mindset shift you need to thrive in a world that's fast changing.
- **Three:** Offers 21st century business nuggets, business lessons and innovative business ideas as more and more young people on the African continent and around the world are rising as thought leaders, inventors, entrepreneurs and innovators.

PART ONE

Part One establishes the baseline and necessity for personal disruption by looking into how cutting-edge technologies and self-service automated systems are reshaping the world of work, as well as the impact of these automated systems on employment.

This raises a few questions:

- Where is the next generation going to find work if the status quo or present trends are maintained?
- Is your job safe?
- Is there something else you can do other than your job?
- What strategies do you have to foster your own disruption and position yourself for the 4th Industrial Revolution?
- Are you prepared for jobs of the future?

Chapter 1

RISE OF THE MACHINES

The rise of the machines and Artificial Intelligence(AI), considered to be the Fourth Industrial Revolution , is a global phenomenon and only a few are prepared for this shift in paradigm. We're on the verge of a major technological disruption to our normal way of life and, in my view; I think this fundamental shift should be on the agenda of everyone. We need to completely discard the notion that this topic of automation or robotics and artificial intelligence is only for experts and nerds. This unprecedented technology requires people, especially youths from diverse disciplines and backgrounds to join the discussion. Machines are coming fast and furious and the future is bleak for those still seeking the jobs of the past. Lest anyone was still hoping for a different verdict, the jury has given its verdict. Technology is transforming our world beyond our wildest imaginations. What you were taught 10-20 ago is fast becoming obsolete.

The term "Fourth Industrial Revolution " was coined by Klaus Schwab, Founder and Executive Chairman of the World Economic Forum in 2016 and published a book titled the same name, Mr Schwab, defines the Fourth Industrial Revolution as "A fusion of technologies that are blurring the lines between the physical, digital and biological spheres."

A growing number of people are becoming increasingly anxious about the future viability of jobs as a result of these fusions of technologies. This is the future we never saw coming, but the writing has been on the wall for quite some time. We were just not paying attention. Personally, I know what job anxiety feels like because I was retrenched at the peak of my career. I'd finally gotten the job I wanted so badly and I was back in school studying for a more prestigious certificate. As you can imagine, I was ambitiously climbing the proverbial corporate ladder but suddenly the ladder was pulled from underneath and I found myself tumbling on the floor, broken, lost and drenched in hopelessness. You'll read more about my retrenchment story in chapter 7 of this book.

The emphasis is that humanity seems to be working hard to remove humans from positions of responsibility and replace them with machines. Rapidly emerging new technologies are generating a huge paradigm shift that is affecting businesses and work as we know it. The process of job loss due to robotics and AI has already begun. This process will continue and speed up in the not-so-distant future. Automation looks set to replace many jobs in the next few decades. While it's difficult to predict the exact extent to which robotics will replace human workers, this process has clearly been set in motion, and it will most definitely affect employment across all industries.

In his 2001 essay, 'The Law of Accelerating Returns', acclaimed author and computer scientist Ray Kurzweil pointed out that 'within a few decades, machine intelligence will surpass human intelligence, leading to The Singularity – technology change so rapid and profound it represents a rupture in the fabric of human history.'

Whether we reach Singularity this century remains to be seen, but Mr Kursweil is right about the profound and rapid change in technology. The impact of increased automation is already upon us and influencing our lives in ways we never imagined. The gravest fear that is rippling through humanity from the technology industry is that, someday, almost all of our jobs might be replaced by computers and robots. While that fear is often laughed off as something that will only happen far into the future, the truth is that it's actually happening right now. Getting into a self-driving car or eating food cooked by a robot chef is no longer a scene in a sci-fi movie but a reality in our world today.

> Job loss due to automation is irreversible. Since automation provides huge advantages to companies that deploy it, it's very unlikely that they will return to using humans for the same tasks.

A multi-tasker robot from a company called *Momentum Machines* in the USA can flip a burger in 10 seconds and could replace the entire *McDonald's* food chain crew worldwide. Sewing robots are turning the clothing and textile industry on its head while robot nurses, surgeons and doctors are on the rise. Robotics and AI is a topic high on the agenda of forward-thinking employees around the globe, yet it is difficult to predict with certainty the extent of job replacements by these systems.

Until now, technology adoption has never been so rapid and versatile. Thanks to robots and chatbots and drones, augmented reality, machine learning, blockchain and much more, our physical space is littered with AI influences. 3D printing and self-driving cars will eliminate millions of jobs around the world, as predicted by Jay Samit. 3D printing is a threat and an impending doom for construction and factory workers. A San Francisco-based start-up, *Apis Cor*, can 3D print a full functional house in one day. Though 3D printing will create human jobs like technicians to design, maintain, use and repair 3D printers, jobs created will be far fewer than jobs destroyed. Even in agriculture, from nursing to planting to shepherding and herding, humans are competing with robot farmers.

The steady loss of jobs and retrenchment happening across the globe will not be reversed, even though many people still hope for the return of these jobs. Job loss due to automation is irreversible. Since automation provides huge advantages to companies that deploy it, it's very unlikely that they will return to using humans for the same tasks. In the past, many companies outsourced jobs to low-salary countries but due to automation, this will no longer be necessary. Automation is causing the loss of both local and overseas jobs.

The *Ball State* study shows that '12.1 million manufacturing workers can now produce at a level that previously would have required 20.9 million workers.'

Automated workers are not only found in factories. They are now found in hospitals, banks, retail stores, mines, law firms, the stock markets, restaurants … and the list goes on. Mass job shedding is on the rise across the globe. In the era we live in, there are no guarantees that going to school and getting a certificate will secure a job in a world where machines are increasingly employable. The employment market is shrinking. A big corporation that needed about 100,000 employees 20 years ago only needs about 50% of those employees or even less today. Although productivity is at record high levels and innovation is at its finest, job-loss rates have never been higher.

In 2004, *Blockbuster* had a whopping 84,000 employees and made about $6 billion in revenue, while in 2016, *Netflix* had only 4,500 employees and made about $9 billion in revenue. We all know what happened next, *Blockbuster* went bankrupt in 2010 and *Netflix* is now worth about $136 billion as of September 2018 thanks to adaptation to technology.

In 1979, *General Motors*, one of the world's largest automakers, employed more than 800,000 full-time employees in its heydays and made about $11 billion, while in 2012, *Google* made about $14 billion with only 58,000 employees. Fast-forward to 2018, and the number of employees at *General Motors* is estimated only at around 180,000: in November 2018, they announced plans to close up to five factories in the USA and Canada and are slashing more than 14,000 jobs over the next two years.

Apple Inc, the first company to surpass a market cap of $1 trillion with about 504 retail stores in 24 countries and only 123,000 full-time employees. You'd think an organisation of this magnitude should employ millions of people, but things have changed. Machines are at work!

You may not like these examples, but global companies like *Google*, *Apple* and *Netflix* are real-life examples currently depicting the state of human workforces. Less is more! Old industries that needed a huge human workforce are running out of steam. Take a look at the automobile industry: when they became significant more than 100 years ago, they created huge employment for people, but today innovation in the car industry does not create as many jobs as before. Electric cars are an outstanding innovation but they won't create millions of new jobs. Robots are now doing more and more jobs in most factories.

But machines stealing jobs is not a new thing. 'Yes, automation has happened before,' says Bhagwan Chowdhry, professor at the University of California, Los Angeles. Chowdhry points to the shifts that took place in factories during the industrial revolution when automation first emerged and other machines took over from human weavers. So what's different this time? According to Chowdhry, 'It is not going to affect only blue-collar workers but also a lot of white-collar workers.'

Hence, if your job involves complex work on a computer, you might be out of work sooner than those who are still hanging onto factory jobs. Automation is no longer just about doing repetitive boring factory jobs but also complex computer jobs. That's what makes the Fourth Industrial Revolution so powerful and so threatening.

According to Erik Brynjolfsson, MIT Professor and Director of Digital Economy, 'Technology has always been destroying jobs, and it's always been creating jobs too, but it's been a wash for the last 20 years. Starting in the 1990s the employment to population ratio started plummeting and it's now fallen off a cliff and it is not getting back up.'

> Human labour does not stand a chance against what's coming. Artificial Intelligence can handle insurance claims and basic bookkeeping, manage investment portfolios, do legal research, and perform HR tasks.

This issue should be the urgent focus of government and policy-makers right now to figure out how to address this problem, but sadly governments are not giving it their due attention yet.

The pace of technological change this time around appears to be unprecedented. Automation today can diagnose diseases, land aircraft, and even trade on the financial markets. We're on the verge of a new age of automation unlike anything we've seen before. The accelerating pace of development in technology continues to di$rupt value chains that were once perceived to be as permanent and unmalleable as a diamond.

In other parts of the world, as opposed to Africa, robots can now flip burgers, take orders and work warehouses. Human labour does not stand a chance against what's still to come. Artificial Intelligence can handle insurance claims and basic bookkeeping, manage investment portfolios, do legal research, and perform HR tasks. There is no question that the speed at which robotics is replacing humans will continue to accelerate. There will be fewer and fewer jobs available across all industries.

Shall we then continue to programme our children the same way our parents programmed us to go to school, get a certificate and get a job? We are seeing more jobs being uploaded to smart software. Fully fledged automation will di$rupt everything – from the financial industry to the electrical sector, to health care, to manufacturing, to mining, to textile, clothing, footwear and automobiles. These industries are bracing for an influx of robots.

Ten years ago, many people believed that self-driving cars were nothing but entertainment in movies. Today, electric cars are a reality. Science fiction is fast becoming science fact. Self-driving vehicles are already in the market and self-driving trucks, aeroplanes and ships are next in line. Rolls-Royce is working on self-driving ships. Many auto truck manufacturers in the USA are already pushing to have fully automated trucks. And if we think we've already seen a lot of change, the real tidal wave is yet to strike.

Why Businesses are More Inclined to Use Robots and Automated Systems Instead of Humans

Cutting costs and making profit while increasing efficiency is a top priority for every business. Robots are seen as an upgrade – more efficient and reliable, and cheaper than humans. Artificial Intelligence algorithms can process thousands of documents faster and cheaper than any human could ever imagine. Setting up automation initially is very expensive but once robots are up and running, they can perform at a low cost for years and years. Automation is free from human biases and this is where the world is heading.

> Machines do not require leave, lunch breaks, smoke breaks, toilet breaks or any breaks for that matter. Robotics do not come late to work. Robots are drama free, they don't organise protest action and they don't complain about workload.

At the rate at which robotics and AI are advancing, machines will soon be able to take over tasks in a variety of industries and do them just as well, if not better than humans. Big corporations are going to employ fewer people to get a lot more done with more precision and better quality. One of the biggest advantages of robots is their ability to work non-stop without getting tired. That's something practically impossible in any line of work with humans.

From a safety point of view, it makes sense for robots to carry out dangerous and laborious tasks previously undertaken by humans, but the use of robotics has since gone beyond safety. Companies designing and incorporating AI argue that the benefits of robotics versus their human counterparts are unparalleled, and they are probably right.

Human error, inefficiency and higher labour costs are eliminated with a robotic workforce. Machines do not require remuneration, medical aid or retirement packages. Machines do not require leave, lunch breaks, smoke breaks, toilet breaks or any breaks for that matter. Robotics do not come late to work. Robots are drama free, they don't organise protest action, won't complain about workload, would not require disciplinary action, or suffer any incapacitating episodes of low morale.

Most interesting, though, is that robots cannot be injured or killed in the line of work, and can be used in situations far too dangerous for human risk. Robots are more hygienic and deliver a finished product at a fraction of the time it takes a human. Faster output leads to increased sales. No matter how cheap human labour may become, buying highly skilled robotics is still cheaper as one pays only once. Robots can work at full speed production with no interruptions except downtime for maintenance, 24 hours a day, 7 days a week and 365 days a year. With machines at work, employee salaries, incentives, annual bonuses and retirement benefits are not only reduced but eliminated.

It's hard to argue against automation when statistics are clearly illustrating its potential. It is obviously cheaper and more sustainable to design machines and systems that check every single detail and do the job all day, all week and all year round.

According to Monetary Watch, a Chinese factory in Dongguan City called *Changying Precision Technology Company* that produces mobile phones replaced 90% of its human workforce with machines, and it led to a staggering 250% increase in productivity and a significant 80% drop in defects. Previously, there were 650 employees, but with the introduction of robots, the number of employees at the factory came down to only 60. Luo Weiqiang, general manager of the company, said in an interview that the number of employees could drop to 20 in the future.

Eight Examples of Cutting-Edge Technologies

The easiest way to understand the Fourth Industrial Revolution is to understand the technologies driving it. So, let's take a quick look into some impressive cutting-edge technologies that are generating a huge paradigm shift in this new economic era. To comprehensively analyse everything about cutting-edge technologies would demand a book on its own, but I believe the information I've shared here is enough to take away some of the mystery. Some of these technologies are already running at full swing while others are still in their early days in terms of tapping into and unlocking the power of their full potential. There are still going to be a lot of experimental fail cases and some of the technologies might take a while to infiltrate Africa, but that they will is a certainty. Automation is here and is here to stay.

When some white-collar professionals hear stories about the robotic takeover, they quickly conclude that they won't be affected. They believe white-collar jobs are off the radar and some professionals have mentally congratulated themselves because they think their 'professional jobs' are safe from the threat of being automated.

Technology is becoming smarter and proving that jobs previously thought to be immune to automation can now be automated. However, there is no need to panic. Chapter 3 of this book gives you a blueprint on how you can upskill yourself, transform your mind into a creative force and take advantage of the opportunities in the new economy.

Understanding the threats and opportunities that these cutting-edge technologies throw up will help ensure that you are sufficiently prepared for the shift in paradigm.

One can do better when one knows better, and so here are some examples of cutting-edge technologies that everyone should know and understand:

1. Artificial Intelligence (AI)

Artificial Intelligence is an area of computer science with the ability to solve problems that are usually done by humans. AI refers to intelligent machines that have been programmed to mimic human action and rational thinking. According to Andrew Kucheriavy, Founder and CEO of *Intechnic*, 'AI learns through machine learning, similar to you and me, by learning from its own mistakes, studying examples and applying the acquired knowledge over time.'

How much of a threat is AI to employment? As already mentioned, AI is cheaper and more productive than humans. It doesn't sleep, need breaks, get sick or take vacations, and it doesn't need health insurance or retirement benefits. It can work around the clock, can instantly scale to levels that a human worker can't simply achieve and can quickly acquire and learn new skills.

Does that sound scary? I bet it does. Even the very engineers designing AI are not safe from AI taking over their jobs. Recent advances in machine learning (or deep learning) allow AI to learn without help from humans and evolve beyond our wildest expectations.

There is no doubt that AI is going to change the face of employment as we know it and revolutionise every industry. But how will this work in practical terms? Effective AI must adjust as circumstances or conditions shift. We look at some of the major changes AI is bringing in the following sectors.

- *Financial Sector*. Bank tellers have already been partially replaced by ATMs, but soon, even higher level bankers, including loan officers, could easily be replaced by AI systems. In a March 2016 report by *Citigroup*, the lender estimated 30% of banking jobs will be lost to AI between 2015 and 2025, mainly due to automation in retail banking. That would see full-time jobs drop by 770,000 in the USA and by about one million in Europe. Algorithms can now analyse financial data and prepare accounts (as well as do tax returns) without the need for accountants. Financial algorithms can spot minute differentials in stock valuations and immediately undertake accurate market transactions.

- *Healthcare.* AI will be a major disruptor in healthcare due to its brilliance at capturing and analysing data. AI algorithms can diagnose diseases and make recommendations about the best treatment, including cancer treatments. People might even have an AI doctor in the comfort of their homes. *Johnson & Johnson* is reported to have an FDA-approved device that can deliver low levels of anaesthetic automatically without an anaesthetist.
- *Architecture.* There are smart software programs that can help individuals design their own homes and products. These make architectural skills, design and even colour choices more automated. As the sophistication of these programs improves, so will the need for human architects and designers diminish.
- *Law.* Being a lawyer is such an interesting high-earning career with bags of social status attached, but a substantial portion of what lawyers do on a daily basis is a lot more routine. The more routine or mundane a job is, the more likely it is that it will be automated. AI algorithms can perform tasks ranging from legal discovery (pre-trial procedure) to creating contracts, arguing parking fines and even handling divorce proceedings.
- *Insurance.* Insurance has been rather a traditional industry for decades but AI is now turning this industry on its head. Customer demand is the key driver for change in the insurance industry. More and more people desire to purchase insurance using their smartphones. Most of what insurance brokers and underwriters do can now be done by computers using AI and big data. At *IndieFin*, a self-service insurance provider in South Africa, getting an insurance quote, being underwritten, and issuing an insurance policy can be done without human intervention in as little as five to ten minutes.
- *Human Resources (HR).* Companies around the globe are already using AI to automate their recruitment processes. Headhunting and hiring are being revolutionised as AI algorithms take on the job of sorting through resumes to find the most appropriate candidates, thereby eliminating tedious administrative tasks usually done by

human HR professionals. *Veriato*, a software company, 'develops AI systems that track and monitor employees' computer activities as well as emails, keystrokes, internet browsing, etc. This data is then analysed to determine a baseline of normal activity patterns in the organisation. Based on that knowledge, the computer is able to flag outliers and report them to the employer. It will also detect changes in the overall tone of employees' communications to predict when employees might be thinking of leaving.'

- *Transportation*. Autonomous cars that can run without any human input have already been developed. Fleets of these autonomous vehicles owned by companies like *Uber* will have an enormous impact on professional human taxi drivers, while autonomous trucks will mean the same thing for long-distance truck drivers. Things don't look too good for driving instructors and licensing departments either. After all, will kids born in 2018 even need to pass a driving test in the next 20 years?

2. Drones Technology

Drones are the second example of cutting-edge technologies and refer to unpiloted aircraft or spacecraft. They are often referred to as unmanned aerial vehicles (UAVs). Drones were mostly used for military purposes because they don't put a pilot's life at risk in combat zones but they are now being used across many different sectors. Drones can be used in monitoring storms and hurricanes without putting pilots at risk. In addition, drones don't require rest; they can fly as long as there is fuel in the craft and there are no mechanical problems. Drones carrying freight will dramatically lower the cost of shipping. Drones over dangerous neighbourhoods will increase public safety in our communities and probably help to eliminate gang violence.

Drones provide many industries with a smoother and easier way of conducting operations. They save considerable amounts of money and time, completing tasks that would otherwise be difficult to accomplish. Many industries are embracing the use of drones and by so doing eliminating humans. From real estate to mining, drones are capturing the attention of every industry. Operations are made easy with these amazing machines. Drones are used for search and rescue missions, photography, videography, wildlife and agriculture monitoring, mineral exploration, surveying, inspecting, delivery, etc.

Drones are equipped with state of the art technology such as infrared cameras, GPS and laser. Drones are controlled by remote ground control systems, also referred to as a ground cockpit. Drones have two parts: the drone itself and the control system. The front part of the drone is where all the sensors and navigational systems are present. The rest of the body is full of drone technology systems since there is neither need nor space to accommodate humans. Some highly advanced drones include DJI Mavic 2, Mavic Air, Phantom 4 Pro, Inspire 2 and Walkera Voyager 5.

Many companies are considering sending drones to deliver goods, which could reduce and even eliminate the cost of using human drivers for door-to-door services. *Amazon* performed its first drone deliveries in Britain in December 2016. *Domino's* also made it to the news when they started using drones to deliver pizzas. We can already see that drones combined with self-driving cars are a big threat to jobs. Africa is not left behind, *UNICEF* is starting to use drones for delivery of blood and medical supplies in disaster struck areas and the world's first airport for drones is being built in Rwanda.

3. Virtual Reality (VR)

Virtual Reality is an artificial environment that is created with a mixture of Head Mounted Displays (HMD), interactive hardware and software. These HMDs are used with headphones and hand controllers to provide a fully immersive experience. You'll probably never go to Mars, go mountain biking, swim with dolphins, sing on stage with your favourite musician or dine with Queen Elizabeth, but if VR lives up to its promise, you might be able to do all these things and many more without even leaving your home. VR makes it possible to literally experience anything, anywhere, anytime.

Immersive VR means that the sensory experience feels so real, that we forget it is a virtual-artificial environment and begin to interact with it as we would naturally in the real world. It convinces the human brain it is somewhere (e.g. underwater or flying over the earth, etc.) when it is really not. A person using VR equipment is able to look around the artificial world, move around in it, and interact with virtual features.

Some of the largest technology companies like *Facebook*, *Samsung*, *Google*, and *Microsoft* are currently investing billions of dollars into Virtual Reality. Companies are now using this technology in their marketing. *McDonald's* introduced new *Happy Meal Boxes* for its customers that can be folded into a virtual reality cardboard headset. *Coca-Cola* has recently introduced a new marketing campaign for a *Drinkable Ad* where you enjoy coke by using the latest technology. To execute this campaign, *Coca-Cola* collaborated with *Shazam* so that users can easily fill a glass of Coke in their smartphones which can be redeemed at any retail store in the United States. The future of VR is set to be a pillar of our everyday lives. Research firm *Gartner* predicts Head Mounted Displays will create $72 billion in revenue for the devices alone in 2019.

4. Augmented Reality (AR)

Augmented Reality technology basically allows you to point an AR powered device like a smartphone at an object and find out detailed information about that object. One can get a sneak peek into what's going on in nearby buildings or nearby museums through an AR powered device. Augmented Reality is the technology that expands our physical world, adding layers of digital information onto it.

Unlike Virtual Reality, Augmented Reality does not create the whole artificial environment to replace real with a virtual one. AR appears in direct view of an existing environment, adding sounds, videos, and graphics to it. Many modern devices like tablets and smartphones already support Augmented Reality.

One of the most popular applications of AR is gaming. AR games provide much better experiences to players and even promote a more active outgoing way of life, as in the case of *Pokemon Go*. But there are much bigger potential areas of use for AR, which include:

- Real-estate: People can benefit from Augmented Reality via 3D tours of apartments and houses.
- Education: Interactive models for learning and training purposes.
- Retail: The retail industry can bring better customer engagement and retention, as well as brand awareness and more sales.
- Medicine/healthcare: Help diagnose, monitor, train, localise, etc.
- Tourism: Gives data on destinations, sightseeing, navigation and

directions.

- Broadcasting: Enhancing live events and event streaming by overlaying content.

5. Internet of Things (IoT)

The Internet of Things is about adding connectivity and intelligence to physical infrastructure and objects to communicate wirelessly. IoT refers to the billions of physical devices around the world that are now connected to the internet through sensors, collecting and sharing data. IoT adds a level of digital intelligence to devices that would otherwise be dumb, enabling them to communicate without any human involvement and merging the digital and physical worlds together.

The term IoT is mainly used for devices that wouldn't usually be generally expected to have an internet connection, and that can communicate with the network independently of human action. A lightbulb that can be switched on using a smartphone app is an IoT device. Adding RFID (Radio Frequency Identification) tags to expensive pieces of equipment to help track their location was one of the first IoT applications. But since then, the cost of adding sensors and an internet connection to objects has continued to fall, making it easier for more objects to be connected and eliminating humans from the process.

6. Chatbots

Chatbots, also known as Visual Assistants, are an answer to customer service in an era where transformation to digital environment is moving at a blinding pace. Bots are software applications that run automated tasks over the internet. They are designed to simplify the interaction between humans and computers and to drastically reduce the cost of routine customer care activities. According to *Expert System*, 'A chatbot is an artificial intelligence software that can simulate a conversation or a chat with a user in a natural language through messaging apps, websites, and mobile apps or through the phone.'

Kevin Ryder, chief marketing officer at software firm *Integrated Research*, says, 'In 2018, we will see even greater acceptance of bots as a legitimate alternative to human interaction for customer service.' *Gartner*, a research firm, predicts the average person will have more conversations with bots than with their spouse by 2020.

7. 3D Printing

3D Printing or additive manufacturing is an innovative technology that lets one create a physical object from a digital model. The development of 3D printing is revolutionary as the technology is already changing how objects are produced, from toys and tools to clothing, foodstuff and even body parts. Scientists in Israel recently unveiled a 3D print of a heart with human tissue and vessels, calling it a first and a 'major medical breakthrough' that advances possibilities for transplants.

3D printers offer amazing results and let one create anything one can imagine at a fraction of the cost. 3D printing is eliminating the middleman and bringing consumers closer to the production process. Consumers can now produce exactly what they need.

In order to print anything on a 3D printer, first one would need a 3D model of the object one wants to print. This can be designed in a 3D modelling program (e.g. CAD – Computer Aided Design), or by using a 3D scanner to scan the object or by searching online for objects already 3D modelled.

Giant industrial 3D printers can print about ten houses in one day and at a fraction of the cost of traditionally building a house. This is a technological revolution in construction, architecture, product design and manufacturing, but it comes at a huge cost of eliminating human labour. Research firm *ABI* expects $75 billion worth of 3D printed products and parts in the USA by 2026. Platinum jewellery is now 3D-printed in South Africa.

8. Blockchain Technology

Blockchain technology is a decentralised ledger that allows a shared set of computing systems to agree and record that a transaction between multiple parties is authentic. In simple terms, it is a public registry of who owns what and who transacts what. These transactions are permanently recorded and consistently reconciled and updated in a cryptographically secure way. Because the ledger is distributed among all transaction participants, it exists simultaneously in multiple places, making it extremely difficult to manipulate entries or corrupt the system without the other parties noticing.

Blockchain technology is used in the bookkeeping for Bitcoin which makes many people equate the two, but blockchain is not Bitcoin. While both technologies originated together, cryptocurrencies are just one of many applications that can be run on top of blockchain.

Blockchain has the potential to eliminate huge amounts of record-keeping, save money and di$rupt systems in ways not seen since the internet arrived. It is one of the most disruptive technologies in decades. The hype around this seemingly new, secure electronic ledger is real. In essence, blockchain represents a new shift in paradigm for the way information is shared and business conducted.

We are fast entering an era of blockchain availability to the mass market. Manipulation of data, scams, lack of transparency and trust are huge problems in society and blockchain is a probable solution to these problems. In the not too distant future, businesses will be required to transfer their business ledgers onto blockchain for transparency, just like businesses are required to have websites for accessibility today.

Other possible uses of blockchain include scenarios where musicians can upload their songs on a blockchain application and specify how they want them to be used – for instance to be available to the public directly, without any large corporation or middle man eating up their revenue. One person could transfer money from their 'account' to someone else without having to go through the bank. The *World Economic Forum* predicts that by 2025, 10% of global GDP will be stored in blockchain technology.

By 2020, the UAE wants all visa applications, bill payments and licence renewals, which account for over 100 million documents each year, to be transacted digitally using blockchain technology. This process will remove middlemen like lawyers, accountants, bankers, immigration officers and government officials. Dubai estimates that by putting its 100 million documents each year onto the blockchain, they will save 25 million man hours and $1.5 billion in tax dollars.

According to *Forbes, Facebook* is planning to launch *Libra* Blockchain by 2020. *Libra* is a secure, blockchain-based cryptocurrency that'll enable people to buy things and instantly send/receive money globally without giant fees. *Facebook* has one primary goal in this project and its banking the unbanked (a global population of 1.7 billion adults).

This move by *Facebook* Corporation in the direction of Blockchain will certainly disrupt the global financial system.

You may ask, how will blockchain affect jobs and employment? The short answer is, probably in ways we have not yet imagined. Blockchain is all about transactions on an open trusted distributed ledger system and that means less need for human verification. The promise of blockchain is a world without middlemen. Combine just AI and blockchain and you'd see how bleak the future of work (jobs) will be.

The Bleak Future of Jobs

Twenty years ago, the workforce was mostly human except for a few computers. You could actually go to school, get a certificate and get a job. There was hope of working in one organisation until retirement. Fast-forward to today, few students are able to find a job after college and few are able to hold down a job in one organisation for longer than five years. Things have changed. Artificial Intelligence and robotics are the new buzzwords. Advances in technology are forcing humans out of the workplace. Businesses are going digital. The world is going digital! Shopping is going digital, banking is going digital, marketing is going digital, insurance is going digital and even dating has gone digital, and much more. Digitalisation simply means fewer employees – fewer cashiers, less book keeping, less trucking and fewer distribution centres. While employees may frown at self-service technologies and digitalisation, it is a dream-come-true for many employers. Every entrepreneur will most definitely embrace technology that saves money and improves efficiency.

Founder and chairman of World Economic Forum, Klaus Schwab compares Detroit in 1990 with Silicon Valley in 2014. He said, in 1990 the three biggest companies in Detroit had a market capitalisation of $36 billion, revenues of $250 billion and 1.2 million employees. But In 2014, the three biggest companies in Silicon Valley had a considerably higher market capitalisation amounting to $1.09 trillion, generated roughly the same revenues ($247 billion) but with only about 137,000 employees, that's about 10 times fewer employees.

And thus, extensive job loss is a reality the world must prepare for as businesses strive towards increased efficiency, flexibility and lower cost. Progress in computing power, software development techniques, and networking technologies have made designing, assembling, installing and maintaining robots faster and cheaper than before. More emerging 'smart software' is likely to simplify robotics even further.

A report by *McKinsey & Co* says, 'Automation systems are becoming increasingly flexible and intelligent with additional capabilities enabling their use in environments that have not been suitable for automation up to now.' An article in *The Economist* says '47% of all jobs globally will be automated by 2034'.

Almost half of all jobs could be automated by computers within two decades and no government is prepared for the tsunami of social change that will follow. The Fourth Industrial Revolution , also known as industry 4.0 puts everything in a constant state of change. At some point in the not too distant future, nearly every physical task conceivable will be done by robots. Some job sectors will shrink drastically and others will disappear altogether. The Forth Industrial Revolution is creating a demand for new competencies and the need for upskilling, creativity, innovation and entrepreneurship has never been more severe than now. The wave of technological disruption to the job market has only just started.

In 2016, Amazon started a chain of grocery stores across the USA, known as *Amazon Go*. The store is the world's most advanced shopping technology as it eliminates the entire checkout process, erasing the need for cashiers. No queues, no checkout – just grab and go! The technology has a high tech level surveillance that identifies people as they walk into the store. It detects when products are touched, taken or returned to the shelf. Customers at *Amazon Go* can walk into the store, grab what they want and walk out. Charges are automatically sent to their *Amazon Prime* accounts.

The pace of change being brought about by AI is unprecedented. Economists across the board predict massive job losses as AI, robotics, and other technologies continue to rise. Not only is the entire concept of work about to change in a dramatic manner, the trend is also irreversible. Jobs being lost to machines are not coming back. The result is a huge amount of uncertainty for both developed and underdeveloped countries. Which raises the question, where is the next generation going to find jobs?

Statistics show that every month more than one million young Indians turn 18 years old, and enter the job market. Most of them will never find a job the way we understand jobs today and these figures are not far different from the number of African youths entering the job market monthly.

> Humanity is working hard to dispose of humans and render them redundant.

According to *The Economist*, 'The effect of today's technology on tomorrow's jobs will be immense and no country is ready for it.' In the good old days, one could get a job in an organisation and work there until retirement but this is no longer the case. Jobs are evolving and technological disruption is age-less, race-less, and gender-less with zero regard for one's social standing or educational background. Automation affects everyone and impacts workers across the spectrum, from low-skilled to white and blue collar jobs.

The Economist ***further reveals***, 'Technological revolution is set to wipe out what looks to be the entire middle class. Technology's impact will feel like a tornado, hitting the rich world first, but eventually sweeping through poorer countries too and no government is prepared for it.'

However, not everyone is persuaded that the future will be as jobless as feared. Some people believe that only the boring parts of jobs, like data entry and filling out forms, will disappear so that humans can focus on more interesting tasks. They believe that no actual jobs will be lost to technology – but that might just be wishful thinking. Some laugh off the idea of robots taking over jobs and others say it might happen but not in this day and age.

Well, it is happening right now in this day and age. Artificial Intelligence is not only capable of mundane routine tasks, but complex jobs too. It is predicted that half of all 'white-collar jobs' might disappear in the next decade or so. Think about that for a moment! The forecasts for the future of work are quite alarming for a continent like ***Africa,*** which is already suffering from a chronically high unemployment rate.

According to data from the International Labour Organisation, Africa has the largest 'youth bulge' in the world and the youth unemployment rate in sub-Saharan Africa continues on its upward trajectory. The African continent has the world's highest rate of working poverty – people who are employed but earning less than $2 a day. The job crisis will only worsen in the future as many companies embrace automation, incorporate AI into their daily operations and continue to cut jobs.

The fight is especially critical for the youth. With Africa as a continent and South Africa as a country already facing a direct unemployment bloodbath, how much worse will things get when manual labour, factory jobs, mining jobs, retail and fast food jobs are done mostly by robots? If we think Africa currently has a high unemployment rate, how much higher is it going to be as robotics continue to invade businesses? The potential retrenchments across the board look dire. But this doesn't mean we are doom, there are new opportunities to be discovered in the new era as you'd see in chapter 5 and chapter 15 of this book.

Be on the lookout for a robo-chef or a self-service kiosk machine the next time you're ordering food at a fast-food joint. Self-ordering kiosks are fast replacing cashiers at fast food chains around the world.

A fully automated restaurant called *Eatsa* was opened in the USA in 2015. No serving staff, and no cashiers – just machines. It is a completely digital, self-serve environment, with frictionless service across all ordering channels. You can order, pay and eat without talking to a single person. *Eatsa's* technology also empowers other restaurants to deliver a magical experience, while serving more customers, faster and more efficiently.

There is also *Spyce*, another restaurant in the USA powered by a robotic kitchen that cooks your food in three minutes with only one human in the kitchen – the employee who tops off each meal with a pinch of garnish. *Spyce's* robotic kitchen is designed to cook, serve, and clean up.

Moley, a German tech company, launched the world's first ever home RoboChef in 2017, considered to be a disruptive force in the food and tech industries. RoboChef is a home version of a robot that cooks. RoboChef has unlimited access to chefs and their recipes worldwide. Chefs and even housekeeping jobs are at risk as these robots become affordable and more available to the masses.

The age of the restaurant self-service kiosks has dawned and *McDonald's*, the second-largest fast food restaurant chain by number of locations in the world, couldn't wait to show off their touch screen machines. If you are a Mc-client, you probably made your recent order via a touch screen instead of a cashier. The self-service kiosk at *McDonald's* allows customers to order food using a touch screen. The touch-screen technology speeds up the ordering process and gives people more control over customising their food, while reducing human error.

According to *The Guardian*, *McDonald's* on 3rd Avenue and 58th Street in *New York City* doesn't look all that different on the outside from any of the fast-food chain's other locations across the USA except that hungry patrons are welcomed not by a cashier waiting to take their orders, but by a 'Create Your Taste' kiosk – an automated touch-screen system that allows customers to create their own burgers without interacting with another human being.

McDonald's is arguably one of the most famous fast food restaurant chains in the world, with about 40,000 outlets in more than 100 countries. In the USA, *McDonald's* already has some outlets that are run entirely by robots and one can only imagine what will happen to humans in the fast food industry if this trend continues. Robots designed for the fast food industry are more hygienic and capable of putting out one burger every 10 seconds.

The rest of the world is behind the global curve when it comes to robotics in the corporate world, manufacturing and restaurants, compared to Japan and China, which are going completely automation and robotic crazy. China is investing heavily in a robotic workforce. Robots are handling more and more aspects of everyday life in Chinese cities. They have been deployed at train stations as security guards. Robots are being used to cook, both in restaurants and industrial kitchens.

In AI and robotics, China is emerging as a global leader. According to figures from the International Federation of Robots, China is already the biggest shareholder of the robotic global market.

Foxconn, a Taiwanese multinational corporation and the world's largest manufacturer of electronic components, plan to deploy an army of one million robots into their factories to cut rising labour costs and improve efficiency in 5 to 10 years. As of 2016, *Foxconn* had about 1.2 million employees and had put in place a three-part plan to fully automate its factories with the aim to achieve 80% automation by 2020. This move is what will put as many as one million people out of work. Foxconn electronics is the company manufacturing some of the biggest electronic brands devices including *Apple* iPhones. In response to President Trump's call to make more products in the United States, *Foxconn* promised to build a $10 billion liquid crystal display plant and create more jobs in Wisconsin State, USA. However, they now plan a substantially different mix of labour than originally projected. Almost all of the actual assembly line work will be performed by robots with only about 10% of employees.

Canon, a Japanese camera-making company, announced the move to entirely phase out human workers from some of its camera factories in an effort to reduce costs back in 2012. Their target has been met and robots are now making the next generation of cameras.

Adidas is also moving towards robot-only factory. In 2016, the footwear giant company unveiled its prototype 'Speedfactory', a state-of-the-art, 4,600 square-meter facility which will automate most of the work.

Futurist Thomas Frey predicts a mind-bulging future. He says 'up to 2 billion jobs will disappear by 2030', that's almost 50% of the jobs in the world. The figures are not too far from those in *The Economist* report that said 47% of jobs in the global marketplace would be automated by 2034.

Nevertheless, technology improves on the existing and brings with it new opportunities. Artificial Intelligence, robotics as well as digital automation will not eliminate everything. Our physical world will always be here. Classrooms, hospitals and physical shops might still be here but the mode of teaching, getting medical help and shopping is fast changing right in front of our eyes. Education is starting to evolve from the conventional classroom experience to digital form.

Technology is being used to facilitate teaching and learning process. Some primary schools already have their school work on tablets, eliminating the need for pupils to carry books. The *Khan Academy*, *Udemy*, *MOOC*, *edX*, *Codecademy*, *Coursera*, *FutureLearn* and other open online course systems are profoundly transforming learning for all ages. We are on the edge of an era of decentralised online learning combined with mentors and apprenticeships which will transform virtually everything we currently assume about education. You'll read more about why the education system in its current state is flawed and broken in chapter 9 of this book.

Jobs Most Susceptible to Automation

According to Wikipedia, 'Automation is the technology by which a process or procedure is performed with minimal human assistance.' This means replacing manual operations with electronics and computer-controlled devices. The end result is that emerging technologies will eventually push up unemployment rates significantly. The question now is, are you ready for this exponential change in work processes?

A wave of automation anxiety has hit the world of work and only few are aware of the changes happening right under our noses. It is business as usual for tertiary institutions and universities, obsessed with rising up the academic rankings while parents are preoccupied with making sure their children get degrees. No one really seems to be thinking of anything other than the usual 'go to school, get a certificate and get a job'. **As AI gains traction,** jobs are at risk and even prestigious certificate might become useless. Turns out we were not stretching our imaginations far enough ahead.

You may have no desire to work side by side with a robot, sit on a bus without a driver, or be served in a restaurant by robots, or get surgery done by robots. But the reality is that it will happen. Allow me to sound the wakeup call that momentous change is here. We are about to face a level of culture shock unprecedented in history.

Unemployment stats are only going to increase. Retrenchment and massive layoffs are going to increase. A lot of the best minds are doubtful many will survive it because we are all raised with the mind-set to go to school and get a job. Millions of youths in Africa and across the world are constantly being fed by the school system with the mind-set that they will all be employed as soon as they step out of the university. What a fantasy!

Until now the jobs most vulnerable to machines have been those that involved routine, repetitive tasks. But thanks to the exponential rise in automation, computers are increasingly able to perform even complex tasks more cheaply and effectively than humans. At this point automation cannot be terminated. No one can put the genie back in the bottle but don't be alarm; you can be part of this revolution if you can apply the mindset shifts laid down in chapter 4 and chapter 9 of this book.

The following areas of work are most susceptible to automation:

White Collar Jobs

Lawyers, doctors, bank managers, bank consultants, accountants, etc. who once felt safe and would usually say 'those stats don't apply to me' are no longer safe. Jobs in banking and elsewhere will become scarcer as banking and other businesses go digital and automation is no longer confined to routine tasks. The world is starting to see fully digital-only banks and mobile app-only banks in operation with no branches, such as *Bank Zero* in South Africa, *Monzo* in UK, *N26* in Germany, *Digibank* in India, *Neat* in Hong Kong and many other digital-only banks across the globe. This new trend in banking is only the beginning. Michael Jordaan, the co-founder and Chairperson at *Bank Zero,* says, 'Banking is necessary but banks aren't.' Digital banks requires no branches and no ATM machines, one's money is with one on one's mobile. Digital technologies offer banking businesses a way out of high fixed and maintenance costs involved in operating bank branches. While these changes are good for the business, they hugely impact employment and spell a bleak future for jobs in the banking sector. Banks are shedding jobs and branch reduction is a global reality.

With AI, digitalisation and automation in place, a bank's efficiency continuously improves, and profits increase with fewer employees. Another big employment decline is currently happening in office and administrative roles. Automated systems are built not just to work alongside humans but to replace humans.

According to Steve Andriola, 'Since 2011, 700 million global consumers have begun banking on their phone.'

Research by *Accenture* reveals that 5.7 million jobs are at risk of total automation in South Africa within just 7 years, this is 35% of all jobs.

According to Dr Roze Phillips, Post Graduate Diploma in Futures Studies alumnus from the *University of Stellenbosch Business School* and MD of *Accenture Consulting* in Africa, 'both white-collar and blue-collar jobs are at risk. Jobs at risk of automation are no longer just manual labour jobs. Accounting, book keeping, and auditing clerks, office administration, tellers, cashiers, farming, food preparation, insurance claims and policing processing clerks, construction, mining, transportation, installation and maintenance are at highest risk of automation in South Africa.'

According to *Accenture*, 'The safest jobs are those that require influencing and advising people, teaching, programming, real-time discussions, negotiating and co-operating with others.'

Technology is everywhere and in high demand. Any country or company that tries to stop AI will be left behind by competitors eager to embrace new things. The business mind-set will be: 'If other companies and countries are using technology to gain a competitive advantage, then we must also adopt it to get ahead.'

There are programs being designed that know all the tax codes better than any human. There are programs that can detect and diagnose diseases more accurately than the best doctors. Accountants, doctors, lawyers, financial analysts, tax analysts, pharmacist technicians, bookkeepers and bank managers are all at risk of automation.

Thousands of financial managers and compliance officers will be laid off as AI-based anti-money-laundering, anti-fraud, compliance and monitoring software fills in. Loan officers will lose their jobs to AI-based credit underwriting and smart contracts technology. The uncertainty surrounding the future of human employment in the age of automation is already apparent, and machines are poised to keep getting better and better at what they do. We already have robot lawyers capable of defending parking ticket violations as well as AI therapists that can outperform their human counterparts in terms of drawing out necessary personal information from patients.

Blue Collar Jobs

Economic experts foresee a massive decline of jobs in mining, manufacturing, construction, textile and production across the world as 3D printing and robotics become part of our everyday life. Millions of people working in the mining industry may not have jobs in the next 10 to 20 years.

The end of checkout lines is the looming crisis for cashiers worldwide as giant retail outlets continue experimenting with cashier-less stores. Retail automation and online stores will destroy more than half of retail jobs. Bricks and mortar retail is having a meltdown. Cashiers, shop assistants and packers should beware.

In 2016, *Pick n Pay* South Africa started testing out their self-service checkout counters. This trend is only the beginning: it is just a matter of time before other supermarket retail chains follow suit.

Then there are autonomous vehicles, trains and aircraft, all set to di$rupt every sphere of the global transport and logistics industry. Although there are still obstacles that must be overcome before autonomous transport becomes available to the masses, make no mistake, it is expanding and will become the norm sooner than we expect. It is predicted that most cities across the world will have fleets of self-driving taxis in the next 10 years.

The privilege of driving is about to be redefined with the technology of self-driving cars. This means drivers will see their jobs dry up as autonomous vehicles hit the road. And it's the ride-share companies who can't wait to rush their drivers out of the car. As *Uber's* CEO said, 'Our service would be a lot cheaper and our profits much greater if we weren't paying for that other dude in the car.' These innovative technologies may take time to reach Africa but make no mistake, it will happen. The delay is an opportunity for Africa to thoroughly prepare for its full-fledged technological disruption.

According to futurist Thomas Frey, in light of transportation going driverless, we won't need as many traffic law enforcement personnel, or the attorneys and judges to deal with cases relating to accidents. Traffic signal production and maintenance will diminish along with the crew that provide those services. Accidents and insurance claims will diminish, reducing the need for claims adjusters, tow truck drivers and collision repair shop personnel. This will also drive down business at the licence departments: needless to say workers at licence departments will face retrenchment.

Elon Musk predicts that 'human driving will be outlawed in the future due to its greater danger compared to driverless technology'. He says it'd be much safer for you, your vehicle and other vehicles on the road to let your onboard AI computer do the driving.

> Technology is ushering in a new economic era, exposing new sources of value and growth. New opportunities, businesses and markets can be created as a result of this new economy.

In the light of these developments, personal disruption starts with a disruptive **mind-set**, the attitude to question and challenge the status quo. Add the desire to reimagine, reinvent and recreate a new way of life, and then the ability to break and rewrite the rules, see new possibilities and new opportunities. Personal disruption isn't about what's happening to you or to the job market. Personal disruption is about how you choose to respond to what's happening in the world.

Technology is ushering in a new economic era, exposing new sources of value and growth. Thus, for you to rise to the challenge you need to recalibrate your mind-set and the conventional way of doing things. New opportunities, products, businesses, services and markets can be created as a result of the seismic shifts bearing down on the economy.

Is the path you are currently on sustainable? Will your certificate be of any use in the next ten years? Look into the future, look within your industry and start making the necessary changes now. Empower yourself, be a pioneer, seek opportunities, check online courses, read relevant books and create value for yourself. You have a responsibility to keep yourself from becoming obsolete, redundant and disposable. Your ability to recreate, perform, innovate and transform is limited only if you're stuck with the old way of thinking. As Newt Gingrich, an author and former speaker of the US House of Representatives, once said, 'The greatest difference in our generation may not be between liberals and conservatives, but between the pioneers of the future and prisoners of the past.'

Chapter 2

IS THE ROBOTIC INVASION COMING TO AFRICA?

Some have chosen to take the pessimistic view that Africa will be left behind by the wave of technological revolution, while others take the naïve view assuming that Artificial Intelligence, digitalisation, robotics, self-driving cars and other disruptive technologies are things belonging to the developed world. However, we cannot afford to be naïve and myopic in our approach to the realities of the current world order.

Some Africans prefer to maintain the status quo, defending irrelevant customs and traditions while sticking to economic activities that keep their poverty intact. But times are changing and Africa will no more be able to avoid the Fourth Industrial Revolution(4IR) than it was able to avoid the Third Industrial Revolution which begun in the 1950s and brought the internet, new information and communication technologies exploding onto the world stage. Indeed, Africa should be driving 4IR emerging technologies and innovation or it will be outpaced by it.

According to CNN, 'about 60,000 robots are imported to Africa every year and the robotics industry in Africa is developing rapidly'. The continent could see its emerging markets and businesses shed jobs to automation much quicker than in countries like Japan and China where the move toward automation has happened more organically through local innovation rather than imported machinery. Nonetheless, I believe the new generation in Africa can rise to this challenge

Do you still think Africa is somehow exempted from cutting-edge technology? Well, let's take a look at the automated teller machine, the ATM. I believe there isn't a single bank in Africa that's not currently using ATMs. This single innovative technology is a robot itself and has displaced thousands of bank employees across Africa. You can now transact at your own convenience. You can make deposits, withdrawals and get bank statements without any help from a bank employee. You enjoy the convenience of doing your financial transactions anytime anywhere, but that convenience came at a cost of thousands of bank tellers losing their jobs.

The ATM is only one example of disruptive technology in the banking sector. I've not touched on smartphone apps or online banking. The smartphone revolution has already shifted the e-commerce landscape, along with sophisticated chatbots and other technological advances in the financial sector. Research by *Citigroup* reveals that 'The downsizing of the bank workforce is about to accelerate as more technology is set to take over jobs humans used to do'. It is predicted that 30% of banking jobs are threatened by AI, digitalisation and blockchain.

Banking is going digital and Africa is not left behind. Digital banking is no longer a mere add-on feature but a fundamental system of banking. With the rise in digital-only banks such as *Tyme Digital*, *Bank Zero* and *Discovery Bank* in South Africa, *CBA Loop* in Kenya and *ALAT* in Nigeria, Africa is leading the world in financial innovation. Chris Skinner says, 'A digital bank is 30–40x more efficient than a leading traditional bank.' Mobile app-only banks incorporate innovative technology to allow them to execute all banking activities from a mobile device without any need to visit a branch or an ATM. This means you skip the queues, red tape and all the monotony that comes with regular banking. With digital banking, it takes only about three to five minutes to open an account and then your bank card will be delivered directly to you. Incidentally, *TYME* simply means Take Your Money Everywhere. Ivory Coast and Uganda already have digital-only banks operating under *Standard Chartered*, a British multinational bank and financial service provider. Research by *McKinsey* reveals 'digital finance could increase the GDP of all emerging economics by 6 percent'.

In a world of instant noodles, fast food, high-speed internet, digitization and emerging technologies, Africa is clearly not exempted. The robotic invasion is definitely coming to Africa as we can see. If Africa can embrace the ATM machines, smartphones, self-service apps, mobile money and now digital-only banks, then it's only a matter of time before Africa embraces everything else that comes with the emerging technology. Nobody wants to stand in queues anymore. People want things done at the touch of a button. The more convenience people demand the more machines will rise and the more jobs will be lost.

> The technological revolution and economy shift in Africa is impending and will happen faster than many are imagining. Kids being raised with technology will work and do business with technology.

Africa has the largest youth bulge in the world. These youths are hungry and curious and – to tweak the saying just a little – 'curiosity skills the cat'. People born between the early 1980s and the early 2000s, now in their teens, 20s, and 30s, are doing things differently. It is important to note that these millennials are the first generation of digital natives, people who have never really known a world without computers and the internet. Children born to millennials are growing up in a world of smartphones, smart computers, smart TVs, mobile money, Wi-Fi, mobile apps and automated systems. While the older generation of Africans may be surprised by these technologies and may even curse them, the new generation can't imagine life without them. Even the day to day running of business has change drastically as you'll learn in chapter 12 of this book.

An older African, say from the sixties, may prefer working in the factory or buying groceries from his usual mini-shop down the street. However, working and shopping are a completely different experience for millennials growing up in the age of the internet. A five-year-old kid today, swiping on his/her parent's smartphone, will demand a much more convenient way of doing business in the next 10 to 20 years – and that's when Africa will begin to experience a real paradigm shift in cutting-edge technologies.

Kids growing up in the digital world with smartphones cannot survive in a brick and mortar environment. The older generation grew up playing down the street and hanging out with friends in the market place, but kids today are growing up with almost all their toys and play things on a tiny screen while hanging out on social media with their 'friends'. This transitioning is happening right now and right here in Africa. This means that the technological revolution and economy shift in Africa is impending and will happen faster than many are imagining. The delay is actually giving Africa enough time to prepare. Kids being raised with technology will work and do business with technology. I believe some of our African kids will build some of the most advanced AI, robotics and digital platforms not yet imagined.

Tech Revolution in Africa

The rapid spread of technological advancement and AI is unavoidable, even for a continent like Africa. The robotic invasion is definitely coming to Africa and it is already here. Necessity is the mother of innovation and as such Africa is an innovation hub. It is quite clear that Africa is ready to start being a key player in the tech revolution. Despite political muscle being wasted on power retention rather than on development and the clearing of economic bottlenecks in different parts of the continent, Africa's newest generation are breaking barriers to write their names on the sands of time, not only in their respective countries but also on the world's timeline.

> Technology, entrepreneurship and the creative economy are Africa's untapped golden markets.

African leaders will have to choose between progress and investing in young creative minds or the old leadership style of protecting bureaucracy and outdated dogma.

It may seem as if nothing is happening on the continent in terms of cutting-edge technology but this is plainly not the case. There are plenty of ground-breaking innovation news reports coming out of the continent every day to support the view that Africa will not be left behind by technology. Africa is rising and there is no shortage of creative minds willing to dig their hands deep into computers to create disruptive solutions for the continent. Not all African youths are baptised with the 'job mentality'. Many are going against the grain, refusing to conform. They are taking the road less travelled instead of the well-beaten path of employment. Technology, entrepreneurship and the creative economy are Africa's untapped golden markets.

African millennials are hungry and curious and their hunger and curiosity are paying off. The tech revolution in Africa has already begun and young inventors are on course to transform the continent for the better. The following are some of the ground-breaking inventions that will fight poverty, diseases and solve a myriad of problems in Africa.

- ***CardioPad.*** Africa's first handheld medical computer tablet that can diagnose people with heart disease. It was invented in Cameroon by a 24-year-old engineer, Arthur Zang. It is expected to facilitate diagnoses and treatment of patients with heart conditions across the African continent.
- ***Pelebox Smart Locker.*** A technology to ensure patients can collect their chronic medication in under 2 minutes instead of waiting hours in queues. Invented in South Africa by Neo Hutiri after he was diagnosed with tuberculosis and faced difficulties collecting his medication. Hutiri signed a contract with the department of health to roll the lockers out in eight of South Africa's nine provinces.
- ***Elikia VMK.*** 'Made in Africa's' first mobile phone – and it's coming out of Democratic Republic of Congo. The Tech Start-up, VMK, founded by Verone Mankou, is blazing a trail for 'made in Africa's' mobile devices.
- ***Biomedical smart jacket.*** A Ugandan innovator, Brian Turyabagye, designed a biomedical smart jacket that can diagnose pneumonia four times faster and more accurately than a doctor.
- ***SALT.*** An acronym that stands for Southern African Large Telescope – the third-largest telescope in the world. It is a ground-breaking technology for space exploration that allows scientists to look many times deeper into space than was previously possible.
- ***Artificial Intelligence Robot.*** Bobai Ephraim Kato, a 24-year-old Nigerian Software Engineer student, built a functional AI machine as his final year project at the International College of Business and Technology in Sri Lanka. He describes himself as a self-directed

learner willing to experiment with new things and will continue to fine-tune his craft to bridge the gap between corporate needs and high-tech machines in his country, Nigeria.

- ***Majik Water***. A water harvesting system that captures water from the air and converts it into drinking water using solar technology. Invented in Kenya by Beth Koigi after going for months without any tap water in eastern Kenya. With the rapid climate change, this could provide a solution for the 1.8 billion people predicted by the UN to have a shortage of water by 2025. Koigi says 'There's six times more water in the air than in all the rivers in the world.'
- ***A Flying Car from Waste.*** It'd be the continent's first ever flying car, an aero-amphibious jet car being built by Kehinde Durojaiye. If he gets it right, his vehicle will fly, float and drive on the road. He started his project to combat the infamously congested traffic in Lagos, Nigeria's largest city. In an interview he said, 'I want the whole world to know it is possible to have a kind of machine that can move on land, on sea and fly, and perhaps move under the sea. That's my ultimate goal.'
- ***The Largest 3D Printer in Africa.*** Built at Nelson Mandela Metropolitan University (NMMU) by a team of student engineers and their lecturers. The five-metre tall printer has an ability to print enormous structures. The first African-made 3D printer was manufactured in Togo and more 3D printers are being manufactured throughout the continent. These machines will revolutionise Africa.
- ***Human-like Traffic Control Robots***. A group of young engineering students in the Democratic Republic of Congo are building robots that control traffic.
- ***M-Pesa.*** The best known innovator in Africa on mobile payment. *M-Pesa* is one of the mobile money apps that have made Kenya an epicentre for the mobile money revolution and a leader in digital payments on the African continent. It has also inspired similar services around the world. According to Chris Skinner, author of *Digital Human*, 'M-Pesa has spread to 10 countries with 29.5 million active users who conduct 614 million transactions per month over the network. There are at least 19 countries with more

mobile money accounts than bank accounts in sub-Saharan Africa.'

- ***EcoCash.*** Zimbabwe's mobile phone-based payment solution that enables customers to complete financial transactions directly from their mobile phones.
- ***Tress.*** An app to share different hairstyles and ideas about hair. It's like *Pinterest* or *Instagram* for hair. Once you have the app, you can follow other people who are sharing their hairstyles and ideas. Invented by three software engineers – Priscilla Hazel, Esther Olatunde and Cassandra Sarfo from Ghana.
- ***Matibabu.*** A swift bloodless malaria testing device which can accurately give blood test results within a minute. Designed by a young Ugandan engineer, Brian Gitta. He recently won the prestigious Africa Prize for Engineering Innovation.
- ***Quiet Cellular Antenna Technology.*** Developed by two South African brains, Gordon Mahew and Paul Van Jaarsveld. It reduces noisy emissions from cellular base stations in the area. The antenna has been tested in other parts of the world and has worked extremely well. It is projected to be 50 to 100 times more sensitive than any other telescope ever built, and an area without much radio emissions is essential for the success of the project.
- ***Charging Shoes.*** Designed by a Kenyan inventor called Anthony Mutua to charge phones using power generated through walking. A perfect solution for people in rural areas with no electricity.
- ***Kiira EV SMACK.*** The first African Electric Hybrid Vehicle designed and built in Uganda by Kiira Motors Corporation, an Automotive Manufacturing Company incorporated by the government of Uganda and Makerere University to champion innovation in transportation technologies.
- ***Drones Airport.*** In the context of agriculture and medical emergencies in remote areas, drones have enormous potential in Africa. As a result, the world's first airport for drones is being built in Rwanda.

Technology is a tool that the African continent will leverage to rise as a world superpower. Anyone thinking Africa will be left behind by the technological revolution should think again. Things are not the way they used to be and will never be the way they used to be.

> Africa's hopeful transformation lies in entrepreneurship. Africa needs more entrepreneurs, innovators, start-ups, disruptors, inventors, pioneers and thought leaders.

Millions of youths are graduating every year in Africa and entering the job market but there are no jobs. The lifeline for Africa as a continent is an entrepreneurial revolution. For Africa to arise and shake off the shackles of unemployment and poverty, it will have to happen through entrepreneurship. Africa needs more entrepreneurs, innovators, start-ups, disruptors and thought leaders.

Whether, you're in Africa or some other part of the world, don't be naïve, times have changed. If you don't take ownership of your life now, automation will force you to do it. You can't afford to fiddle at the margins, you can't sit back and wait for government or someone else to hand you success. Graduates across the globe need to find new ways to adapt their academic qualifications and skills in an economy that's rapidly changing.

The Rise of Robots in Africa

Five years ago, The *African Robotics Network* launched a $10 Robot challenge to encourage students to produce their own robots. There are also over 20 African organisations encouraging participation in robotics.

According to *CNN*, 'Although robots in Africa are still in its infancy, with under 60,000 imports a year, the robotics industry in Africa is developing rapidly.'

A policy brief by the United Nations conference on trade and development reveals that 'robots will take away two-thirds of jobs in developing countries'.

Another study from *World Bank Research* states that 'more than half the jobs in parts of Africa are at risk of automation, with Ethiopia leading the global list with 85% of existing jobs at risk'.

In Africa, robots are already mining, controlling traffic, doing customer service and fighting deadly diseases.

- *Nedbank* South Africa launched the first humanoid robot in one of their branches. It's called '*Pepper*', and could possibly do away with thousands of employees in the future if the trend continues. No longer just the objects of fascination in science fiction, robots are beginning their invasion of banking even here in Africa.
- *Vodacom,* a South African mobile communications company, also decided to take *their* innovative ways to another level and have added a new member to *their* team, a humanoid *r*obot also named *Pepper.*
- In Kinshasa, DRC, robots are already a part of everyday life. Eight foot tall, solar-powered '*Robocops*' have been brought in to direct traffic. These robots have eliminated the need for human traffic wardens as they can detect pedestrians and are designed to withstand all weather conditions.
- In Tanzania and Uganda, drones with sensors have replaced the need for some farm workers because of their ability to detect stress in plants, ten days before humans can.
- In South Africa, robots now replace humans to access depths unsafe for humans in the country's gold mines.
- The situation in Botswana closely mirrors that in South Africa. Robots are now employed to mine diamonds at depths that are unsafe for humans.
- In the wake of the 2014 Ebola crisis, Liberia took full advantage of the 5×5 foot robot, TRU-D, to beat the deadly virus. *TRU-D* had the ability to disinfect rooms where Ebola patients were treated, a feat too risky for humans.
- Rwanda, a country where there is one doctor to every 16,046 people, is building the world's first drone airport to deliver medical and emergency supplies, and much more, to its rural areas. Rwanda is steadily moving towards its vision of becoming an information-rich, knowledge-based economy and Africa's tech leader.

Chapter 3

A THREAT TO THE STATUS QUO IS AN OPPORTUNITY IN DISGUISE

Emerging technologies do bring a sense of gloom and doom, but the good news is that technology also brings opportunities. Businesses of the future cannot operate fully without humans. There'll be great need for machines and humans to work side by side, supplementing each other. Artificial Intelligence, like every other tech revolution before it, will create new opportunities. Humans will always be needed to come up with innovations on how to use robotics.

Engineers and programmers will always be in demand to programme the machines and tell them what to do. We'll still need humans to create bigger, better robots and to make sense of the data the machines generate. Innovation has always killed jobs but it always creates new and better opportunities, as a more productive society becomes richer and its wealthier inhabitants demand more improved goods and services.

Today, the pool of secretaries and admin staff has shrunk, but there are ever more computer programmers, web designers, cyber security officers and app developers. People with skills required to design, install, operate and maintain robotic systems are becoming more widely available. Robotic engineers were once rare and expensive specialists, but this is no longer the case. Experts foresee a strong employment growth across cyber security, science, engineering, computer and mathematical job families in future. Emerging technologies like drones, chatbots, 3D printers and the blockchain will need experts who can ensure these systems work effectively. As the world becomes more digital, there's a bright future in cyber security careers.

When confronted with the right mind-set, disruptive technology is not a roadblock, but a catalyst for creativity, a pathway for growth and an opportunity to create a better life. As Abraham Lincoln said, 'The best way to predict your future is to create it.' You don't stumble into the future.

While some jobs will be lost because of robotics, other jobs will be created by the rise of new technologies. Companies that implement robotic automation will need specialists to monitor, analyse, and run the technology, and someone to train their staff in running it. The new technology will thus create a whole new field of expertise that will be highly sought after, and well paid, I suppose.

AI will destroy millions of jobs but will also create new jobs that are technical and more sophisticated unlike anything we're familiar with today. AI will create a new ecosystem of jobs that aren't in existence yet. However, jobs created by AI will be fewer in number compared to jobs destroyed by AI.

According to research by the World Economic Forum, the rise of the robotic will eliminate more jobs than it will create. The numbers indicate seven million lost to two million gained.

According to research by the *World Economic Forum*, 'the rise of the robotic will eliminate more jobs than it will create. The numbers indicate seven million lost to two million gained.' And this is where the challenge and the opportunities lie. Five million jobs will be lost forever, never to be seen again. We're looking at a dire future where seven million people will have to fight to occupy two million vacancies.

The effects of cutting-edge technologies will spread right across the hierarchical structures, from top management right down to the cleaners and security guards. The new way of doing things will affect everyone. You will be left behind unless you're willing to let go of the traditional way of doing things. By embracing personal disruption, you will be able to transform your mind-set and unlock your full potential. If you can get your mind-set right, you can gather the resources and knowledge that you need to upskill and be successful. Upskill and recreate yourself, because you're either being disrupted, or you're the disruptor. Which would you rather be?

The biggest challenge for the future will be defining ourselves outside the notion of a 'job'. For everyone whose job is already displaced or yet to be displaced, the biggest concern is what to do for an income. But all hope is not lost. Opportunities in this new era are not only 'job' related. The future belongs to creatives, risk-takers and non-conformists. Those who cannot imagine life outside the cubicle are in for a rude awakening as there simply won't be enough jobs to go around.

Certificates are no longer a guaranteed ticket to success, you can do more today with your life having just a smartphone and an internet connection; and that's an opportunity our parents and grandparents never had. When people don't have work then people will have to pursue their passions. There are so many opportunities online. You might just be a *Google* search away from an entirely different life. They are so many smart, talented people working just to pay bills and survive. These people could be researching, inventing, innovating and developing disruptive systems that'll change the world, but some are too afraid to step into their own greatness.

This is the time for us to try new things and find new pursuits. This is the time to partake in creative enterprises and start new ventures. This is the time of the flowering of humanity. Instead of being stuck and working just to pay the bills, you can pursue your passion and make a difference in the world. If the analysis of the robotic takeover as predicted is halfway correct, the social effects will be huge. Anyone not willing to di$rupt themselves and own their future won't be able to survive what's coming, even with the most prestigious certificates.

Our world is changing fast, but all is not lost in the race to automation. With the rise of the robotic, the focus is shifting from people power to intellectual capital. With or without a certificate, a disruptor's mind can foresee limitless opportunities in the newly emerging economy. You can create your own path, based on your ability to draw on all the pockets of information stored inside your brain to make clever decisions at every turn. With each technological disruption, wealth shifts from the entrenched to the disruptor and innovator.

Personal disruption means removing blindfolds you've imposed on yourself by trying to fit into shackles imposed by parents, teachers and society. Irrespective of the changes happening in the world today, there are more opportunities to make it on your own today than they were in the past. What a time to be alive!

The internet has changed the game; with just a click you can reach millions of people online. We are all on mobile and we can leverage big data to create opportunities and solve new problems. There are no more gate keepers blocking your way to success. Thanks to the internet and mobile connectivity, it now takes less capital to launch a business than it did a decade ago. It doesn't matter whether you're in your room, in the village or in the biggest city in the world. You still have access to billions of people.

> The future will not seem so scary if talent is put to use.

You can launch a global business even from the comfort of your home. You can create systems that will solve problems and di$rupt industries. Anyone can take advantage of these opportunities by capturing the values released through disruption. Thanks to technology and disruptive innovation, businesses like *Uber* were born. The sharing economy is an opportunity for many to leverage on global businesses and to create your own! The sharing economy – also known as collaborative consumption – is a system whereby assets or services are shared between private individuals for a fee, typically by means of the internet.

You are the missing disruption. Africa needs more entrepreneurs, idea makers, innovators, and disruptors to fill the new gaps. The world today envisions developing next-generation systems that work side-by side with humans, accelerating our ability to create, learn, think and make decisions. Disruptive innovation will help us architect the future with the most advanced AI platforms. If you can engineer your own personal transformation, you will welcome a life of exciting endeavours and possibilities. The future will not seem so scary if talent is put to use.

Opportunity for Personal Growth and New Careers

The bleak future of jobs should be the concern of everyone: the employed, unemployed, graduates, non-graduates and even children in primary and high school. The question of 'what can I do to create a better future' should be on everyone's mind. But sadly, very few are thinking in that direction. As usual, many are waiting on government to wave the magic wand and solve everyone's problems. But government will always do what it does best, put you on life-support. This might tempt you into a parasitic economic situation where you are neither legally alive nor legally dead.

Well, given the growing trend of cutting-edge technologies and robotics, governments across the globe have come up with some potential solutions to address massive job loss and employee displacement. Among those solutions is something called Universal Basic Income, a system in which all citizens of a country receive an unconditional amount of money on top of their basic income. The question, however, is simply: will this be sustainable? Can people live a comfortable life or build legacies on government stipends? I'll show you in chapter 11 how governments and freebies has never helped anyone succeed.

The most fundamental unit of disruption is you. Instead of waiting on government to rescue you, ask yourself: 'What can I do to rescue myself?' Instead of being afraid of losing your job, kindly ask yourself, 'Is what I'm currently doing the only contribution to society I have to offer?' What if you could start that business you've always wanted while planning your escape? As more robots enter the workplace, you'll need to teach yourself how to be creative, innovative and entrepreneurial. The freedom of choice and creativity is one trait the machines can't take away from humans.

So you'll need to choose to be proactive, to seek opportunities. There are tons of books out there; there are YouTube tutorials on different skills and free online learning you can take advantage of to add more value to your life. By embracing the power of personal disruption, you can create value for yourself where it didn't exist before and make yourself indispensable. There's no doubt that AI and other cutting-edge technologies are going to change the face of employment as we know it. Educate yourself now and understand how it can impact your job or business. The Fourth Industrial Revolution also known as industry 4.0 or 4IR is an historical event that is currently being understood only by experts. You are ahead of the curve and pioneering change if you can study what is being regarded by experts as the biggest threat to the human workforce. Don't fight emerging technologies, you will lose every time. Instead, embrace them and become part of the revolution. You cannot fight technology but you can use it to safeguard your future employment or whatever skills or talents you have that need enhancing. By educating yourself about AI today, you can help amplify your work abilities tomorrow, making yourself an irreplaceable asset to your organisation.

> Educating yourself about technology and automation now gives you an excellent opportunity to future-proof your job and skills. It helps amplify your potential and work abilities thereby making you an irreplaceable asset.

According to research findings from *Accenture*, 'hard-to-automate jobs include tasks like influencing people, teaching people, craftsmanship, creativity, and programming, real-time discussions, advising people, negotiating and collaborating.' The future of work will be unlike anything we're familiar with. That's why re-skilling, re-training and re-learning are imperative for anyone to thrive in this new era.

New skills encompass the cognitive abilities, aptitudes and dispositions needed to stay relevant and thrive in the fast-evolving digital economy, as well as the specialised knowledge or craft skills. These are capabilities that individuals can learn at any age and hone over time.

Many will be required to learn new skills and find new work; others to switch occupations completely. You must use your mind and come up with some really great ideas. That way, you'll never have to worry about automation or being made obsolete. The future will not seem so scary if talent is put to use. The future certainly has the potential to draw more on an individual's talents than certificates.

Creativity and originality are no longer going to be only nice extras. Creative solutions and original thinking are the basis of innovation. Skills that are least vulnerable to automation are creativity, social intelligence, the ability to use your mind and connect with people, collaboration, critical thinking and problem solving.

AI and automation are handing us an opportunity to change how we've always done things and to get better at our craft. Take the opportunity and don't sabotage it. If you do, you'll only be sabotaging yourself. Disruptors don't see only one way of doing things. They are forward thinkers and open-minded and often start moving well before they fully understand what they are doing. When you've been doing the same things for so long, it's easy to think you know it all, have seen it all and have tried it all – but disruptors disagree. There's always another way, a better way, another approach, and something untried that may just work.

Many of us bought into society's social contract of success, which states – go to school, get good grades, get a job and live happily ever after. But this doesn't work anymore. At the most basic level, disrupting yourself will demand that you breach this contract of social conditioning and conformity.

Robotic takeover, machine intelligence and many others yet to be considered are not yet on the radar of our politicians or even fully on the radar of our economic planners. Therefore, if you are to survive this socio-economic challenge, you need to find a way to upskill and empower yourself regardless of whether or not you have a job. Own your future! Create your own version of success through profitable, purpose-driven and innovative thinking without depending on the system or bureaucratic policy makers.

The government must embark on an extensive education reform of the school system from primary through university to meet the demands of tomorrow's economy because the school curriculum is currently failing to prepare students for jobs of the future.

But you are gifted and you can learn how to build a better

tomorrow by taking steps today. To own your future is to become your own successor, keep yourself in demand and in control of your destiny. There is no formula. Make your own rules – try them, tweak them, push them, or even reject them. You must believe you can do it and not depend on the system. Small actions can trigger big changes.

Disruptors aren't bogged down by the day-to-day routine. They learn how to be leaders instead of followers. They learn how to demand of themselves the very things they demand from the government or the system. They learn how to give 100% to the job and still think outside the box. They're ready for major changes in the landscape because they're deeply engaged in what's going on around them. They know themselves inside out, they know their industry inside and out, and they're always looking for ways to learn, improve, expand and develop themselves.

> No one is more motivated, innovative, resourceful, and more self-reliant than a broke person who has decided to 'make a way for himself/herself out of no way' in a difficult economy.

No one is more motivated, innovative, resourceful, and more self-reliant than a broke person who has decided to 'make a way for himself/herself out of no way'. Complaining and manufacturing excuses are not part of a disruptors' vision. Disruptors recognise the trends and the inevitable changes that come with them, and work out how to surf the wave instead of getting dumped by it.

> There has never been an opportunity for personal growth than what confronts us now. Those that are disruptive and purpose driven will not only survive but thrive in the new economic era ushered in by technology.

The key to disruption is motion. Get out of your head into the real world. Fearful or not, you keep going forward, you keep evolving and never stagnating. That's how life is. Be ready to try a new way of singing a song you've performed for years, a new way of doing business, a new way of satisfying your customers, a new way of doing your job, a new way of showing your significant other your love for him/her, a new way of cooking, a new way of doing your hair, and even try out a new road home. Don't keep playing the safe card by doing things the same way year after year.

Power is moving to the people in the new economic paradigm. We are moving from a world where things were closed to an open world. There have never been opportunities for personal growth like those that confront us now. Those people who are disruptive and purpose-driven will not only survive but thrive in the new economic era ushered in by the emerging technologies. Be open-minded and ready to reinvent yourself. The new era demands a more self-reliant spirit and a greater emphasis on entrepreneurial thinking. Hence chapter 15, the last chapter of the book offers 25 innovative business ideas for you to create your own economy.

Upskill Yourself: Money Grows on Skills, not Trees

You should get ready for a globalised economy and a lifetime of relearning, reskilling and retraining. This does not necessarily mean going back to mainstream school, as some people will presume. Education goes beyond the classroom and education should never stop when schooling stops. Specialist training should not limit you to that specialisation alone. Most people think of disruption only in relation to business, but it is best to think of yourself as your own business so you use disruptive thinking to transform yourself. You can add value to yourself by broadening your knowledge and perspective beyond the cubicle in which you might find yourself.

On the other hand, discovering what you are good at is no longer a luxury or a hobby in a world that's changing faster and more furiously than ever before. It's a matter of urgency, as you add value to yourself, to find a market niche in which you can excel. You need to pinpoint what it is that you have a passion for and market your services/products accordingly. This is the only way to stay relevant and ahead of technological disruption, although an even better way might be to have two market niches – just in case. Be willing to turn your hobbies, talents and even academic qualifications into thriving ventures. Your ability to recreate, perform, innovate and transform is limitless.

You don't need to be an engineer or a tech wizard, but you must have a basic knowledge of how AI and robotics work, their applications in your life, business, industry and what the future holds. Upskill, recreate and add value to yourself. Read as many books and articles as you can, take online courses, attend conferences and webinars to learn about emerging technologies and their applications to your life and work.

Educating yourself about technology and automation now gives you an excellent opportunity to future-proof your job, skills or business and helps amplify your potential and work abilities, thereby making you a valuable asset that may be difficult to replace. The secret to growth in this new era is being willing to 'learn and relearn' even if what you knew previously brought you success.

As futurist and philosopher Alvin Toffler wrote way back in 1970 in his famous *Future Shock*: 'The illiterate of the 21st century will not be those who cannot read and write but those who cannot learn, unlearn and relearn.'

Put your future in good hands – your own! Personal disruption means not waiting for the government or your family members to hand something to you. It means rethinking the parameters of your life, and perhaps even of your community, maybe even your country. It means looking forward instead of staying mired in the present. It means making things happen instead of waiting for things to happen.

Things like sex skills are not taught in mainstream school but most people are pros and gurus in this department. They'll do whatever it takes to get the skills and perfect them. The same energy, time, research, money and practice should also be poured into gaining other more valuable skills that will make you indispensable in your career, your business and your community at large.

Risk taking, hustling, resilience, sales, negotiation, creative thinking, creative writing, self-awareness, networking, communication, personal development, financial intelligence, emotional intelligence, leadership, public speaking and much more are skills many people lack but do nothing about. Sometimes these same people resort to complaining, or blaming the government and/or their parents. Yet no parent or government department has ever been credited for their spectacular mind-blowing skills in bed.

Same goes for fashion and make-up. Every woman out there, young or old, knows how to draw the newest eyebrows on fleek. People know what's trendy in fashion and what's outdated without someone running after them and forcing them to learn these things. And let's not forget dancing. Some people can watch one video 30 times to master a particular dance move but can't watch even a 20-minute tutorial on *YouTube* that teaches skills like how to build a computer, how to develop an app, how to fix cars, etc.

Just because school is over, doesn't mean you should discard your brain or put it in shutdown mode. The end of school should be the beginning of your greatest curiosity and that means learning new things, lots of them, and all the time. We're in the middle of the Fourth Industrial Revolution and those who don't update their minds will be left behind. We have the amazing gift known as the internet whereby you can learn pretty much anything you want and whenever you want: from writing to the various art-forms, to programming, to coding, to learning the dynamics of AI and anything else you can imagine. *YouTube* especially has got you covered on almost every 'how to do this and that'. *YouTube* is the second most used search-engine in the world after *Google.*

There is no excuse whatsoever. If you really want to do something with your life, you'll find a way to make it happen. No excuses! You didn't wait on anyone to give you your sex skills, you made an effort, you took the initiative to get the skills yourself. So, what's stopping you from taking the initiative with other aspects of your life? What's stopping you from learning other skills? 'Energy flows where attention goes' and opportunity avoids those whose minds are empty!

More than anything, personal disruption is a mind-set. It is an attitude and a desire to take your life into uncharted waters. Personal disruption isn't change for the sake of change but it is understanding that change is inevitable if you are going to survive and flourish. The goal is to never become obsolete. You're doing yourself a major service by expanding your horizons and finding new ways to do things. This means getting past fear, stepping out of your comfort zone and creating value for yourself in areas where it didn't before exist.

As Klaus Schwab, Founder and chairman of World Economic Forum said, "Technology is not an exogenous force over which we have no control. We are not constrained by a binary choice between "accept and live with it" and "reject and live without it". Instead, take dramatic technological change as an invitation to reflect about who we are and how we see the world. The more we think about how to harness the technology revolution, the more we will examine ourselves and the underlying social models that these technologies embody and enable, and the more we will have an opportunity to shape the revolution in a manner that improves the state of the world."

PART TWO

Personal breakthrough is the vehicle through which success and economic growth travel. As an anonymous writer once said, 'Personal development is a major time saver. The better you become, the less time it takes you to achieve your goals.'

This part of the book offers the blueprint on how you can shape your own future, discover your unique talents, take hold of opportunities and the mindset shift you need to thrive in a world that's fast changing. You can escape the shackles of conformity, reinvent your thinking and stand out in the ever changing tech world.

Here are some questions to ponder on as you delve deeper into the blueprints for personal disruption and mindset transformation:

- What is the one thing you would hope to change about yourself?
- Do you find fulfilment in what you do daily?
- Are you worried about your future?
- Do you have dreams/talents buried deep inside you?
- What is holding you back from making a change?
- What do you risk losing if you di$rupt yourself?
- What could happen if you don't do something about your life now?
- Is there anyone telling you that you can never be more than what you are right now?
- Are you willing to revolutionise your mindset and adopt an unconventional approach to life?

Chapter 4

THE MINDSET REVOLUTION

Before you can change yourself or impact the world, you must first change your mind. The concepts, trends and solutions I've offered in this book will be of no value if they don't influence any major changes in your thinking. A shift in mindset amidst emerging technologies is the new imperative for anyone hoping to thrive in this new era. The way we think directly impacts on our growth. Change begins in the mind before it can manifest itself outside. The mind is where the revolution begins. Don't wait for things to fall off the cliff before you start thinking differently. Transformational thinking is a key requirement to survive and thrive in a world that's fast changing. We are at the beginning of a major disruption to our way of life. The rise of the machines is challenging everything school taught us, as we saw in part one of this book. What you were taught 10 or 20 years ago is fast becoming obsolete. Upskill and recreate yourself.

> "Most people go through college and learn to read virgil and master the mysteries of calculus without ever discovering how their own minds function."

Forward motion begins when an awakening takes place in the mind. In order to provide something different to the world, you must be different and that requires a big shift in mindset. The world is constantly looking for what is new because it remains hungry from being fed the same thing repeatedly. Your mind is your most powerful resource. The mind controls the destiny of man. As Dale Carnegie, an American writer and lecturer said, "Most people go through college and learn to read virgil and master the mysteries of calculus without ever discovering how their own minds function."

Irrespective of where you are in life, you can alter your circumstances for good by altering your mindset. Your certificates can become outdated but your mind will never become outdated. If a Robot can succeed without a certificate, so can you. It's all about programming! Business as usual is dead. Only those who can di$rupt their thinking, learn and relearn new skills can pivot themselves towards new opportunities. Creativity, innovation, invention and transformation are not sparked in the classroom but in the mind. Your life ticks the way your mind thinks.

As Bishop TD Jakes said, 'There is nothing as powerful as a changed mind. You can change your hair, your clothing, your address, your spouse, your friends, but if you don't change your mind, the same experience will perpetuate itself over and over again because everything outwardly did change, but nothing inwardly changed.'

> Many people are suffering not as a result of a rigid economy but as a result of a rigid mindset.

Your mind doesn't think its own thoughts. Whatever you allow into your mind is what will sit there. Being a disruptor is a state of mind and having the ability to challenge the status quo. It is an attitude and a desire to take your life into uncharted waters. Personal disruption isn't change for the sake of change but the understanding that change is inevitable if you are to flourish and succeed. Disruptors overturn conventions and that's what sets them apart. Every successful person who has skilfully transformed themselves, their job, their business or relationships, started with a shift in mindset.

Personal breakthrough is the vehicle through which success and economic growth travels and this cannot happen without a change in mindset. The single most important secret to success is not what you do, it is how you think. The results you get are only as good as the thoughts in your mind. The more energy you invest in cleaning up your mindset, the better your life will be. You cannot win in life if you are losing in your mind. Many people are suffering not because of a rigid economy but as a result of a rigid mindset.

You don't need to be trapped in your way of thinking or society's way of doing things. If you are unhappy with your life, your business or your job – do something about it! Don't conform but di$rupt. Regardless of what society has told you or what everyone else has accepted as normal, you can di$rupt the shackles of conformity and reprogramme your mindset. The most disruption will happen within your mind rather than in an economy because businesses don't di$rupt, people do. Therefore, be a change agent in ***your*** own life. The day you change your mind is the day you change your life. Embrace what *Stanford* researcher Carol Dweck calls a 'growth mindset', which to me is the best way to get ahead in today's turbulent economic environment. According to Carol Dweck's theory, a 'growth mindset' revolves around the belief that we can improve intelligence, ability and performance, while a 'fixed mindset' assumes that our character, intelligence, and creative ability are static traits which we can't change in any meaningful way.

Think Outside the Box

Among some of the well-beaten phrases in the business world is this phrase: 'think outside the box'– but thinking outside the box is more than just a business cliché. It is about approaching problems in an unstructured and innovative way. It means thinking creatively, freely and off the conventional path. Thinking outside the box is about dispensing with constraints and structured thinking. It's about conceptualising problems differently and understanding your position in relation to any particular situation in a way you'd never thought of before.

Outside the box thinking doesn't discount things simply because they seem unconnected. According to Wikipedia, 'thinking outside the box is a metaphor which means to think differently, unconventionally, or from a new perspective.'

A mindset that assumes ideas are carved in stone leads to actions that linger within the box. On the other hand, a mindset that assumes new ideas can be explored differently takes us down an entirely different trajectory of possibilities, discoveries, innovations and success. Thinking outside the box is the ability to develop ideas that are different and unusual. It is the openness not to stubbornly persist on your own opinion and the willingness to change your opinion when another person proves you to be wrong or mistaken. Even though it sounds simple, many people stubbornly persist in their own opinions and linger only within their own box for the rest of their lives. Being oppressed by your own mind is the worst kind of oppression.

According to blogger Steve Mueller: 'Thinking outside the box would mean that you cast off the atmosphere that envelops you, step out of the box, leave all your experiences, mindsets and attitudes behind and start to view things from a completely different perspective. Outside the box thinking is unfiltered, unbiased, open for suggestions, willing to empathize with others opinions, but also ready to swim against the flood and to think what no one else has ever thought of. It also means that you abandon everything you thought you knew, everything that was taught to you in school, and start to approach specific situations and problems from a completely different point of view.'

In a world that is increasingly polarised economically, there simply won't be as many jobs to go around. A lot of people will find their job prospects dimmed and wages squeezed. Depending only on the traditional way of success which for centuries has been attached to having a 'job' will leave many deeply disappointed. Retrenchment is fast becoming the order of the day. As a result, a mindset revolution is needed. Develop the ability to look at things differently from the way you typically look at things. Sometimes when you are losing in a game you have to stop playing by the rules, switch it up, and change the game itself. Instead of waiting for a job, you can turn your unique strengths or academic qualifications into a thriving business venture.

With regard to retrenchments and job losses, the solution is not to protest and burn properties but to reprogramme our mindsets and think outside the box. Protest actions will only accelerate the shift from human workers to computers. As we are already aware, robots don't go on strike, burn things or skip work, thereby causing millions of dollars' worth of losses to an organisation.

Do not take facts presented to you by family, friends, teachers, professors and experts as the one and only truth.

Times have changed! Don't depend on any politician or government to fix your life. Don't depend on any organisation to employ you and keep you till retirement bells rings. The only way in which any government can help its people is through education. Relevant education will give you an excellent opportunity to future-proof your skills. The school system should foster individual talents and creativity as these will set humans apart from computers. But while the education system is yet to catch up with this reality and reform itself, you should get the ball rolling in your own life through self-education and personal development.

Make it a habit to question things and discover new and better solutions or facts about life, business or career. Thinking outside the box gives you the freedom to change your point of view. For example, 'the glass is half full' would then be an improved version of 'the glass is half empty'. Apply this change in thinking in today's world and you'll see opportunities are everywhere.

Outside-the-box thinkers question things and do not accept things as predetermined straight away. Thinking outside the box means that you do not follow given instructions and mandatory paths. This might be a daunting task for those with a dependency mindset who always rely on instructions, policies, the media or people's opinions to get things done. Some people prefer the pleasure of working with whatever ideology is presented to them. But if you are to grow, do not take facts presented to you by family, friends, teachers, professors and experts as the one and only truth. Be curious!

Outside-the-box thinking is a deliberate decision to challenge the status quo and revolutionise your thinking. Let your gaze wander through your environment to discover all the new things you haven't noticed before. If you are sitting in your house you could pick up whatever object looks interesting to you and discover it all over again. You might notice something different about the object that you haven't noticed before. In this way, you can step into another world to discover insights that before had remained completely unknown to you.

Stepping into another world in this way will generally allow you to look at problems differently, which will also increase the possibility of new solutions beginning to emerge. You can step into another world by meeting new people or studying something outside your academic qualifications and certificates. Some people have never read anything outside the school curriculum and as a result of their ensuing rigidity, they end up being obsolete.

Major Pitfalls to Avoid: Entitlement and Victim Mindset

Entitlement is the idea that you deserve or are owed something or are in some way privileged or superior. This type of thinking is a dream killer. It manifests itself in several ways. Maybe you are expecting to get a raise or a promotion at work, recognition for an achievement, or money from your parents/friends to start a business. Expectations of this sort are entitlements. They strangle growth, innovation, success and personal transformation. Instead of actively seeking improvement, the entitled are usually too busy waiting for rewards, handouts or recognition. It's not a bad thing to get these things but it's hideous to put your life on hold if you don't get them.

Entitlement is a mindset but never forget that you have the freedom to choose how you experience and interpret life. There are lots of people in our world today plagued by the 'gimme, gimme, gimme' attitude. It is necessary to ask yourself if you are a part of this group. Do you perhaps feel that the world owes you something? Do you perhaps feel entitled to the good treasures of life? Do you think the world owes you happiness, fairness, shelter, friends, etc? The sooner you come to terms with the fact that nobody owes you anything, the sooner you will take your life into your own hands and begin to chart a course for yourself.

You shape your own world! Yes, you are the power tool that shapes your own world. You might have been programmed by society that things are to be handed to you, that for example the government is supposed to give you a job, a house, electricity, food, or that your family owes you a good life. But in actual fact, you are the architect of your own life. You can overcome all self-imposed assumptions and provoke a mindset revolution that will transform your life. A person who is crippled by a sense of entitlement waits for recognition or reward instead of actively seeking solutions to the problems by which they are confronted. As Bono, the musician and businessman, once said, 'The world is more malleable than you think and it is waiting for you to hammer it into shape.'

> An entitled person waits for recognition or reward instead of actively seeking solutions to their problems.

A victim mindset on the other hand is just as counterproductive as an entitlement mindset. It stifles progress. A victim mentality is a psychological term that refers to a type of dysfunctional mindset which seeks to feel persecuted in order to gain attention or avoid self-responsibility. When you carry a victim mindset, you are basically filtering your entire existence through a narrow mental lens that you have adopted as your primary way of perceiving the world. People who struggle with the victim mentality are convinced that life is not only beyond their control, but is out to deliberately hurt them. This belief results in constant blame, pain, finger-pointing, and pity parties that are fuelled by negativity, distrust, fear and anger. Simply put, having a victim mindset means that you blame other people and circumstances for the unhappiness you feel and any failure you've experienced in your life.

Maybe you were sexually abused as a child, raped, abandoned, ignored, betrayed, rejected, mocked or emotionally and physically abused by someone you loved, or have been a victim of human trafficking, starvation or war. These are horrible things that can happen to anyone. But healing is possible if you can shift your perspective on life. Whatever your case might be, your own long-term response to them can make or break your life. As Joyce Meyer, an American preacher and author, once said, 'You can be powerful or you can be pitiful but you can't be both.'

While it's important that you come to terms with what happened to you, you cannot move on with your life unless you step out of the victim role and into the survivor role. What happened might have been so horrible you feel you have every right to hold onto your anger, but responsibility lies with you to use your own power and reclaim your life. It's okay to feel angry, but it's healthier to let go. You cannot start the next chapter of your life, if you keep re-reading the old one.

> Listening to a survivor is more refreshing and inspiring than listening to a victim wallowing in blame and self-pity.

A victim argues with life, a survivor embraces it. A victim dwells in the past, a survivor lives in the present. Victims believe they're helpless; survivors take back control over their lives. Although the victim mentality can be addictive, the survivor mentality is much more empowering in the long run. Once you start seeing yourself as a survivor, you'll begin to feel better about life and you'll attract other people for the right reasons. Listening to a survivor is more refreshing and inspiring than listening to a victim wallowing in blame and self-pity.

Most people harbouring a victim mindset refuse to turn to themselves for help. But, in fact, you are the hero you are looking for. Step out of the victim role. Be kind and compassionate to yourself. Practise being sincerely thankful, even for the smallest things. Gratitude can save you from drowning in self-pity. Change your mindset and invite positive good things into your life with the right words. Use affirmations. Whatever comes after the words I AM, the mind believes it to be true. So, use the power of I AM to rescue yourself. For example, 'I am amazing, I AM extraordinary, I AM creative, I AM beautiful inside and out, I AM enough, I AM wealthy, etc.' The choice of words you use to describe yourself will ultimately shape your reality. If your choice of words sounds something like 'I am not smart like others, I am not good at this or that, I am very slow, etc.' these descriptions cannot empower you. You can transform your life by changing what you say about yourself and how you think.

As Bob Moawad, a prolific author, said: 'The best day of your life is the one on which you decide your life is your own. No apologies or excuses; nobody to lean on, rely on, or blame. The gift is yours – it is an amazing journey – and you alone are responsible for the quality of it. This is the day your life really begins.'

Victims often carry with them a list of possible explanations as to why their life is the way it is. They blame the government, their parents, friends, the weather, taxes, inflation, the media, interest rates, the economy, immigrants, negative relatives, their bosses, company policies, and their salaries. But it is not circumstances that define the person you become. It is your choices! You become weaker not stronger when you keep blaming other people or circumstances. Everyone has the power to fight back when at their lowest point. As the saying goes: 'Rock bottom has created more champions than privilege.'

The opportunity to live an extraordinary life lies in chaos rather than in bland normality. As William Arthur Ward, a poet and writer, once said: 'It is wise to direct your anger towards problems not people. It is wise to focus your energies on answers not excuses.'

What really matters is not what happened to you but what happened *in* you. Nothing on earth has as much power to make a choice as an individual human being does. Be a willing participant in whatever goes on in your life. No one magically wakes up successful with no idea how it happened. The world is waiting for your appearance as a courageous person. The world won't care otherwise. So, don't be a victim. Your pain, conflict and heartache are challenges that can be turned into lessons to shape the world for the better. With your contributions the world won't be the same. Your struggles are the platform through which some people will experience healing.

As black American poet Maya Angelou has said, 'Someone was hurt before you, rejected before you, mocked before you, wronged before you, was hungry before you, frightened before you, abused before you, humiliated before you, betrayed before you, raped before you. Yet, someone survived. You can do anything you choose to do.'

Yes, it's hard growing up without a father or a mother; it's hard growing up without basic education or basic needs. It is hard being a single parent. It is hard fighting an illness that has invaded your body or an addiction that has taken over your life. It is hard getting over abuse or rape. It is hard getting over the death of a loved one – but it's not impossible. You can rise above your circumstances. What destroys some also makes others to shine. Listen to Joyce Meyer one more time: 'You can be powerful or you can be pitiful but you can't be both.'

Lack of a formal education is a death sentence to some and an opportunity to explore for others. Divorce or a breakup can be the end for one and the beginning for another. Pain is the reason some are so broken, bitter and angry but also the reason some are so powerful and successful. Learn to make lemonade out of the lemons life throws at you. Nothing is more powerful than a man or woman determined to rise.

Steve Maraboli wrote, 'Today is a new day. Don't let your history interfere with your destiny! Let today be the day you stop being a victim of your circumstances and start taking action towards the life you want. You have the power and the time to shape your life. Break free from the poisonous victim mentality and embrace the truth of your greatness. You were not meant for a mundane or mediocre life. Do not dilute the truth of your potential. We often convince ourselves that we cannot change, that we cannot overcome the circumstances of our lives. That is simply not true. You have been blessed with immeasurable power to make positive changes in your life. But you can't just wish it, you can't just hope it, you can't just want it. You have to live it, be it and do it.'

The Story of William Kamkwamba

William Kamkwamba, a Malawian self-taught engineer, is a perfect example of one who did not allow himself to become a victim of circumstances. At 14 years old, William dropped out of school due to poverty. Though his parents could not afford his school, his mind did not stop working. While his friends were at school, William decided to use his mind, his time, his hands and his curiosity at trying new things at home. He was not in the classroom, but he nevertheless began his journey onto the world stage. William continued to think, dream and learn new ways to improve his life outside the classroom.

An awakening took place in his mind. Armed with curiosity, determination and a book he discovered in a nearby library, William embarked on an audaciously daring plan to build a windmill to provide electricity to his parents' home. He eventually built an electricity-producing windmill from spare parts and scrap parts. His windmill did not only provide electricity, but also provided water to his home in rural Malawi. Since then, he has built a solar-powered water pump that supplied the first drinking water in his village and two other windmills.

William's windmill attracted international attention. He spoke about his grit and invention on *TED Talk*. His story was chronicled in the 2013 award-winning feature-length documentary titled 'William and the Windmill' He also wrote a book, an autobiography, titled *The Boy who Harnessed the Wind,* which was selected as a required book for all incoming students at the Auburn University, Alabama, United States. William's remarkable story is being turned in to movie. The film, set to debut on *Netflix* early 2019, was shot in Malawi.

You too can turn your wounds into wisdom!

Reinvent Yourself

As economic change accelerates, so must the pace of your own personal strategic renewal. Challenge subconscious beliefs that may be holding you back from living your full potential. The only person whose life doesn't need change is the one whose life is dead. You ought to build within yourself a revolutionary advantage. For most people, profound change is almost always crisis driven. People resist change until breaking point and that's where change becomes convulsive, traumatic, episodic and often expensive. But you can initiate your own disruption and change ahead of the curve without the force of crisis breathing down your neck.

We live in an era where giant companies can topple almost overnight. Brands like *Nokia* and *Blackberry* were once household names but today little to nothing is heard of them. Don't wait till retrenchment knocks at your door, don't wait till your company files for bankruptcy, don't wait till your boss hands you that dreadful letter, don't wait till you have a robot for a colleague before you start thinking about reinventing yourself.

Do something outside the norm, learn a skill within or outside your academic qualification. Be more open-minded to opportunities around you. Facing your inner self is an exercise you can no longer avoid if you truly desire change. Change is one of the hardest things any of us will ever try to do. It needs a deeper level of self-awareness to successfully transition.

Are you happy with your life? If the answer is no, that's a clue that reinventing yourself is critical. An unhappy person cannot be productive or creative. Your personal power is unleashed when your emotions and purpose are in alignment. Look within yourself and see which areas of your life are crying out for change. As the great Russian novelist, Leo Tolstoy, once wrote: 'Everyone thinks of changing the world but no one thinks of changing himself.'

Allow these questions to guide you as you embark on reinventing yourself:

- Are you living to your fullest potential?
- Are you living with a version of yourself that has lost the zeal for life and is downright depressed and unhappy?
- Who are you becoming?
- What is the one thing you would hope to change about yourself?

Reinventing yourself is about personal transformation and becoming the person you truly want to be. As American essayist and philosopher, Ralph Waldo Emerson, once said 'What lies behind us and what lies before us are tiny matters compared to what lies within us.'

One way to reinvent yourself is to play to your strengths. Again, consider the following questions:

- What are you good at? Be honest and really give yourself a hard look over.
- What are the attributes that will help you achieve your success or whatever your desired outcome is?
- What are the attributes you admire in others that you wish you had?
- What are the challenges that limit your ability to change?
- What vision do you have for your life?

More often than not, I hear people complaining about lack of support and external resources. However, the key to success is never in finding external resources but in being resourceful. Don't allow your attention to dwell on what you lack. Don't complain about lack of education, certificates, money, lack of family support, or any of the lacks that stop people from stepping out. Simply look for ways you can become more resourceful and valuable.

Being more resourceful will give you access to the things you thought you lacked before. Look deep within yourself, what can you pull out from within that can benefit you and others? You might be naturally gifted in something. Reinventing yourself is all about creating value for yourself where it didn't exist before. No matter the circumstances you were born with or born into, you can reinvent yourself and create massive value for yourself and for those around you.

The internet is a school on its own. What skills have you always admired or desired to have? You might just be a *Google* search away from learning it. The more things you try, the more skills you learn and the more valuable you become. Yesterday is too expensive for you to buy but if you make the necessary changes today, tomorrow can be yours.

Throughout your life, you yourself will remain your greatest project. The goal is not to be better than anyone but to be better than the person you used to be. Reinventing yourself is not about conforming to society's norms or trying to meet someone's expectations of you, but to make sure you are in alignment with your purpose. Sometimes, when you are trying to make a positive change in your life, the voices in your head will not be in agreement, but you have to make the conscious decision to keep going. You'll question yourself as to why you have to take an online course, or watch *YouTube* tutorials, or read books or attend seminars. As the old adage says: 'The toughest battle is over self; old habits die hard.' When you're on a journey to personal transformation, the old version of yourself might come swinging at you like Muhammad Ali in his prime, but be ready and put on your gloves.

Be willing to do something you've never done before if you want something you've never had. Instead of reading romance novels, read books on personal development; instead of watching music videos laced with nudity and vulgarity, watch motivational videos; instead of attending musical concerts, attend seminars and workshops. Instead of partying every weekend, attend business networking events and associate with great minds. That's reinvention. Write affirmative notes and stick them on your mirror or wall. Make a dream board, write down your vision and speak it out loud.

Where do you see yourself in five years? Do you plan on quitting your job to embark on your dreams? If yes, when? Be specific about what you want and when you want it. Just like you can never fully realise the power of water when it's standing still, same goes for you when you're standing still. Don't limit yourself because of fear, or because of people's opinions or insecurities. Move! Be like liquid and enter into space. You don't necessarily have to change your environment. Change starts from within.

You can completely reinvent yourself and create a new wave of existence and meaning for your life. You can rise from anything. Nothing is permanent except death. You can think new thoughts. You can learn new things. You can take up new hobbies. You can create new habits. All you have to do is decide today and never look back. Instead of saying 'I can't do it' why not ask 'how can I do it?' Instead of 'I don't have the money' why not ask, 'how can I raise the money?' When you say you can't, your brain shuts down. But when you ask 'how?', it puts your brain to work. Solutions begin at the how!

> Success happens when you change, not when other people change.

You can transition from one form of life to another. It may take a period of cocooning yourself, a time of withdrawal so that you can regroup and begin to build yourself a new foundation. But when the time is right and you emerge from your cocoon, you'll be a complete new person. You'll be unstoppable! You'll be able to spread your magnificent wings and fly into the vistas of your own design. The journey to reinventing yourself is not a one-time fix but a constant consistent action. You're going to slip off your action agenda a dozen, even a hundred, times. But if you keep going, one day you will meet the person you are busy becoming. Success happens when you change, not when other people change!

My Personal Disruption and Reinvention

Most people think of disruption only in relation to business, but it is best and even safe to think of yourself as your own business enterprise so that you can use disruptive thinking and actions to thrive and flourish. Di$rupt yourself and step into the life of your dreams – or at the very least, set the wheels in motion.

Now I would like to tell you my personal story. I am a product of the self-disruption and reinvention I've been talking about in this book. As I have said, there are the high achievers and the average Joes and Jills, those who take action and those who merely dream, those who make things happen and those who wish for things to happen, and they are all mixed together in the melting pot of life. Which one are you? For many years, I was the latter. As an adult, my life was twisting along and I felt lost in the path of nothingness; barely reaching the speed limit on my journey to nowhere.

I was caught between unhappiness, accepting whatever was thrown at me, pleasing people, following conventions, conforming and going through life on auto-pilot. But a time came when the feeling of dread became unbearable. I knew something was missing. I had a deep hunger for something but had no idea what. I couldn't discuss my emptiness or hunger with anyone for fear 'that no one will understand'. Life was unfair, stagnant, and devoid of purpose. And so, I did what normal people do: I decided to go back to school. Finally I can have bragging rights of going to the university too, I secretly thought with a smile on my face. My family and friends were thrilled with the decision. 'It's the right thing to do,' they reassured me. Well, it's what my peers were doing. I didn't know any better. There was so much chaos in my life at the time. And so going back to school was the perfect escape.

In hindsight, that decision was the beginning of self-disruption for me. What I do today is not related to those three years at the university, but taking that step to actually do something with my life opened a whole new world for me. However, things got worse than I'd anticipated.

I got retrenched the same year I completed my studies. So much for going back to school, I sighed! My new diploma couldn't save me from retrenchment. Once again, I was lost in the abyss of nothingness. My hopes were dashed against the wall. Instead of searching for another job, I made the painful decision to part ways with the corporate world. I disrupted myself again. One thing led to another and the rest is history. I fell in love with entrepreneurship, I fell in love with writing, I found my purpose and today you are reading my book that came as a result of chaotic circumstances and my own personal disruption. Since then, I've had the opportunity to meet great people, speak at conferences, business seminars, and have my voice on radio. I interact, engage and empower thousands of people on the internet across the continent of Africa via my *Blog (www.nickyverd.africa)* and social media platforms. And this is only the beginning of my journey.

My story might look rather cute in retrospect, but you should have seen me back then. I was a mess – and then I reinvented myself.

The Story of Helen Keller

Through the centuries many people have reinvented themselves, but if there is a person in the history of humankind who has shown us the power of rising above circumstances even when all odds are against you – that person is Helen Keller. Helen was born in Alabama at the end of the 19th century. She was born a healthy child with no complications or physical disabilities but when she was sixteen months old, she developed an illness that left her deaf and blind. Very few people believed there was any future for young Helen, not even Helen herself. What kind of future would she have being deaf and blind? Helen became a very wild and unruly child as she grew but her life started to change when her parents brought a woman named Anne Sullivan to be her private tutor.

Anne Sullivan believed in Helen and not only did she teach her extraordinary ways to read and write but also taught her to believe in herself and reinvent her thinking. She taught her that there was nothing impossible if she could tap into her inner abilities. As a consequence of this extraordinary encounter with Anne Sullivan and the revolutionary shift in mindset, Helen changed her negative outlook on life. She took her future into her own hands and went on to become the first woman in history to graduate with an Honours Degree from

Harvard University and first deaf-blind person to earn a Bachelor of Arts degree. Sullivan's extraordinary work then became the blueprint for teaching the deaf-blind to this day.

Helen went on to become a powerful woman in history who authored great books, fought for the rights of physically disabled people and lectured throughout the world. Helen Keller was appointed Counsellor of International Relations for the American Foundation of Overseas Blind. She was honoured around the world and harvested many awards for her achievements including the Presidential Medal of Freedom and election to the Women's Hall of Fame. She associated with world leaders, presidents and some of the greatest people of her time, including Mark Twain, Andrew Carnegie, Eleanor Roosevelt, Albert Einstein, Henry Ford and Alexander Graham Bell. Through her many speeches and appearances, Keller brought inspiration and encouragement to millions of people around the world. By overcoming her adversity with a great deal of persistence, she grew into a respected and world-renowned activist who laboured for the betterment of others.

One day in an interview, a news reporter asked her: 'Ms Keller, is there anything worse than being blind?' She answered: 'Yes, the only thing worse than being blind is having sight but no vision.' Before her death her name had become a worldwide symbol of what the human spirit can accomplish despite severe physical limitations. Her legacy still lives on. Some great quotes are attributed to Ms Keller. My two favourites are: 'What I am looking for is not out there, it is in me,' and 'Avoiding danger is no safer in the long run than outright exposure. The fearful are caught as often as the bold.'

Chapter 5

PAY ATTENTION TO THAT NAGGING FEELING

Once upon a time, back in high school, you were the best athlete, best dancer, best poet, best writer, best public speaker, best comedian, best in cooking, best soccer player, best in design and art, etc. Then you left school and held onto a certificate. A certificate that had nothing to do with your talents. Why? Because society says 'go to school, get a certificate and get a job'. Why? Because your friends got the certificate, got the job and you also want to fit in. But why? Because your family says it's embarrassing for you to be a comedian, a photographer, a writer, or a dancer.

And so you've convinced yourself that people will think you are weird if you take the road less travelled or follow your heart. For this rather flimsy reason, you've abandoned your God-given talents, talents that could've put you on the world map. You decided to 'fit in' and be 'normal' but there is that nagging feeling in the gut that keeps saying you don't belong here. There is a voice inside screaming at you to step into the world and be heard.

But you are now in a job you hate. You feel sick just thinking about going to work. Sometimes, you get to work and instead of going in straight, you drive around the building because you don't even want to get into that office. You're at constant war with yourself and the people around you. Happiness has become a foreign concept. You are paying the biggest price for silencing your calling. You have no inner peace. You bought yourself a nice car and a nice house. You even got yourself a nice spouse and you have produced really nice children. Yet you're still feeling empty inside.

To the rest of the world, you're an epitome of success but deep down you feel lost and unfulfilled. You feel as though your identity has been stripped away and all you're left with is a name tag – a lawyer, a teacher, a nurse, a doctor, a manager, a supervisor, etc. But still, you'd rather conform than di$rupt the status quo. A salary has aborted many dreams and slaughtered a great many more first class talents. But if your biggest dream in life was to have a job and earn a salary then nothing has been aborted. However, if you long for more, then it's time to start paying attention to that nagging feeling, because no number of awards, luxuries or accomplishments can fill that void or silence that nagging voice.

> A salary has aborted many dreams and slaughtered a great many more first class talents.

Maybe your case is different. Maybe you don't have such a nice problem as to have a job you hate. You actually wish you had the job – at least it'd pay the bills. You wish you had a boss you could curse in your heart and colleagues you could gossip about all day. You've visualised the day you'll finally update your social media status with 'Hey guys, I got the job' and phone home to give your family the long-awaited good news. You want to wipe that smug expression off the face of your ex and everyone else who taunted you for being unemployed. You've applied for jobs even outside your academic qualifications, you've prayed, you've sowed seed, you've shouted in church 'I receive', you've attended interviews, you've cried, you've laughed, you've given up, you've joined the queue again and again, yet you remain an unemployment statistic.

> Pay attention to your calling and the world will pay attention to you.

What's wrong? You secretly wonder! You did as you were told from childhood: 'go to school, get the certificate, and get the job'. Why doesn't this formula seem to be working? Well, it seems someone lied. Society is not always right. You are gifted, you have great potential – why are you only holding on to a certificate? A job is just one way to success; it's not the only way. You could've been far down the pathway to success if you'd put that energy of looking for a job into your talents or some other ventures. We all have talents and dreams that fall outside society's definition of 'normal success'. Many people with great potential are sitting on their talents. We've been programmed from childhood that the only way to make a living is to go to school, get a certificate and get a job. This might have been true 200 years ago, but it's no longer the case. Times have changed. Machines are now employable and companies are doing more with fewer employees ... hence the rise in retrenchments.

Whether you are employed or not, the new way to success is to embrace your individual unique abilities and giftedness. Don't drown yourself in the ocean of certificates, conformity and societal norms. The cubicle is not for everyone. Some were called to stand out. Your passion, creativity and gifts will make room for you and bring you before great men and women. Even if you are in the cubicle, have something else going on the side. Some have built empires and great ventures while holding a job in one hand and their passion in the other. Pay attention to the rhythm of your soul, pay attention to those nudges: they are divine inspiration calling you out into greatness. Pay attention to your calling and the world will pay attention to you.

The challenge with corporate life is that creativity, dreams, talents and innovation can easily get locked-up in the closet. The rule of thumb is 'do as you are told' – but not everyone is built to follow this rule. The average workplace is a buzz killer. Petty rules, pedestrian goals and pyramidal structures drain the emotional vitality and creativity out of people. Maybe that didn't matter in the old economy, but it does matter enormously in the creative and innovative economy we're moving into now. Being forbidden to use your brain is suicidal. Fulfilment, happiness and influence are the fruits of a righteous discontent with the status quo. If you are educated with the best certificates from the best universities, but you are not exercising your unique individual talents, you're probably going to be miserable. You might end up being depressed, burned out and unfulfilled if you ignore the nagging feeling that keeps calling you towards your purpose. Most people hate Mondays simply because they are guilty of trading in their talents for a salary.

Most people are not happy with their lives, yet they are out with friends every weekend. If you are not happy with your life, what exactly are you celebrating every weekend? For some, partying is a temporary escape from the emptiness they feel inside, while others are just preoccupying themselves with normal daily stuff like breakfast, going to work, having lunch, getting home, cooking, watching TV, and going to bed. This is living in auto-pilot mode and it's where the majority of the world resides.

According to statistics, people who start life from the platform of their talents find more fulfilment than those who start life from the platform of their academic qualifications. There is more inside you than you think, but you won't know just how much until you slow down and ask yourself some deep questions like: Who am I? Why am I here?

Who Are You?

Who are you? Many people dread this question, especially those who have opted to conform. Some choose to live in the shadows while others choose to do what they think is right so as to be most accepted by their peers. But who are you? Seriously, this is one of life's most important questions. What usually bubble up as answers are the labels that society and the culture have piled on us, like: wife, mother, husband, boyfriend, girlfriend, son, daughter, etc. But these are just labels very similar to the titles we use when people ask about us and we start to describe what we do. I am an engineer, a manager, an accountant, a doctor, a teacher, a nurse, etc. But is that really who we are?

Mark Twain, the great American writer, lecturer and publisher, said: 'The two most important days of your life are the day you were born and the day you find out why.'

As humans, rarely do we ask 'WHO AM I?' Rather we are always asking 'who are you'? We are more interested in knowing about other people than knowing ourselves. More often than not, this is because we are afraid to face our own truth. We are afraid of how friends, family, society will react if the answer is different from what they've told us about ourselves.

But wait. Aren't you tired of living in the shadows? Do you have the courage to ask the person in the mirror: Who are you? Real freedom lies in knowing yourself!

Who are you? Usually when faced with this question hundreds of thoughts run through the mind. 'Should I say my name? Should I refer to what I do for a living? Or the family I come from?' But the real answer to this question can only be unearthed through self-discovery. Self-discovery is the hunt to find the treasure buried deep inside you. It is the process of getting to know who you really are and not who you've been told you are and certainly not what your certificate says you are. To truly answer this question, you need to look deep within yourself to discover things about you that make you unique, different and special. Failure to embark on the pilgrimage of self-discovery will cheat you of an opportunity to know what you really want out of life, as well as how you can add value to others during your time here on earth.

Self-discovery is for individuals willing to question themselves, their beliefs and their inner structures and, most importantly, to find the answers for themselves. Self-discovery allows you to burst through self-imposed restrictions, tackle issues you were once afraid to admit even to yourself and discover the person you truly are. Self-discovery allows you to break free from social conditioning that can so easily create self-loathing and self-rejection. Only by seeing yourself as that small core of life right at your very centre can you discover your unique soul-print.

For some people, self-discovery can happen entirely by accident, usually through some tragic event or extraordinary challenge. For others, it requires a conscious solo journey deep into themselves. You came into this world naked, but you did not come empty. You were carrying something great within you: it was your inbuilt purpose. Finding your purpose can be a painful process or it can be almost like a spiritual revelation. What is important to understand is that it stands as a central duty to all of us. It is more than a duty; it is our uniquely human privilege that should never be neglected.

People who neglect to find their purpose and discover who they truly are end up searching for themselves in the wrong places. Some scratch about in extra-marital affairs, some search for themselves in the bottle, some search in drugs, some search in acquiring multiple certificates and academic qualifications. Some search on gambling tables, some search in nightclubs and all sorts of places. But this form of searching only increases their emptiness and widens the hole in their hearts. Rest assured that life has more meaning for any man or woman who has found the deep purpose in their lives and is walking towards fulfilling it.

You can use the following questions as a guide to discover what sets you apart as you take the journey into yourself:

- What makes you tick?
- What makes you come alive?
- What wakes you up?
- What do others say about you?
- What do you want in life?
- What compliments do you shrug off?
- What are your non-negotiable core values in life?
- What are you willing to fight for?
- Do you like to connect with people?
- What are you a natural at?
- What life did you dream of as a child?
- What are you most afraid of?
- Does the life you are currently living feels like it belongs to someone else?

Answering these questions honestly requires digging deep into your shadows or childhood experiences and revealing deep-seated beliefs that have shaped you – for good or bad – until the present. Everyone has to discover their purpose in life for themselves. So, get a diary and write answers to the above questions. Doing so will help you discover your unique soul-print. Marianne Williamson, an author and entrepreneur, once said, 'It takes more courage to endure the sharp pains of self-discovery than to choose to take the dull pain of unconsciousness that could last for the rest of our lives.'

It is only through self-discovery that you can identify your purpose and actualise your potential. Purpose is not a mystery. Most people are very much aware of their purpose. It haunts them every day. Hence I urge you to pay attention to that nagging feeling. Purpose is always nearby. It's been hanging around the fringes for years waiting for you to gather the courage and strength and energy to tackle it with two hands and with your whole heart.

Personally, I didn't always know I wanted to be a writer who connects with people in a meaningful way. I stumbled into my purpose when my world fell apart, as mentioned in the previous section. I was going through one of the most devastating periods in my life. Writing became a way to escape my suffering, but I soon discovered it offered freedom to others and tremendous fulfilment to my soul. I've never looked back ever since.

Studies show that 'A sense of purpose makes you more resilient, improves health, increases life satisfaction and, according to one medical study, even helps people with chronic conditions feel less distressed.' *Pew Research* found that: 'People who said they had a sense of purpose lived longer than those who didn't – regardless of what age they found their purpose.' Do you still need any more convincing to find your purpose?

'Your calling will never stop calling.' -TC Maila

Everyone has a purpose. It is your responsibility to find out what that purpose is. Your purpose is embedded in the thoughts that keep coming back even after 40 years. Firmness of purpose and finding it is one of the most necessary muscles of success. Without it, geniuses waste their efforts in a confusing pathway of inconsistency. Having purpose gives you direction. Purpose decides the friends you keep, chooses who you date or marry. Purpose decides which books you read and the TV programmes you watch. Purpose gives you something to look forward to and to yearn for – a reason for being. As TC Maila, a South African travel photographer, once said 'Your calling will never stop calling.'

Try different things or hobbies. Paint, draw, colour, cook, read, sing, write, sketch, knit, craft, build, code, deep-dive, research, volunteer in your community, meditate, do gym, take pictures, start a business, travel, etc. Try new things and soon your real passion or purpose in life will start to reveal itself to you.

Things fall into place even when your purpose is bigger than you and has an impact that is way beyond self-serving. It feels effortless, like it's the most natural thing in the world for you to do. It shouldn't be something forced. People who force things are those who hate what they do. Once you sink into your purpose and are deeply in love with what you do, you'll be absolutely amazed at how your life shifts and how incredibly new doors open up. Opportunities you hadn't dared to even dream of suddenly fall within reach. When you find your purpose, everything changes, like it seemingly happened out of nowhere, but the more you reflect on it, the more it makes absolute sense. It'd be exactly what you'd been unconsciously building towards your entire life.

The career you chose, the skills you learnt, the mess-ups you made, the failures you faced, the betrayals, the heartbreaks, the rejections and everything else you've experienced haven't been wasted. Every little thing you have worked at, started, experienced, loved, learnt from and been challenged by: all of these experiences were meant to be, culminating together in one perfect bundle to form your purpose.

Never dislike anyone or any experiences you've had on your journey. So what if you wasted 10 years in a job you hated? Who cares if you took the wrong career path or chose the wrong university degree? So what if your relationship or marriage didn't work out? So what if the one you thought was the one walked out on you? So what if you were betrayed by someone you trusted? So what if you had a bad childhood or your parents abandoned you? Stop feeling sorry for yourself or wishing things were different. Everything that happened was meant to happen so that you could arrive at where you are today.

Sometimes struggles, agony, and hardships are exactly what you need so that you can grow. Pain is meant to produce purpose, not kill it. Man was created and programmed to live creatively and with purpose. The most miserable and bankrupt people in the world are not the poor or even the penniless, but those living lives without purpose. What do you stand for? Forget what other people say about you. The million-dollar question is, what do you say about yourself? If someone were to hack into your heart, what will immediately stand out? To answer these questions and find your purpose, you have to di$rupt yourself and overturn conventions. Personal disruption is an integral part of finding your purpose. Identify what you do well. Identify what you do particularly well – even if it's outside your certificate. Or maybe you are one of the few whose academic qualifications are in sync with their life's purpose. This could be in any field whatsoever. For instance, what a joy if your training was in writing or speaking and then you discover that this is also your purpose!

You don't necessarily need to be an entrepreneur. You could be a stay-at-home parent, a teacher, a sportsperson, an artist, a writer, or an employee in the corporate world. The key is that you should feel that your contributions, whatever they are, in your corner of the world, matter and help to impact someone's life in a positive way.

Are you still struggling to pinpoint your purpose? Try imagining conducting your own funeral. I mean in a positive way. Ask yourself, when all is said and done and you've breathed your last breath, what will people remember you for? What legacy will you leave behind? Are you currently doing something that will outlive you? What will people say about you? What contributions or difference would you have made in this world? These are big questions that can be very difficult to ask and even more difficult to answer. But you can't avoid them if you truly want to live a purposeful life. While the answers can be uncomfortably revealing, they can also be incredibly empowering. That's because the best thing about imagining your own funeral now is that you are still alive and have the power to change things. Don't waste a single day living someone else's life. Find your purpose, discover your unique soul-print and live a meaningful life. Your heart is beating on purpose and so should you.

Find an Outlet for Your Talent

We are hearing a lot about doom-and-gloom surrounding the future of jobs, but who's at risk? Well, the honest truth is that everyone is at risk, not just warehouse workers, manual labourers or cashiers but, as we have seen, so are office workers, accountants, lawyers, inspectors, doctors, etc. Even bartenders and chefs should be on the lookout as cocktail mixing robots and kitchen robot-chefs are entering the market.

However, this is not doom but an opportunity to tap into your creative side. There is an increase in demand for creative skills as machines invade the workforce. When was the last time you had the opportunity to really use your brain at work? I'm talking about actual creative brains, not simply the application of mundane tasks. Most jobs require a series of steps and actions that have to follow a certain standard and pattern. Using your own brains (creativity) is usually frowned upon.

You are now a human resource manager but you were a singer before you ever heard the words human resource. You were a great poet, writer, singer, athlete, etc. What happened?

Dr Wayne W Dyer, in his book *The Power of Intention,* writes: 'If you bring forth what is inside you, what you bring forth will save you. If you don't bring forth what is inside you, what you don't bring forth will destroy you.'

A lot of people go to work every day, they clock in, clock out and never have a moment of happiness. But what every human being truly wants is to be challenged in such a way that they can feel they are making a difference based on their contributions. This is why following your heart is usually more fulfilling than maintaining the status quo. People like actors, athletes, writers, musicians, etc., generally have a more fulfilled life. Yes, there are miserable ones of course, but generally, people who start life from the platform of their talent are more fulfilled than people who start life from the platform of their certificates. As Maya Angelou said in *I know why the caged bird sings*, 'There is no greater agony than bearing an untold story inside you.'

Statistics show that more and more people are unhappy with their jobs. But if you have a job that you genuinely enjoy then congratulations are in order. You're one of the few lucky ones. Sadly for most people, job fulfilment is a foreign concept and the reasons are different for different people. The big question is if you are not enjoying your job, what are you doing about this dilemma? As Warren Buffet once said, 'Don't settle for anything other than your passion.'

Real financial security and freedom is not in your job but in your passion. Emotional, social, spiritual and financial prosperity lies in your passion. Discover why you are here on earth and be willing to pay the price for it. Some people slave away at their office job or whatever they do for a 'living' but secretly wish for another life. These are the people this book is written for. The people who are not inspired by what they do. They simply bought into society's social contract; but deep down they carry an untold story inside them. It could be in music, sports, writing, business, art, fashion, technology or any type of creative outlet. They long to tell this story and show themselves to the world. There is a soul passion and purpose deep within longing for an outlet but sadly some have chosen to live in the prison of their own creation.

Your life is 100% your responsibility. The act of showing up, engaging and putting your talents to use is the most important activity you can ever engage in. It is not the government's responsibility, your employer's responsibility or your parents' responsibility to make you successful. It is your own responsibility. Do you desire to create something of your own? What do you want to express to the world so badly? Finding an outlet for your talent can bring more joy into your life.

> You can get fired from your job but you can never get fired from your talent.

Jay Shetty while growing up with his middle-class parents had three options: to become a doctor, an engineer or a failure. He chose none of the above. But today, Jay Shetty is regarded as one of the most influential persons on the internet. He was featured on *Forbes* Under 30 in 2017 as a game-changer in the world of media. He is an entrepreneur, an award-winning story teller, host and viral content creator. He achieved all these by following his heart, not his certificates or what his parents wanted. Jay Shetty found an outlet for his talents and gives this simple advice to us all: 'Build a life not a resumé.' Hence, I say one can get fired from one's job but never from one's talent.

In a world that's fast changing, having a talent is more powerful than having even four university degrees. Therefore, allow the talents and dreams in you to leap out into the wild. Giving your talent the attention it craves will ignite a fire in your heart never to be put out again. The power inherent in talent is that it can awaken a wild vein of passion in you that will never go back to sleep. Listen to your intuition, the nagging feeling and the thirst within you. Imagine something bigger for yourself, imagine the change you can bring and the lives you can touch. This is what life is all about, not just surviving and paying bills. Magic happens when you're in alignment with your purpose.

You may ask, why give an outlet to my talents? The answer is because the people who follow their hearts are the ones with an incredible rare spark. It's not what they say, or even how they say it. There is something about them and it's indescribable. It's their energy; it's their aura. It can be argued that everyone has it but most people will never get to know. Conformity and a yearning for security have caused many to lock their talents inside themselves.

Throughout history, you find people who took the road less travelled and stepped into non-traditional paths. These people are sometimes referred to as 'nonconformist'. Their talents, their work, their influence, and their ideas were their heart. These people come from all walks of life, and they have one thing in common – they are unconventional. They are the game-changers, life-changers, path-changers, rule-breakers, thought-leaders, innovators and pioneers.

Pause and think for a moment: who are the most influential people in your own community? Who are the people everyone looks up to? Who are the people you watch on TV, read about in books and see on magazine covers? Are they those who conform and live according to society's script or those who di$rupt? When you begin to stand out, people around you will not understand you, some will think you've gone crazy while others might even avoid you. But that's okay. Greatness is not the product of convenience. Conforming to the status quo is the surest way to live a life of mediocrity and defeat. As Hans F Hansen, a retired football player, once said: 'It takes nothing to join the crowd. It takes everything to stand alone.'

Yes, of course not everyone among us can escape the cubicle. However, I seek to address those whose purpose lies outside the cubicle as well as those whose vocation in life lies outside their academic qualification. As Abraham Lincoln, the 16th president of the United States, once said, 'The dogmas of the quiet past are inadequate to the stormy present. The occasion is piled high with difficulty, and we must rise with the occasion. As our case is new, so we must think anew and act anew. We must disenthrall ourselves, and then we shall save our future.'

The Story of Paul Desmond

'I quit my job and picked up my guitar six years ago and heard all the naysayers said – It's too hard to learn, you will quit after a couple of weeks, you will never be a star, etc. I didn't listen to any of their negativity but followed what was in my heart. I'd finally had the courage to do what I wanted to do since I was a kid. I took lessons and persisted in my passion for music and guitar with a vengeance. Today, I am in my very first rock 'n' roll band at the ripe young age of 50.

'I am living my dream and couldn't be happier than I am at this point in my life. I am having so much fun playing with others and learning along the way. Never say never! Never give up on your dream. I will be playing until I can't anymore. This is what I should have been doing all my life but I wanted to please my family. I tucked my dream away until the pain became unbearable. Whatever life throws at me now, I just look at my guitar and feel the pure bliss that it gives me.'

The Story of Celine Dion

Celine Dion, the youngest of 14 siblings started her music career from a young age (12 years). Her parents saw her gift and nurtured it from an early age. She dropped out of school and informally perfected her English language so it could enhance her music career. Today, she's #6 on Top 10 Richest Musicians in the World and the top wealthiest music artist in Canada of all time after selling over 200 million records! She is known as one of the best female selling artists of all time.

Celine Dion has won countless awards, and has the record for the highest concert residency of all time, where in Las Vegas she can command $500,000 per show and she's performed her 1000th show in Las Vegas in 2016 – take that info and do the math. She is currently richer than both Barbra Streisand and Beyoncé as of 2018. Celine Dion is by far the most influential, committed, talented entertainer, mother and wife of her generation all thanks to the fact that she took the road travelled.

Chapter 6

DI$RUPT YOUR COMFORT ZONE

Greatness is not scripted in comfort. Growth happens when you operate on the edge of your comfort zone. The comfort zone is safe, comfortable, easy and familiar. Most of us are wired to avoid discomfort, but the world we now live in demands that we di$rupt our comfort zones. The biggest move you can make to grow as a person is to step out of your comfort zone. Life begins at the end of your comfort zone. It's sad to see people choose comfort over freedom. Some are not happy where they are but would rather stay there than take a leap of faith into the unknown. The place of discomfort is the place to discover your unique strengths and your power to create a new you.

Become comfortable being uncomfortable. Put yourself in purposeful counter-intuitive situations so you can grow. You can start out with simple non-threatening things like eating at a new restaurant, ordering something from the menu you've never ordered before, learning a new recipe, taking a different road home, adding new and unfamiliar music to your playlist, watching motivation and business seminars on *YouTube* instead of prank videos and movies, reading books outside your normal genre, adding a different flavour to your wardrobe or setting out to make a new friend – and then continue from there.

When you notice that these little changes didn't kill you, you'll realise that there's a lot more of you visible and functioning when you're outside your comfort zone.

There is nothing unique or extraordinary about you if you only operate within the boundaries of what you are comfortable with. So start making changes to your routine life and be willing to fumble through it until you eventually find your way out of the place of comfort. Getting out of your comfort zone is the key to thriving in a world that's fast changing. The world needs people who are on fire about life, not those that have died inside and are now simply awaiting burial.

What have you settled for? Maybe you've got a good job, a good salary, a good car, a good house, a good spouse and good children. Yes, these are definitely great achievements, but don't you want something more? Why limit yourself to basic achievements? Don't you want to write your name in the sands of time and give the world a reason to remember you? History makers operate outside the comfort zone. Disruptors are people willing to move past good to great. Disrupting the status quo fuels creativity, innovation and success.

Do something that stretches you beyond what you are comfortable with. Stretch your mind, spirit and goals. Take hold of that dream in your heart and make it happen. History is staring at you. Your power lies outside the comfort zone. Nurture within yourself a growth mindset that says 'there is more for me' – more life, more love, more money, more houses, more cars, more to learn, more to experience and more to achieve.

Whatever your aim is, keep in mind it is okay to suck at new things. It is okay to sing or dance off-tune. Embrace the flops, the falls, and the challenges that come with stepping outside your comfort zone. You'll get better with time. When you challenge yourself to stretch towards a higher level of your abilities, you also increase your overall well-being. Do not settle for good enough – a good job, good salary, good car, good house, etc. There is more for you out in the world. You can drive a better car than the one you're driving now, you can live in a better house than where you're living now, and you can make an impact on people way beyond your immediate family.

Nothing will change if you don't change. You are the only person who can improve your life and create massive success for yourself. Don't wait on the government, the economy, and certainly not the company you're working for, to change your life. Your potential is limited only by your own imagination. As a man thinketh so is he.

Maybe you are comfortable slaving at a soul wrenching job and eating crumbs. You have convinced yourself it's better than nothing – at least it pays the bills. You are comfortable waking up at 4 am every day to get a taxi at 5 am so you can get to work by 7 am. You are comfortable standing on your feet all day. You are comfortable getting home at night. You live with your family yet you are absent. You are comfortable leaving home while your children are still sleeping and getting back home after they've gone to bed. Perhaps you've convinced yourself that success and a good life are for other people and not you. Someone might have told you this is all you can ever be – and to add salt to injury, you've accepted this as your reality, hence you've settled. But is this really the life you *really* want?

> Walking around isn't proof of life. If everyone that is this dead were to be buried, there wouldn't be enough room for all the graves.

Perhaps your case isn't that of settling for a good enough life or slaving at some soul wrenching job. Perhaps you really have nothing to settle for; no car, no house, no bicycle, no wife, no husband, but still you've settled. You still live at home with your parents. You've got zero plans for the future. You are comfortable sharing one room with your five siblings. You are comfortable queuing for your own share of pension money from your parents. You are comfortable queuing at government offices for social grants. You are comfortable that your children belong to the state and the government is paying for you. You are comfortable washing your clothes with your mother's washing powder. You are comfortable watching your parents' TV and using their Wi-Fi. You are comfortable getting into your mother's kitchen, eating her bread/tea, cornflakes/milk and eggs for breakfast every day. You are comfortable eating lunch and supper that you contribute nothing to. You are living life on other people's budget/plans and you are comfortable with that.

You are grateful that at least you are alive. But walking around isn't proof of life. Life is contained in the battles, the sweats and daily challenges you are able to overcome. Life is contained in facing your struggles head on:

- How long will your aging parents continue to take care of you and the grandchildren you're making almost every Friday?
- How long will you continue to be a weight on your family members?
- How long will you be a liability to the government?

- What plans do you have for your own life?
- When was the last time you did something out of the ordinary?
- When was the last time you pushed yourself or tried something new?
- When was the last time you searched the internet for opportunities that could improve your life?
- When was the last time you learnt a new skill?
- When was the last time you went out hustling?
- What steps are you taking to ensure you step out of your comfort zone?
- When was the last time you worked on your dreams? Wait. Do you even have dreams?

Stop playing poker with your life! Stop blaming the government, the economy, and above all stop making excuses. The more excuses you make, the less progress you make. Stop spending most of your valuable time watching television, listening to music or doing things that add no value to your life. Let go of bad friends, unproductive conversations, idling about, and all the other frivolities you indulge yourself with. Stop leaving life to chance. Instead, begin taking uncomfortable but profitable, practical and productive steps, steps that will be beneficial to you in the near future. This is called intentional living. Step out of your comfort zone. Nothing grows in the comfort zone, not even comfort. Depression, negativity, hopelessness, complaining and sickness are things that flourish in the comfort zone. Everything you want in life lies outside of that toxic comfort zone.

Stop living your life as a joke. You are not here only for entertainment. Think about the next generation, not just about next weekend or next month. Some who are reading this need to start businesses, some need to write books, some need to pursue their music careers, some need to join an athletic club or soccer club or poetry club. You are precious as an individual, and valuable – we should say 'hugely so' – as a member of a group. You are like an enriched seed that is meant to yield bountifully, for yourself and for others. You are gifted, your potential is limitless. There is always a choice, you can either watch life from the side-lines, or actively participate. Di$rupt yourself and refrain from the playful, unambitious and unproductive lifestyle you've been living. Restrain yourself from too much aimless entertainment. Even comedians who make entertainment their career, approach it seriously, certainly if they aim to achieve greatness and make a name for themselves.

Challenge the status quo, dare life, and live your dreams. Trouble your troubles. Cheat on your fears and face them with courage until your fears fear you. Take a chance on something worthwhile and have a bust-up with doubt. Hope against hope and, no matter what happens, keep on keeping on. Challenge your challenges, pity your pity, reject rejection and tie the knot with your dreams. Endeavour to make a way and make a name for yourself before you breathe your last breath. Many people, who no one could ever have imagined would amount to anything, woke out of their slumber and created great success. People who fulfil their highest potential are not always the ones you'd expect.

As Myles Monroe, the late Bahamas televangelist and leadership consultant once said: 'Potential is hidden talents, dormant ability, reserved power, untapped strength, unused success and capped capabilities. It is all you can be but have not yet become, all you can do but have not yet done, how far you can reach but have not yet arrived, and what you can accomplish but have not yet accomplished.'

Believe in yourself and never doubt your abilities. You become what you believe yourself to be. If you keep on saying to yourself that you cannot do certain things, it is possible that you will end up really becoming incapable of doing them. On the contrary, if you have the belief that you can do it, you will surely acquire the capacity to do it, even if you may not have it all figured out in the beginning

You can stretch beyond the parameters of opinions and labels people have put on you. The position you are in right now is not the problem. The problem is that you've settled. You've accepted 'your lot' as the only realistic option for your life. But it's time for you to fight. Think of yourself as a lioness going after another lioness that has robbed her of her cubs. There is no such thing as failure. You will fight until you reclaim what is rightfully yours: your cubs, or, to explain the analogy, your natural power and potential. Provided what you do is honest and respectful of others, push as hard as you can until you become fully yourself, and in that way an asset and not a liability to the human race.

There's nothing quite like holding your head up high. That is what brings us our human dignity and purpose. It can also bring us great joy.

> Chase your dreams even when the world laughs at your guts. Struggle now and shine later.

You were not put here on earth to pass through this life unnoticed. You were sent here to be one of the leaders, the movers and shakers. The earnest expectation of the world is waiting for your transformation. Do not disappoint your Creator, do not disappoint your family and do not disappoint your soul. God created you, gave you a mind, invested talents in you and put you here on earth for a purpose. You have a responsibility to give back a good return on God's investment (talents). Put the naysayers and sluggards to shame.

Rock your life's boat. Kiss mediocrity goodbye. Invest in your dreams. Struggle now and shine later. Stand on your own if you have to. Chase your dreams as far as the pathway leads, even when the world laughs at your foolishness. Life is a mysterious game of innumerable mishaps. You have to figure out how to escape between the gaps and just once taste what success is like. Then it's almost impossible to turn back, especially when the world stops laughing at your foolishness and begins cheering your guts.

One thing is certain: nobody comes out of this life alive. You might as well live fiercely with all that you have and with all that you are. The difference between those who become victims and those who step up to the challenge is that the victims tend to work themselves into a frenzy of self-pity, while those who opt to live their lives are deeply rewarded, not necessarily by instant fame and riches but certainly with the satisfaction and the sense of self-worth that comes with knowing that we are giving it our best shot. Despite the hard knocks life has served you, you can still fill the length of your days with wonder and amazement. When the struggle is over, those who have distanced themselves from you will line-up to re-introduce themselves. Step out of your comfort zone, live your dreams and share the richness of your soul with the world because profound success (in all its guises) is what you were sent here on earth to experience.

Feel the Fear and Do It Anyway

One of the biggest obstacles that keep people in their comfort zone is fear. Everything goes on lockdown mode in your brain when you are afraid. We're all afraid, but you have to get to the point where you understand that fear doesn't mean you can't be brave. Courageous people are not free from fear, they proceed in spite of their fears and do it anyway. Fear by definition is an 'unpleasant emotion caused by the threat of danger, pain or harm'.

But for me, 'unpleasant' does not cut it. Fear is a horrific, gut-wrenching, crippling, sickening, and a teeth-shattering emotion that shows up when you're attempting to do something new. However, fear is commonplace. To succeed in business or relationships or anything in life, you must have an unwavering, insatiable, tenacious courage and bravery. You have to be able to back yourself; to harbour that kind of unbridled faith in what you believe that will stop at nothing until you achieve your goals.

When you feel fear, acknowledge its presence and ask yourself – what would the best version of myself do in this situation? The best version of yourself usually won't run away. Fear produces adrenalin and that has the potential to catapult you into superman mode. Thus, face your fears or they will choke your creativity, evaporate your promising ideas, imprison your mind and stop you from realising your dreams. Personally, I had to adopt the mindset that fear is normal and that real failure is giving up without trying. My life got way better and I've made more progress since adopting this mindset.

Dale Carnegie, the famous self-improvement writer, said, 'Inaction breeds doubt and fear. Action breeds confidence and courage. If you want to conquer fear, do not sit home and think about it. Go out and get busy.'

To win the war against fear, you have to start playing more often in your fear zone instead of avoiding it. There is no honour in staying average. Greatness is in us all but it's up to us to bring it out. The only way to live life to the full and bring your greatest contribution to the world is by shining brightly and expressing your talents freely. Do it while afraid and get so involved in the process that you forget you were scared. Whatever new project you want to undertake, fear dissipates the moment you get the ball rolling. It's magical! But if you hold back because you are afraid, fear only breeds fear. Action is the antidote for fear. Fear is an opportunity to get to know yourself better and be more in control of your actions and reactions.

Marianne Williamson, an author and entrepreneur, once said, 'Our deepest fear is not that we are inadequate. Our deepest fear is that we are powerful beyond imagination. It is our light more than our darkness which scares us. We ask ourselves – who am I to be brilliant, beautiful, talented, and fabulous? But honestly, who are you not to be so?'

If you are not afraid to fail then you've already won. To really conquer fear, you have to go through it not around it. The negative effects of fear go beyond keeping you in your comfort zone. When fear takes over, it locks you up in a self-defeating mindset and a perpetual mood for repeated defeat. You become used to looking at life through the eyes of fear. You can choose to see poverty, lack, scarcity, deprivation and injustices or you can choose to see opportunities, abundance, success and wealth. What you see is what you get. A fearful person is often a negative person.

A negative mind can never give you a positive life.

When fear inhibits you, it makes you become so pessimistic that nothing positive can grow in your mind. Your negative thinking might translate into words like this: 'If I start selling candles, the sun will stop setting or people will stop dying, or electricity will never be off. If I start selling baby clothes, all women will go barren or the government will pass a law limiting fertility to one child per woman. If I take a long-term investment, the company will collapse or I'll die before my investment matures.' This is what fear does to a person's mind. This type of thinking cannot produce success.

The fear of failure, rejection, success or simply the fear of the unknown can render you powerless. You end up boxing yourself into a mouldy corner, feeling unfulfilled, unworthy and frustrated. In order to destroy fear, be willing to rewire your brain. Replace the negative thoughts with the positive ones. Stop feeding your mind with negativity and unproductive junk. Be careful what you watch on TV and read in newspapers. Rather read books on personal development. Listen to music that is transformational and motivating. Watch videos that are educational and positive. A negative mind can never give you a positive life. You become what you watch, listen and expose yourself to.

Interrupt the negative committee that conducts negative meetings in your head! Take action towards a meaningful life. Fear creeps in when you don't take action towards what you really want. In every phase of your life, you will be confronted with something that scares you. But you have to be brave and march forward as a valiant. As Ralph Waldo Emerson said: 'Do the thing you fear the most and the death of fear is certain.' Suzy Kassem, a poet and writer on the topic of fear, also said: 'Fear kills more dreams than failure ever will.'

Bravery is not the absence of fear. The only proven method to triumph over fear is to face what you are afraid of. Those who are not afraid to go after what they want in life are the ones who usually turn out to be successful. Fear will always be present but you are the one in charge. Fear is something that rules everyone, but you can control how much influence it has in your life. As Hafez, a 14th century Persian poet, said: 'Fear is the cheapest room in the house. I'd like to see you in better living conditions.'

Take a look at these scenarios. Many people are afraid to go to their doctor for medical check-ups; some are afraid to write an exam; some are afraid of heights or travelling in an aeroplane, some are afraid of escalators at shopping malls while others are afraid of using lifts in tall buildings. All these are common fears people often experience but they don't let it stop them from writing an exam, travelling or taking a medical test that could be the determining factor between life and death.

Feel the fear, but do it anyway. Fear does not pay the bills. Fear does not win any awards. The fear of what people will say has never stopped people from talking about you behind your back. The fear of failure has never prevented anyone from failing. So, whether you do it or not, you'd still fail by default. People will still talk about you whether you're the richest, poorest, most average or most miserable in your community. Don't surrender to the emotion of fear if you want to be successful or make a difference in the world. Waiting for the right time will not eliminate fear. Procrastination generates nothing but more fear. If there is a mountain before you, waiting will not make the mountain become smaller.

Think Solutions not Problems

Stepping out of your comfort zone requires that you shift from problem finding to problem solving. It's easy to spot problems first, that's human nature. Viewing problems as obstacles to be solved and not seeking further irrelevant problems is the mindset switch that disruptors invariably adopt. Those who find problems in everything are those who make excuses for everything. Change cannot happen if all you see are problems. You can't step out of your comfort zone or fear zone until you're willing to start solving your problems.

Disruptors create unconventional solutions to problems. Two guys had a transportation problem one night and thought to themselves, how cool it'd be to tap a button and get a ride. These men went on to create an unconventional solution to transportation inconvenience that's now serving the entire world – and that's how *Uber* was born.

> Many failed at things I've accomplished simply because they were busy finding problems and excuses while I was busy finding solutions.

As a society, we need more solution-based thinking over problem-based thinking. Everyone is capable of identifying problems, but identifying solutions that address these problems is what really makes the difference. It's hard to see opportunities when all you see are problems, but avoiding your problems makes things worse. Life becomes interesting when you focus on finding both your problems and their solutions. Take time to figure out what's really going on in your life, find the source of the problem and find the solutions. Some people stop at only finding the problems. Then they start blaming others. They blame the government for their unemployed status. They blame their parents for their alcoholism and drug addictions. They blame their disadvantaged backgrounds. Problem finders and excuse makers blame everyone and everything else for their problems – except themselves.

I stopped blaming people for my problems and started searching for solutions on how to improve my life. In so doing I've improved the lives of others as well. Problems and solutions depend on your outlook and perception of life. Success is not a product of convenience. Many have failed at things I've accomplished simply because they were busy finding problems and excuses while I was busy finding solutions. Success requires that you be stingy with excuses.

Some people don't have a job or any source of income but you hear them say things like 'I don't like selling, business is not my thing, network marketing is not my thing, I am not an entrepreneur or a hustler, etc.' These are excuses they cook up for not trying to make something of themselves in a difficult economy. The million-dollar question is, what is your thing? Is being broke your thing? Is being a weight on your parents your thing?

The irony here is that if entrepreneurial abilities, advanced selling skills and creativity were listed as a necessary requirement on a job advertisement, the same people who say 'selling is not my thing' would rush in their numbers to apply for the job. Clearly, anyone can train themselves to be whatever they want to be. If you can automatically find the solution to your lack of selling skills in order to get a job then there are many more solutions you can find to other problems in your life. The reason people shy away from finding solutions to their problems is because most people are too terrified of standing on their own two feet. They can commit to almost anything as long as it is within the confinement of a job. They can see themselves acquiring any skills virtually overnight and becoming whatever the job description demands just so they can find comfort as well as this illusion of 'security' in a job.

Many are baptised with 'a job mentality'. Their minds are married to this idea that success can only be achieved through having a job. This isn't something that comes from deep within. It is simply conforming to societal norms, hence the infamous hashtags #ThankGodItsFriday and #IhateMondays. If someone can work at a job they hate for 10 long years, a job they feel sick just thinking about, why can't that same person go through temporary discomfort and take the leap of faith into the unknown to create something they really love doing and build a better future for themselves?

Many people dream of becoming better people but only a few attain it. Only those who focus on finding solutions make things happen. Hence, be stingy with excuses and open your mind to the opportunities around you. The most unprofitable thing you can ever manufacture is an excuse. You could be the next Nelson Mandela, Bill Gates or Aliko Dangote; you could be the most talented singer in the world, but if you let problems and excuses stop you from expressing your gifts, it's game over! No one will ever get to dance to your song.

The American poet Henry Wadsworth Longfellow once wrote: 'Excuses are tools of the incompetent. They build monuments of nothingness. Those that often use them seldom build anything.' Many of us are way too generous with excuses, but disruptors find very few. Here's a list of classic excuses compiled by an anonymous writer. Do any of these excuses sound familiar to you? How many have you used to thwart your own progress?

What is Your Excuse?

- I am afraid. (Well, who isn't? No one is immune to fear. It is a regular fight even for the strongest and the bravest.)
- I don't have the money. (Who has?)
- I don't have connections. (Really? Everyone starts as a nobody.)
- I'm not smart enough. (You've just crowned yourself 'a stupid'.)
- I can't talk. (Are you dumb?)
- I don't have the time. (Yet you have the time to watch TV and finish an entire season of your favourite series without missing an episode.)
- I am too busy. (Doing what exactly?)
- It takes too long to build a business. (But you envy Aliko Dangote and Patrice Motsepe. You even make suggestions on how they should use their money.)
- It is too risky. (Name one thing that is not risky. Is life not risky? Is crossing the road not taking a risk?)
- I don't like dealing with people. (Mr Island, I greet your Excellency.)
- I'm too old. (But you said you were too young a few years ago.)

- I am waiting for the lights to turn green. (The lights will turn green when you press the button.)
- My husband, my wife, my parents don't support me. (They don't support you being broke either.)
- I'm not good at marketing. (Yet you are good at forwarding chain messages and sharing numerous silly posts on social media.)
- I am not a professional. (Who was born a professional?)
- I had a bad childhood. (Few people on Planet Earth had a flawless childhood.)

George Bernard Shaw, Irish playright and intellectual, said: 'People are always blaming their circumstances for what they are. I don't believe in circumstances. The people who get ahead in this world are the people who get up and look for the circumstances they want, and, if they can't find them, they make them.'

He Makes Four Times More Money Driving an Uber than He Did Working a Job

I recently had an interesting conversation with an *Uber* driver while returning home from an event at which I was speaking. We started a casual chat and it quickly turned into an interesting, inspirational and educational conversation. He told me a time came in his life when he desperately needed a change. He was tired of being broke all the time even though he had a job. He was scared out of his wits, yet he decided one day to quit his job and became an *Uber* driver. He said, 'My father nearly had a heart attack when I made the decision to quit my job. My father was disappointed in me and told me he regretted the money spent to put me through university. Nevertheless, I stood by my decision.'

He went further to tell me about his old job. He was earning about $1200 every month from his job but was always broke. Sometimes he'd wait for his salary at an ATM to draw out all the money before the debit orders went through. After quitting his job, he started as an *Uber* driver with the one car he had. Things were very slow in the beginning, he started wondering if he'd made a mistake but he didn't give up. He said he felt so much freedom just being outside the office environment and being in control of his life and his time.

As time went on, he started to understand how things work in the *Uber* world and he picked up momentum accordingly. After one year, he bought a second car on auction. Having two cars on *Uber* was a great accomplishment for him. He kept pushing and today he has four cars on *Uber*, three driven by other people he employs. All the cars combined make about $1050 per week, which makes is about $4200 per month. Which is almost four times what he used to earn in one month with his job. He told me being an *Uber* driver in South Africa brought him in contact with so many VIPs that he could never have met in real life if he'd stayed stuck in the office. Networking with these people has opened his eyes to bigger opportunities and he's now starting to branch out into other businesses.

There is another world out there but you'll never know until you step out of your comfort zone. Retrenchment is on the rise. Companies are employing fewer and fewer humans. Yet, many people are sinking in self-inflicted poverty because they cannot afford to lose their social status and reputation. They cannot imagine life outside the notion of a job. Students are deep into debt even before they earn their first salary – all in pursuit of a 'steady job'.

Those who are the most educated are sometimes the most trapped by this mindset. I'm not against education, but the truth is there is another life outside a certificate. Street-smart people make more money and progress faster in life than classroom-smart people, or should I say office-smart people. Street-smart people are open minded and willing to hustle even from the boot of their cars.

Financial freedom starts outside a salary.

Street-smart people are willing to step out of their comfort zone, fear zone and start at ground zero to build their way up. Street-smart people are willing to start any business no matter how undignified it may be viewed by society. Street-smart people don't care about having a dignified job title yet who are borrowing money for petrol or taxi every month to get to work. Financial freedom very often starts outside a salary.

Street-smart people are creative and open minded, willing to try anything until they find their big break. The most influential, powerful and wealthy people of this world found their big break outside their certificates and academic qualifications. Whatever your situation, you can create change if you really want change. A graduate should not be imprisoned by certificates, an employee should not be imprisoned by salary, and the unemployed or uneducated should not be imprisoned by their circumstances.

Chapter 7

ESCAPE THE SHACKLES OF CONFORMITY

Society's unrelenting grip has brainwashed the masses into attaining one singular goal: conformity. This grip is so strong on people, young and old, rich and poor, privileged and otherwise, from fashion, food and entertainment to education and success. We are expected to look a certain way in order to pass the success test. We are expected to carry corporate suitcases or CVs. There is always an idealised depiction of an 'idyllic individual' that doesn't really exist. Yet society is on a mad rush to be like this utopian person. On almost every street corner are flashing lights, blinking promotional ads, neon posters, people rushing to or from work, fast-food deals, ripped-up clothing passing as 'haute couture', and other extraneous ephemera that seem to scream: Succumb! Conform! Be like everyone else!

But John F Kennedy, when he was President of the United States, said: 'Conformity is the jailer of freedom and the enemy of growth.' Conforming to society's trends is like a steel prison that suffocates your personality and freedom. Like a thief, it steals from you the ability to mature as your own person. Conformity is the destruction of dreams and talents.

It's easier to conform and shut up than to di$rupt and stand out. To conform is to align your attitudes, beliefs, and behaviours to those of people around you. Conformity is a powerful force that can sweep you away from the life God designated to you. Even though society is more liberal than ever before, there is still tremendous pressure to conform. Stifling traditions, glass ceilings, suffocating expectations from family and friends, limiting labels, restrictive stereotypes, school conditioning, climbing corporate ladders, and other impossible standards, can be difficult to avoid. However, the problem is not in their existence, but in our lack of conscious engagement with these social pressures. Your life's purpose becomes cloudy and diminished when you conform, thus failing to give yourself sufficient space to connect with your own unique soul-print.

> When you set an ambitious goal, many or most of your friends and family members may scoff. People will try to get you to stay in the little box they created for you.

There is always a choice to step into the murky uncharted waters or become a casualty of conformity. The status quo is a swamp! Stagnation and conventions are slow death. You are hard-wired for unique self-expression. Hence, design your own life instead of trying to squash yourself into a tiny box. When you set an ambitious goal, many or most of your friends and family members may scoff. People will try to get you to stay in the little box they created for you. But once you can see your vision clearly, other people will see it too – eventually. As a wise man once said, 'the greats knew they were great before anyone else did'. So, create the life you want and step into it.

Don't live your life according to society's script. The future that's coming, and is already here, will demand more self-reliance, more risk-taking, more entrepreneurial ideas and more creativity than anything we've seen before. Companies will continue to employ machines, preferring them to large human workforces.

But this new era needn't be a disaster, filled with smiling chatbots and disgruntled human beings. The responsibility to create value for yourself and design your own code of success in the Fourth Industrial Revolution lies with you. As Mandy Hale, a prolific writer and best-selling author, once said: 'Be bold enough to live life on your terms, and never, ever apologize for it. Go against the grain, refuse to conform, take the road less travelled instead of the well-beaten path. Laugh in the face of adversity, and leap before you look. Dance as though everybody is watching. March to the beat of your own drum. And stubbornly refuse to fit in.'

Those who shift their mindset will reap the benefits of not

following the status quo. Look around you. Who is the richest person in your community? Who is the most respected or influential person you know? Who is the person everyone strives to become like? Is he or she a conformist? Is he or she following the rules and maintaining the status quo? Usually the most successful, influential and powerful people in society are those who do not conform to society's norms. That's what makes them stand out. As a result, for you to make an impact in your community, you'll have to be unconventional and different.

> You become the co-author of your own misfortunes, the moment you go through life dancing to the tune of family, friends, co-workers or the community at large.

We live in an era where machines are employable. It is therefore necessary to figure out how to create your own opportunities. More people are transitioning from employee to entrepreneur. More people have a side hustle. That's how things are working in the new economy. More and more people are stepping out of their comfort zones, fear zones and pain zones. The traditional way of defining success – go to school, get a certificate and get a job – is fast becoming obsolete. Don't do things because others are doing them. Don't go back to school because your colleagues and friends are going back to school. Don't get a job because others are getting jobs. When you go through life dancing to the tune of family and friends, you become the co-author of your own misfortunes.

Between a Dream and Insanity: The Story of Paulo Coelho

Paulo was born in Rio de Janeiro, Brazil, to middleclass parents who had plans for him to become a lawyer. As a teenager, Paulo wanted to become a writer. Upon telling his mother his dream, she responded, 'My son, your father is an engineer. He's a logical, reasonable man with a very clear vision of the world. Do you actually know what it means to be a writer?' At age 17, Coelho's opposition to following a traditional path were seen as rebellion. When his parents' attempts to suppress his dreams of becoming a writer failed, they took it as a sign of mental illness and had him committed to a mental institution, where he endured sessions of electro-convulsive therapy. He escaped from the institution three times before being released at the age of 20.

Following his parents' demands, Coelho enrolled in law school but one year later, he dropped out and became involved in drugs and a rock star lifestyle while working as a songwriter. This led to him being arrested and tortured due to the content of some of his songs. The experience affected him profoundly and he decided he had had enough of living on the edge and wanted to be 'normal' just like his parents desired.

He joined a theatre group as an executive and also started to work as a journalist at age 26 but deep down Paulo was always a non-conformist and seeker of the new. 'For seven years,' as he says, 'I was living a life of routine encounters, regular meals and stable pay checks.' But it soon turned out that 'I could not stand to be normal.' Mr Coelho then left his lucrative career and his country behind to travel the world with his wife.

In 1986, he had a turning point in his life while in Spain which led to him writing his first book, *The Pilgrimage*. And one year later he wrote *The Alchemist* at age 38. *The Alchemist* was discontinued after an initial print run of just 900 copies but Paulo did not give up. He approached a different publishing house, which printed the book and *The Alchemist* became a worldwide phenomenon that has sold over 65 million copies, an unprecedented number exceeded only by a handful of classics. *The Alchemist* is one of the biggest bestselling novels ever written, published in more than 170 countries and translated into 80 languages. All in all, Coelho has authored about 30 books and sold over 150 million copies. He holds the Guinness World Record for being the most translated living author.

Create a Compelling Future for Yourself

As the world becomes more automated, more and more industries are relying on machines to deliver simpler, faster, and more efficient performances. Machines are increasingly taking over the workforce, from simple jobs such as packaging in factories to taking orders from customers in fast-food chain restaurants and doing more complex jobs like accounting. Automation is no longer confined to routine tasks.

A recent *PwC* study reveals 'that up to 38 percent of existing jobs in the United States are susceptible to automation by the 2030s, followed by Germany (35 percent), UK (30 percent), and Japan (21 percent). The survey notes that compared to other sectors, humanity will see the highest transformation in transport, manufacturing, wholesale and retail. Meanwhile, education, health and social work can expect lower penetration of robot workers.'

Is technological disruption a bad thing? Well, it depends whether you are the disruptor or the disrupted. Hence, don't fight technology, embrace it and become part of the revolution. Don't hope for your organisation or the government to save you. One of the greatest lessons you'll learn as you grow in life is that you are responsible for your own life, whether it's a success or a failure. Your life and future belong to you. You are the one to decide what direction your life takes. You cannot control technology or the government but you can control your own life.

Neither the present nor the past will decide your future, unless you decide that it should. Did your parents abandon you as a child or didn't they? Has your husband/wife left you for someone else? Has a business partner or friend betrayed you? Have you been retrenched, or never ever had a job? Are you the most loved or the most hated person in your family, your community, your country, the world? All these circumstances don't really matter. The most important thing is that you are here now. You are alive. Therefore, you have within you the power to change things. You can parent yourself and undo some of the damage your parents, spouse, employer, the government or society in general have done. You can recreate yourself and fashion a compelling future for yourself.

The full story of my life, the obstacles and tragedies I've had to deal with might someday demand its own book – perhaps. In the meantime, here is another snippet. I've had my fair (unfair) share of rainy days. I've had many ups and downs, and I've hit rock bottom a few times. Then drop a few levels lower when I thought the worst was over. I had a tough childhood. I never knew my Dad, never saw him and never spoke to him. To say it was hard growing up without a father, not even knowing what he looked like, would be an understatement. A fatherless daughter, while still trying to make sense of how a person called 'Dad' could just walk away and never look back, life served me another misfortune. My Mom, the only parent I knew, died when I was 14 years old. Fast-forward to 16 years later. Even as an adult, I found myself in an environment that was surrounded by abuse, betrayal, lies, loneliness and pain. I felt like a nobody, trapped and lost. To add salt to injury, life served me another curved ball. I was retrenched from a job I had held on to for dear life.

But I grew through the pain and stopped cursing or blaming others for my circumstances. Through it all, I knew there was more in me than I had ever realised. Instead of playing victim, I decided to create a different reality for my life. I needed a champion and so I became one!

You are just one decision away from a totally different life. You can create something that pulls you into the future. The future is not something you tumble into or some event you're waiting to attend. The future is something you create.

> 'Never stand begging for that which you have the power to earn.'

Don't think your time will simply come of its own accord. Your time starts when you decide to put your journey into gear. Don't wait for the green light; you'll only have the green light when you turn on the switch. Some people wait to take action only once they know what is ahead and that's why they never go anywhere in life. To see what's ahead you need first to take action. Only when you've taken that first step can you truly begin to see what lies ahead. Believe in yourself. As Spain's greatest writer, Miguel de Cervantes, wrote in *Don Quixote*: 'Never stand begging for that which you have the power to earn.'

Never feel guilty for wanting more out of life. Be different! Conventional thinking promotes mental slavery and destroys talents. Students are shocked, some even sink into depression, when they come face to face with the reality that certificates won't save them. They are shocked to discover there are no jobs as they were promised. Some are drowning in student's loans because the system encouraged them to buy on credit a certificate that might not help pay their student loan.

Some students even took courses they hated because they were told their job prospects would be rosier if they acquired such and such a certificate, only to discover that in the real world things aren't that easy – not even with a Law, Accounting or Engineering degree. This leaves many youths angry and frustrated. Maybe that's why you are reading this book. So let me repeat the good news. You can di$rupt yourself, overturn all conventions, overlook your certificate and depend on your amazing brain for solutions. You can create your own future rather than wait on the promises of the government or politicians for a job. You are remarkably talented, gifted, passionate and intelligent. You can start life from the platform of your talents and passion rather than from the platform of your certificate. Many have found their big break outside their academic qualifications.

Human beings are creative by nature. As a child, before you were told to go to school and get a job, what did you dream of becoming? What are you good at? What comes naturally to you? We live in an era of unprecedented opportunities. You cannot depend only on your certificate as the only road map to success. Technology has broken barriers and made things easy for us all. Even kids are showcasing their talents online and being picked up by the big brands. Many people are becoming rich and famous through their creative outlets thanks to the power of the internet and social media.

Don't wait to be spotted. Push yourself to the front and let the world know you too were here.

For some celebrities and business moguls, using social media proved to be the key to their success. Thanks to platforms like *YouTube*, *Facebook*, *Instagram*, *Twitter*, and even blogs, it's now easier than ever for you to share your talent or business venture with a global audience. In this digital age, one post can change your life. Justin Bieber, a Canadian songwriter and singer, was discovered on *YouTube* – and there are many more examples.

From comedy to fashion, singing to modelling, art, cooking, poetry, photography, acting, dancing, designing, writing, launching a business venture to even raising capital, you can use the internet to kick start your dream and create a life more fulfilling and successful. If you can think creatively you can create massive value for yourself in this digital age. You don't have to start with a huge plan. You only have to start with a huge dream and take little steps towards achieving it. With consistent little steps you'll be surprised how much your life will change in three to five years if you keep at it. Create a better future for yourself. Don't wait to be spotted. Don't wait to be rescued. Push yourself to the front and let the world know you're alive and here you are!

Got Big Dreams?

You've got big dreams, haven't you? Your dream is perfect, safe and comfortable. It's untouched, stuffed in a box on a shelf, tucked away safely, far from the world it's supposed to operate in. When will you bring that dream to life? Dreaming is an inalienable right. We knew this as children, we believed we can be or do anything we imagined. A singer, dancer, writer, astronaut, photographer, doctor, ballerina, business mogul, president – and sure, why not!

Unfortunately, as social conditioning, schools and society hand us what's expected of us, we often tuck our dearest dreams safely away under the pillow of life. At this point, dreaming becomes a dare. We then succumb and conform to the norm, hence sentencing ourselves to a life of complaining, blaming and paying bills until we die.

What is your dream? Some people dream to be employers while some dream to be employees. Some dream to be philanthropists while some dream to have three meals a day. Some dream to be on TV while some dream of buying a TV. Some dream to change the world while some dream of someone to change their situation. Les Brown, author and speaker once said: 'Most people fail in life not because they aim too high and miss the target but because they aim too low and hit the target.' And Norman Vincent Peale, an American minister and author also said, 'Shoot for the moon, even if you miss you'll land among the stars.

There is no glory in small dreams. Thinking small is mediocrity not humility. You may be living in this shadow, settling for a mediocre life. But is that who you really are? Are you okay with being average? Are you okay having your whole identity wrapped up in your job title and pay cheque? Some people's salary doesn't last for a week. Many adults are extremely tired of working constantly yet being stressed out, unhappy, broke and drowning in debts. Disruptors dream big, visualise big and plan big.

Things may never change as long as you follow rules. You may never amount to much if you stay within the confinement of what you are comfortable with. You can di$rupt yourself and follow your heart instead of abiding by the customs of your industry, profession, geographic location, associations or affiliations.

> The cost of not following your dreams is spending the rest of your life wishing you had.

Move from being a passive bystander who's accepting whatever happens and start contributing to your own life. **Live life** with a sense of urgency. Unleash your next level. Start something on the side even if you have a full-time job. Consistent drops of rain can cause a tidal wave. Don't be afraid to follow your dreams. If it happened for someone else it can happen for you too.

The cost of not following your dreams is spending the rest of your life wishing you had. Believe that you can achieve your dreams. It matters not what your idea or dream is, be it art, fashion, technology or business, what matters is that you have it. One day, if you don't give up, you will bask in the glory of your dreams. Do not let any of the stuff that happened or didn't happen affect the size of your dream. If you wait for other people's approval you are missing the real meaning of being a dreamer. To be a dreamer often means to be in conflict with others. You are the only person who can give yourself permission to be great. You are designed to stand out, not to blend in.

As writer Charles F Glassman once said, 'The danger of venturing into uncharted waters is not nearly as dangerous as staying on the shore, waiting for your boat to come in.' Most people seek approval and safety their entire lives, ultimately dying with no approval and nothing to show. Don't wait to rally the troops or everyone's support before stepping out.

Dream big. Dream beyond what's expected of you. Dream beyond the parameters set by society. Be unreasonable. Great people in history were nearly always unreasonable. Dream, even if everyone else around you thinks it's ridiculous, too simple, too complex, or too boring. Keep going even if they think you are too young, too old, too black, too white, too educated or too dumb to achieve your dreams.

> You can't bake a cake without breaking some eggs. Don't water down your dreams to make others comfortable. People will talk about you no matter what you do.

Dream with your eyes wide open. Day-dreaming without day-doing is a strategic blunder. Do whatever it takes to fulfil your dreams. Teach yourself to do things that add value to your life. Learn a new skill, get tutorials on *YouTube* on skills you need, read books, attend seminars to learn and network with like-minds. You can't bake a cake without breaking some eggs. Don't water down your dreams to make others comfortable. People will talk about you no matter what you do.

Throw your entire weight into your dreams. Don't become a casualty of conformity and don't let 'lack of funding' stop you. Provision never comes before vision. Most people think they need money before they can start their journey, some believe they have to start big but you have to start small with whatever you have and build up from there. Instead of waiting to start big, start small so you can grow big. When you have a dream and you are thinking only in terms of money, you might never start. Skills are more important than money.

You need to absolutely remove the lack-of-money barrier from your mind if you truly want to be a game-changer. Instead, go into the mindset of 'If I had all the money in the world, how would I do this?'

This way, you can get really clear on where you want to go. Once you are clear and excited about that, more often than not, the money has a way of coming. Always go with the visionary big picture first, and then work back to figure out how you are going to make it happen. By approaching your dreams this way, it removes all barriers and eliminates concerns about the groundwork you'll need.

Two key questions you should always ask are, 'If money was no object, what problem would I like to solve?' and 'How would my dream improve someone else's life?' Once you find the answers, you can do big things. You can start re-kindling the flame you once had for your dreams. Little sparks can grow into larger-than-life flames. Open yourself up to deeper conversations; make peace with the mistakes or bad decisions you might have made in the past, and start connecting with your dreams instead of avoiding them.

However, not everyone has to abandon the traditional path. Some people are in the cubicle by divine calling. Some accomplished their greatest life's dream when they got employed. Consequently, if you absolutely love your job and are excited each morning to go make a difference at work, then there's no need to worry about dreams or entrepreneurship. If you're working toward a potentially achievable goal, such as being a manager at your company or winning a 'c-suite' job in your industry; if your biggest dream in life is to buy a house, a car, pay bills on time and have a comfortable life, then personal disruption or dreaming big dreams is really not necessary for you. But if you want to impact the world and create something that will outlive you, then take a good hard look at your life. Ask yourself: 'Is my life fulfilling or am I running away from myself? What do I need to change in my life in order to accomplish my dreams?'

As India's famous non-violent game changer, Mahatma Gandhi, so prophetically stated: 'You must be the change you wish to see in the world.' All the problems in your life are waiting for you to di$rupt yourself. The solutions are within you! Disruptors are problem solvers who see all problems as business opportunities waiting to be discovered. Many people came about their businesses as a result of various personal problems they were experiencing, and in solving these problems for themselves they solved them for others too, and so a business was born.

Disruptors don't allow the economy to decide their fate. Yes, there is a lot of economic anxiety due to rapid technological advancement. But people are still expanding new frontiers. The problem is not lack of opportunity but lack of vision.

The more the economy goes down, the more some people flourish. You can sit around playing the 'what if' game or you can begin to get your hands dirty and do the hard work of getting your dream out of the box and into the world.

You've had a great business idea for years yet you do nothing about it. Nobody gets changed by only an idea. Dreams don't work if you don't roll up your sleeves. Don't just dream of writing a book, begin writing. Don't just dream of being an actor, put yourself out there, have a *YouTube* channel to show the world your acting moves, sign up with an agency and attend auditions. Don't just dream of being an entrepreneur, start something – even if it's selling stuff on the street or from the boot of your car. Whatever you do, don't get discouraged with initial results. As Irvin Chauke, an author once said, 'If you stop because you don't see results, you will never see the results.'

Hold tight to your dreams no matter how unreachable they seem and keep believing even in the face of overwhelming obstacles. Never stop dreaming. Once you're in a place where you're no longer dreaming, learning, and creating new things, that's death! Average people die at 25 but get buried at 60 or 70. Because of lack of dreams, there is nothing else to look forward to once you've got the education, the certificate, the job, the car, the house, the spouse and the kids. This is where life comes to a halt for most people. This is the survival wiring passed down to us by our forefathers. But pioneers of the future are disrupting the status quo. Being satisfied with daily needs, monthly bills and yearly holidays is how some have buried their potential and are going through the rest of their lives on autopilot. Thomas Edison, America's greatest inventor and father of the electric light bulb, said: 'Show me a thoroughly satisfied man and I will show you a failure.'

Theodore Roosevelt, a conservationist and 26th President of the United States, once said, and I quote: 'Far better is it to dare mighty things, to win glorious triumphs, even though mocked and checkered by failure, than to rank high with the poor spirits who neither enjoy nor suffer much, because they live in the grey twilight that knows not victory or defeat.'

There is an Economy in Your Mind

Machine intelligence is quickly replacing human cognitive power in the same way machines replaced muscle power in the Industrial Revolution. As Tony Seba, an author and lecturer on disruption, once said, 'The Stone Age did not end because we ran out of rocks. It ended because a disruptive technology ushered in the Bronze Age.'

Similarly, jobs in our own era are not disappearing because of lack of qualified workers but as a result of better technology that does the work more accurately than humans. Employment is losing its former status, and along with it is diminishing the value of climbing the corporate ladder. Young people who choose only this path are becoming increasingly disappointed. But as employment is undermined by automation, new opportunities also rise. To make use of them, or even to see them clearly, the new socio-economic realities require you to think creatively rather than to take comfort in conventional wisdom, false solutions, or unrealistic promises from politicians.

According to Erik Brynjolfsson, Massachusetts Institute of Technology Professor and Director of Digital Economy: 'We are going to see an increased demand for creative skills as we automate a lot of the repetitive work humans do. We are also going to see an increased demand for those with social skills, interpersonal skills, negotiating skills as well as nurturing, caring, coaching, persuasive and selling skills.'

There is a new generation of young people which is breaking trends, going into entrepreneurship and making a living in fundamentally different ways from their parents. They work and play around the clock in a myriad of galleries, fashion outlets, app development studios, bookshops, publishers, theatres, culture, media, internet start-ups and cafes. These young people are, generally speaking, operating in creative business modes. They are motivated both by the desire to pave their own path and also to make their own rules. They can be described as artists, designers, musicians, actors, writers, start-up superheroes, photographers and tech gurus.

Entrepreneurship is the biggest and most exciting economic

development segment in the world today. The possibilities are endless. If you are looking to remain competitive in the future, you have to bring something extra to the table and that's your creativity and unique talents. Ideas and imagination are the new currency. These are skills that Artificial Intelligence cannot render obsolete. Entrepreneurship and the creative economy are Africa's untapped golden markets. The greatest asset in the creative economy is your imagination. The more you can imagine and think unconventionally, the more valuable you become in the market place.

> Having only one skill or holding only to your academic qualifications in this new era makes you economically vulnerable.

One of the central features of this new era is the explosive growth in the number of people making a living through entrepreneurship, creative art, online stores and social media platforms. This new generation is now able to reinvent themselves for the increasingly global markets that are available. Disruptors are self-reliant and their efforts cannot be hindered by the administrations of government entities.

AI is taking over jobs and entrepreneurship is the only way forward for some people. 'Start your own business and be free to do your own thing. Live and work like an artist! You can make it if you really want it.' While this may sound like a cliché, it is the reality for millions of millennials in Africa and the world today. The employment market is shrinking and this trend is irreversible. You can jump on the moving train of entrepreneurship and explore opportunities in a connected and networked global economy. There is an economy in your mind. If you can change your mind, your economy will change. Having only one skill in this era or holding only to academic qualifications makes you economically vulnerable. Educate yourself, learn skills outside your certificate.

If you keep doing the same thing year in year out, your economy remains the same. Everyone is creative but creativity cannot survive in a lifeless environment. Don't be afraid to put yourself out there and try things. You could be the next programmer who'll build a tech solution to an important problem in society – but you'll never know until you try.

From Caterpillar to Butterfly: Evolve

According to Merriam-Webster's Learner's Dictionary, to evolve is to change or develop slowly often into a better, more complex, or more advanced state: to develop by a process of evolution.

Evolve comes from the Latin word *evolvere,* which means 'to unroll'. When something is unrolling or unravelling, it is doing so gradually, not all at once. Evolve describes a development that is taking its time to reach its final destination. When something evolves, it changes, or develops over time, like your taste in music and clothes, which evolves as you get older. Your taste in music evolved from the nursery rhymes you loved as a little kid to whatever you like today. Even places can evolve, like the old-fashioned coffee shops that evolved into internet cafes as people began to bring their laptops with them. If you look around you at the physical universe, you will see that its nature is growth. Everything from technology to business models to the cells in your body to the planets orbiting the sun is constantly growing, constantly changing, constantly evolving. Nothing stands still. Nothing remains the same. Everything changes. So think about it – why would your life be the exception? Why would you be the only thing that exists in all of creation whose purpose isn't to grow?

Everything on this earth is in a continuous state of evolving, refining, improving, adapting, enhancing and changing. In life you need to come to that point where you explore, experiment and evolve. Like a caterpillar through a season of loneliness and isolation develops and evolves its wings into a beautiful butterfly. Evolving is a type of transitioning and disruption happening on a deeper level. To evolve is to grow and mature. Adaptation to change is a characteristic of all living organisms. Thus, all living things must grow, adapt, evolve, or die.

Evolution is nature's creative way of pushing living organisms to higher degrees of complexity, and humans are no exception. Evolving and disrupting is not arrogance. It is confidence that says: 'I will not become obsolete, stagnant, afraid or pulled backward by circumstances.

Evolving recognises that the risk of staying the same is far greater than the risks involved in changing. All your relationships, pain, predicaments and all of your challenges are opportunities for your soul to evolve. Evolving and disrupting increases your value.

> You can live according to society's script or you can escape conformity, reinvent yourself and rise above the norm.

Stop delegating progress and success to others. You too can be successful. Stop following the crowd and start participating in your own life. Your challenge is to adapt up, not to compromise down. Never stop disrupting the status quo. Your potential should not be decided on by policy makers. It's okay to be different. Defy your own stereotype, grow your brain, evolve and rise above societal norms. Feast on life! After all, everyone gets disrupted by something or someone.Hence, disrupting your own life can be the most exciting, liberating and empowering thing you can ever do. You can live according to society's script or you can escape conformity, evolve and rise above the norm.

My Retrenchment Story

Job security is an illusion. One day you may get to work, content in the knowledge that you are safe and secure in your job. Then you'll get a call from your boss, he wants to see you in his office. Yes, that's right – your guess is as good as mine. You'll get told the company is restructuring or some other nicety or not-so-nicety story and that will be the end. That contract you signed for permanent employment means nothing. There is always a possibility that you will no longer have a job if you don't perform, do something outrageous or fall behind certain criteria. Sometimes you may not have done anything wrong. Your employer might just need to downsize and get rid of some staff, and because you were the last one in, you are the first one out.

I know this too well because I experienced it myself. I always thought that retrenchment was something that happened to old people. Yes, I was that naïve. I had an illusion of job security like many people who are working today. I was a permanent employee with a permanent contract of employment nicely kept in my cupboard until that fateful morning when my boss called me into his office. It was nothing unusual as that was what usually happened whenever he'd been away and then returned to the office. And so I walked into his office suspecting nothing and sat down with this big smile on my face. He looked at me and took a deep breath that felt like he took my soul along. Immediately I knew something was wrong, my smile faded as I was waiting for him to drop the bomb. He went silent for about 20 seconds which felt like eternity. I could feel my heart pounding against my chest.

Finally, he looked straight at me with this pale look and said 'I've been wondering how to tell you this but there are some changes going on and we've decided to let you go.'

In that moment I felt my heart drop into my stomach.

That's how I got retrenched. It felt as if I had just been hit by a train. This turn of events was completely unexpected and shocked me to the extent that I sat there, open mouthed, struggling to comprehend what I'd just heard. His eyes stared at me intently; his inability to grasp the chaos he had just unleashed was astounding. Yet I couldn't respond. I was rendered speechless. My mouth was dry. I could feel my heart forcing its way out of my chest.

This was a watershed moment in my life and I knew life was never going to be the same again. I've just lost the very job I held on to for dear life. My identity, my bills and my children's futures were wrapped around that job and it was gone in an instant. As a single mom I felt my world crashing into tiny little pieces. To say that day and the weeks that followed were some of the worst days of my life would be an understatement. I cried myself to sleep for weeks. Anxiety was the order of the day.

As time went on, the raging storm inside me began to subside. I had no idea what I wanted to do with my life, but still I made the tough decision never to return to the corporate world again. I decided it was time to pave my own path. One thing led to another. The journey has been littered with teeth-shattering challenges. It took a lot of resilience and persistence to get to where I am today. Depending on your own self for your own bread and chasing a dream only you can see is not a walk in the park.

The struggle landed me in hospital at one point but I never gave up. Believe me when I tell you that I'm very fulfilled and satisfied with the path I took. My life is not devoid of struggles and challenges but I've found something that is uniquely me, and we can weather the storms of life together. That is purpose!

Looking in hindsight, getting retrenched was the best thing that happened to me. I was 'released' and 'set free' to find something better – and I did. The very fact that you are reading this book is proof that there is beauty in chaos. Dealing with nearly insurmountable challenges can sometimes turn out to be the best thing that ever happened to you, as was the case for me. Don't run away from pain. More often than not, a best-seller, best business model, an award-winning song or start-up of the year are usually born out of deep pain. Suffering without something to show for it is nothing but wasted pain. You can take the pain, the frustrations, skills and experience you have inside you and package it into something that the world will pay for.

Never waste your pain! As Oprah Winfrey said: 'Turn your wounds into wisdom.' Your most meaningful and impactful accomplishments will be born out of your deepest pain if you use pain wisely.

Pave Your Own Path

As anxiety about the Fourth Industrial Revolution grows and retrenchments loom, it may look like a dark time in history. In fact, though, this is the best time to be alive because disruptive change brings more opportunities. Many people still believe that the idea of success and having a job are interconnected, but the world is full of successful people who never took the employment route. They paved their own path.

A great example I saw recently was that of *The Coca-Cola Company's* CEO, James Quincey and *Coca-Cola's* investor, Warren Buffet. Coke's CEO is an employee and earns a net salary of about $1.3 million annually excluding bonuses. Warren Buffett, Coke's investor, earns about $1.5million a day from Coke stock dividends.

According to Wikipedia, *Apple Inc*, one of the most valued public company in the world, has 504 retail stores in 24 countries, 123,000 full time employees and is the world's first trillion-dollar company as of 2018. This would never have been possible if Steve Jobs took the traditional path. We would never have known anything called apple, except for the fruit.

These two scenarios show that one can achieve great success outside the traditional path. The pursuit of a salary has aborted many dreams and slaughtered uncountable first-class talents. In pursuit of a safe life, some have doubtless abandoned an idea that could've changed the world. It's funny how most of the world is brain-washed into believing that you are doomed if you don't have a job. Nothing hurts like the system which seems to work on the law of averages and the lowest common denominator. Many are consumed by the system. In the system, you can be under people who are supposed to be under you. You could be led by people you should be leading. The system is sometimes so myopic that greatness is shelved and mediocrity promoted.

Depending on the system, policy makers, governments or your boss will schedule your life for you. This deprives you of the joy of paving your own path. It deprives you the sense of freedom and fulfilment that running your own life invariably brings. Hence, the need to create your own security instead of hoping for job security or some other external security beyond your control. It is not security if you cannot control it. I have learned that real security is when you are your own boss or earning money doing things on your own terms. Using your creativity, motivation and application to create money is a skill which you can always enhance and improve on thereby increasing your earning potential. This to me is the biggest security and freedom anyone can have. You don't need to rely on someone hiring or firing you.

Life becomes miserable when you conform to societal norms neglecting what your heart longs for. Why are you trading the only life you've got for something you hate? The thought of tearing yourself away from the comfort of your bed reduces you to tears each morning. You rise like a zombie, shuffling around this metaphorical wasteland in the hope of being put out of your misery. 'Hey, at least I've got a job,' you sternly tell yourself while weeping bitterly inside.

I understand that everyone needs an income and right now you may not be able to give up everything, and that's fine. What I do say, though, is that you owe it to yourself to have a 'think moment' about paving your own path, especially if you know deep down in your heart that there is more in you and you don't belong in the cubicle. You can get fired from a job but you can never get fired from your talent and your determination to use it.

> You can get fired from a job but you can never get fired from your talent.

Don't conform, never fall in line. It's suicidal to do things contradictory to what you feel inside. Are you going to keep waking up every morning dreading the day ahead, or are you going to take control of your life and go for what sets your soul on fire? Too many people live life in comfortable ignorance, unaware of their true potential. They spend their lives counting down the days until the weekend so they can forget about work that becomes drudge because it doesn't inspire them. Then it's right back on the hamster wheel on Monday.

You end up hating Mondays, but Mondays don't suck: your life does. And it's not just in employment that people are miserable. Some people are in business but have no business being in business. Some are preachers but have no business being in the pulpit. Some are occupied with one thing or another but deep down they know they don't belong there.

Conformity has robbed many of their ambition, drive and childhood dreams. Conformity offered to take care of them with its lure of acceptance, protection and security, but at the same time it dampened their senses, stripping away their self-worth, dignity and purpose. Machines have already infiltrated our daily lives and it will only get worse. As a result, break free from conformity, look around your country, your continent and see what problems you can solve. Many join the status quo out of fear of having to think for themselves. But thinking can no longer be avoided. The world has gone through a seismic shift.

We look for patterns we understand and feel safe with. This means that all too often we miss blatant outliers. We've conditioned ourselves to be safe. So in the end that's all that matters. We wake up, go to work, deal with the boss (or if you are the boss, you deal with everyone else), come home, dabble in a personal life for an hour or two, go to bed, wake up, and repeat. That's how life is set up for a majority of people. That's what society accepts as normal. But seekers of the new, the pathfinders and creatives, see a different perspective on life that others miss completely.

Self-disruption will help you to pave your own path, to step out and embrace your passion. Write your book of life and let the world read it.

Risky Is the New Safe

Don't wait to be ready. No one is ever ready enough, strong enough or tenacious enough prior to starting something new. An impossible journey is the one you never began. You will never be able to leave footprints in this world if you keep tip-toeing around people. When you're afraid, your susceptibility and natural survival instincts will lock you up in a state of self-protection, like a tortoise in its shell, and this robs you of your creative abilities. History makers aren't afraid to live their dreams and take a risk. The odds are often better than you think.

As philanthropist JA Shedd once said, 'A ship in the harbour is safe, but that's not what ships are built for.' The only reason ships exist is to go places. In a harbour they are almost useless. Out of harbour, they are at risk but risk is what ships are built for. Safety is nice, but when you are completely safe, you cannot really do much. To make a lasting impact in your life and on those around you, you have to at least leave behind some of your safety and take risks. While caution has a prominent role in balancing safety and risk, what you have in the absence of risk is hardly much of a life. Risk, be it in business or life in general, is not meant to be avoided but to be managed.

Myles Munroe, author, preacher and leadership consultant, said: 'The wealthiest place in the world is not the gold mines of South America or the oil fields of Iraq or Iran. They are not the diamond mines of South Africa or the banks of the world. The wealthiest place on the planet is just down the road. It is the cemetery. There lie buried companies that were never started, inventions that were never made, bestselling books that were never written, and masterpieces that were never painted. In the cemetery is buried the greatest treasure of untapped potential.'

Doing nothing is far worse than taking a risk. Your life slows down when you're trying to avoid risk and failure. Whatever makes you angry is what you were born to solve. Take a risk, go after that dream and sing your heart out on live stage. Start that business you keep thinking about. Write that book you've been talking about. A small business today could turn out to be a global conglomerate tomorrow. A simple audition could turn you into the next best thing on TV screens. A few online courses today can upskill you, save your job or lead you to your future self.

You are the one who determines how your future turns out. The future that you envision requires you to take action. Small changes today can have a big impact tomorrow. Take some risk today towards the changes you want to see in your life. You'd be surprised at how much of a difference even a single step in the right direction can make.

> The more you protect yourself from getting hurt, the more you protect yourself from progress.

Unchain yourself from people's opinion and push against everything anybody ever did or said about you. Now more than ever the world needs your brilliance, your unique voice, your creativity, and your particular genius. Di$rupt yourself and let the world know you too are here, and you're going to live your life to the maximum. **The more you protect yourself from getting hurt, the more you protect yourself from progress.**

The Story of Kate Drummond

Kate Drummond is living proof that it is possible to escape conformity, risk it all and follow your heart. After 12 years as an elementary school teacher, Kate left the classroom and her life as she knew it behind. She sold her house and all her possessions, packed up her dog, and moved to a new city to pursue her lifelong dream of becoming an actress.

Little did she know that making this change would change her life forever. Since embarking on that path, Kate Drummond is not only a successful *Hollywood* spotlight actress, but also a film producer, director and writer – a journey that started as a result of an innocent question from one of her students.

One day, during a class project, one of her students asked her what her dream was, if she had always wanted to be a teacher. This question opened up a dream that was buried deep within her soul for twelve long years. Kate could no longer carry the pain of ignoring her dream. She loved her students but she had to make a decision. 'Big dreams can take big bravery and the acting bug could only lie dormant for so long', she said in an interview.

Today, Kate is an inspirational woman who has shared her story on global stages like *TED Talk*. Her journey, and the many lessons she learned as a result of taking her biggest leap of faith through film, inspires many to do the same.

Show Me Your Friends and I'll Show You Your Future

Life is a like a theatre, invite your audience carefully. Not everyone is worthy to have a front seat in your life. Surround yourself with people who enhance you rather than constrain you. Relationships that matter are the ones that add value and inspire you towards fulfilling your purpose. The best support system in the world, apart from your family, is your good friends. Really good friends are rare to come by. You do not randomly stumble on them. They are something you create. So, be deliberate in your efforts to seek, preserve and nurture good relationships. They become an invaluable asset in making, shaping, developing and connecting you to your destiny.

> 'The key to keeping quality people is to become a person of quality yourself.'

Who stays in your life is just as important as who left. There are those among us who fertilise the gift and give wind to the open sails, and then there are those who take the air right out of the balloon. Relationships are an integral part of life, so it is important that you seek to build relationships that will develop, challenge and transform you, rather than those that would prefer you to remain static and afraid.

Your dreams should decide your associations. Your vision should decide who you date and who you marry. Your vision should decide the books you read, the shows you watch and the places you go to. Some relationships are irreplaceable. Losing them could mean losing key destiny partners. One is such a small number to achieve greatness. Only irresponsible and egoistic people neglect essential relationships. However, hanging with the right people does not always eliminate conflict or disagreements. You should develop the mindset of a leader. Great leaders fight in the boardroom and still go out for lunch together. The purpose of your relationship should be greater than your arguments and disagreements. Take nothing personally, and never apply jealousy where you are supposed to draw inspiration. As an anonymous writer once said, 'The key to keeping quality people is to become a person of quality yourself.'

Success is not a one man show. You need people, the right people. Yes, it is entirely up to you whether you will be successful or not, but your associations will determine how far you can go. If you hang around the wrong people, you will not get to where you want to go in life. You cannot change the people around you but you can change the people you choose to be around. You can't just hang around anybody hoping by some chance they'll understand your mission and support it. You have to consciously build your network. The people you get involved with will have an impact on your life, values and even income.

What are you into because of friends? What are those things you never would have dreamt of doing but you are now doing them? These could be good things as well as horrible things. Never underestimate the power of influence! There is a saying that deserves consideration: 'If you hang around four losers, you'll become the fifth and if you hang around four winners, you'll also become the fifth.'

Friends who make you feel good are not necessarily good for you. What kind of content do your friends forward to you on *WhatsApp*? Friends who feed and nurture your dysfunction or weaknesses are enemies to your progress. You want to quit smoking, drinking, doing drugs or whatever addiction you are struggling with, but instead of your friends supporting you, they laugh at you and call you weak. It is better to be alone than with the wrong people. Some people think being alone makes you lonely, but being surrounded by the wrong people is the loneliest place in the world. So, build relationships that are in alignment with your dreams. Build relationships that challenge and inspire you to be the best version of yourself.

As author Wilferd Peterson once said, 'Walk with the dreamers, the believers, the courageous, the cheerful, the planners, the doers, the successful people with their heads in the clouds and their feet on the ground. Let their spirit ignite a fire within you to leave this world better than when you found it.'

Surround yourself with friends who can tell you when you are wrong, friends you can pray with, friends you can call when you need advice, friends who can raise your kids if something were to happen to you, friends you can trust with your life and your secrets. Find friends who have goals and work hard towards them; friends who share opportunities, their wisdom and their experiences because they want to see you grow. Genuine friends are those you can gladly grow old with, friends who toast to each other's successes without jealousy, friends you can laugh with even when the world laughs at you.

Delete toxic people from your life. Some people operate on a deep level of hate and complaints. They hate life, they hate their jobs, they hate their boss, they hate business, they hate getting out of bed, they hate the traffic, they hate their wife/girlfriend/husband/boyfriend, etc. They only enjoy partying, getting drunk, getting high, gossiping, slaying all and sundry in the most expensive outfits. If you are in such a pathetic and negative environment all the time, you'll start to take on that lifestyle as well. You won't even realise when it rubs off on you. Everyone then becomes a grumpy bunch dragging each other down. People with no dreams and no ambitions are an obstacle in your way. You need to arrive at a place where your destiny becomes more important than the pleasures you get from partying and hanging with wrong friends.

Pay close attention and observe the relationships in your life. Check which ones uplift, and which ones drain? Which ones encourage, and which ones discourage? Which ones are on a path of growth, and which ones are going downhill? Which ones always have drama and don't really understand how to appreciate you and the gifts that lie within you?

If you want to take the next step in your life or want to try something new or want to follow your dream but you are afraid of what your friends will think, that's a sign that you are with the wrong friends.

There are handsome and beautiful people in the world but their looks are all they've got. There are no more surprises from them other than their looks. They have no interest in or hunger for knowledge; they are wise in their own eyes and clever in their own sight. Whereas there's another type of person who keeps moving, learning and changing. They are fluid. They keep developing their minds and having new rendezvous with life. Their passion keeps them young and ready for new opportunities. When you are with the wrong people, they make you feel like something is wrong with you. It is amazing what you can accomplish when you minimise the time you spend with certain people or let go of them altogether.

If you want to take the next step in your life or want to try something new or want to follow your dream but you are afraid of what your friends will think, that's a sign that you are with the wrong friends. The path to greatness has a price tag on it. Walk away from arguments that lead you nowhere but to anger. Walk away from people who deliberately put you down. Walk away from opinions that decrease your self-worth. Walk away from people who choke your dreams. The more you walk away from things that poison your soul, the more successful and meaningful your life will become.

Chapter 8

DI$RUPT FALSE SYMBOLS OF SUCCESS

From ancient times, people have felt the need to set themselves apart from others in the community in which they lived. This in itself is not a bad thing. I am an advocate for being unique and different if you want to make an impact in the world. The problem, however, is that this desire in some people takes only the form of acquiring material things to symbolise their distinctiveness. These material possessions then become a benchmark by which success is measured. Common examples include houses, cars, expensive watches and jewellery, designer clothing, having children at private schools, shopping in Dubai, and even owning a dog. Having a nanny is also emerging as a success symbol in today's modern society.

Let's take a quick look at a car – an automobile, a machine designed as a mode of transportation to easily and conveniently move you from one place to another. But the advertising industry and some insecure people have hijacked the car as the ultimate symbol of success. Some people think they've made it in life simply because they have a car. Some will do just about anything to own a car. Some prioritise owning a car above everything else.

Back in ancient times, history suggests that owning a horse was the same as owning a car today. If you were an equestrian (horse rider), it meant you were successful. Despite the fact that humans have evolved through the centuries, there is still a primitive mindset in today's society as regards what symbolises real success.

The majority of people associate owning a car with being successful. Sometimes, the type of car doesn't really matter, especially here in Africa. You only need to own anything with four wheels and you're automatically elevated to the elite rank in your community. With this type of mindset, some people then go out of their way to make others feel like aliens and complete failures for not owning a car. Some look at you with pity and whisper among themselves whenever you arrive at work, functions, or any social gatherings in a taxi.

A fancy car with leather seats and designer clothes means nothing if you own no assets, no investment portfolios, and no businesses.

This is the reality in today's materialistic culture. Well, you have two choices: you can sign up for the competition or run your own race even if it's on foot. A car is a false symbol of success. Yes, many successful people own cars but not all car owners are successful. Successful people own cars but they also own assets, investment portfolios, and even businesses that will outlive them. We suffer from a disease the chief symptom of which is needing to look rich even if we're not. It's a shallow satisfaction, because you know you're indulging in deceit.

In his book, *Capitalist Nigger*, Chika Onyeani said, 'We are a conquered race and it is utterly foolish for us to believe that we are independent. The black race depends on other communities for its culture, its language, its feeding and its clothing. We must abandon the belief that whatever is white is better. We abandon our own businesses to patronise those of others.'

I therefore believe we still have a lot of catching up to do in regard to what real success is. When some black folks fail to achieve real success, they tend to cover up with what is perceived by society to be the symbols of success. That includes fancy cars, designer clothes, expensive weaves, jewellery and watches. However, disruptors, innovators and world changers are driven by something much bigger and they emancipate themselves from these false symbols of success. They understand that what drives you is more important than what you drive. If you follow your purpose in life, you stand a good chance of achieving real success. But if you follow cars, you might never taste success at all.

A fancy car with leather seats and designer clothes for yourself means nothing if you own no assets, no investment portfolios and no businesses. Owing the latest *BMW* means nothing if any of your family members are still receiving food stamps and queuing for social grants at government offices.

History makers and world changers are not car owners but dream owners and visionaries. Not everyone driving a car is successful. Not everyone driving a car sleeps at night. Some of the cars are owned by people who can barely afford them. Some of the cars are acquired through loans. As the saying goes, 'modern slaves are not in chains but in debts'.

Some countries around the world with booming economies promote cycling. People use bicycles as a mode of transportation. They use them to go to work, drop children at school, and cart around groceries, but here in Africa a bicycle is a symbol of poverty. A bicycle rider is considered the poorest of them all. Countries that are way richer than Africa use bicycles to commute. But Africa, considered the poorest continent in the world, wants only cars. In Africa, you are a laughing stock if you walk or take public transportation like taxis, buses or trains.

According to a *World Bank Blogs* article, 'In China, 37.2 percent of the population uses bicycles. In Belgium and Switzerland, 48 percent of the population rides. In Japan, it is 57 percent, and in Finland it's 60 percent. The Netherlands is known as the nation with the most bicycles per capita. Cyclists also abound in Norway, Sweden, Germany, and Denmark. The Danish capital, Copenhagen, is considered the most bicycle-friendly city in the world. Bicyclist commuters are generally healthier than those who drive motor vehicles to work and they are unaffected by crude oil production or the price per barrel.'

I am in no way against owning a car or having nice things. My point here is the mindset around purchasing those things. It's better to delay buying liabilities and invest in assets first. It is pathetic to define success as based on owning a car or having a house that gives you zero return on investment. Being a home owner definitely elevates your status among your peers, offers comfort and convenience, but being a home owner is not a wealth creation strategy unless the house you bought is for commercial purposes. Even some business owners take huge amounts of capital they could've put in business and pour it into buying/building a house as though owning a house is a wealth creation strategy. Now they have what society regards as a sure sign of success but deep down, they themselves know they are far from successful.

When success is attached only to material things, we are simply encouraging a culture of consumerism. It's all about buy, buy, buy and buy some more. Buying more stuff serves only as a distraction from looking inward and facing the emptiness that so many people are feeling today. Many people are not fulfilled, a piece of them is missing, but things will not change until they reach breaking point, where suffering becomes impossible to avoid. And when there's nothing left but to face it, then they can either change or break.

The black community is the epitome of this culture of consumerism. You could be drowning in debts, behind in your bills, unable to provide basic needs for your family, but as long as you drive a car, black folks will celebrate and even envy you as a success!

Let's be real, apart from the convenience of having your own house and mode of transportation, does your house/car really fulfil you or make you extra happy? Do you feel like you are making a difference? Are you a better friend, better parent, better spouse or better human being simply because you own some nice expensive things? At the end of it all, nobody will remember the clothes you wore, the car you drove, the neighbourhood you lived in, or your Rolex watch. People will only remember how you made them feel and the impact you had on others.

Luxury Cannot Cure Poverty

The rich have more assets than liabilities, but the reverse is true for the poor. Due to low self-esteem, some people believe they can only add value to themselves by what they put on themselves instead of what they put in themselves. That's why some spend so much money on luxury. The outfit, the handbag and the shoes have to scream 'I've got money!' But poverty is too deep a wound to be covered with luxuries. Luxury cannot cure poverty.

According to statistics, only 4% of people born into poverty will ever make it out. However, this does not mean that you are doomed if you were born into poverty. It only means that you have to work triple hard to get yourself out. The world's richest people don't always come from rich backgrounds. Some of the wealthiest people on the planet came from nothing. The rags-to-riches stories may sound like a cliché, but many of them are definitely grounded in reality for some famous billionaires.

Some of world's richest people grew up working as waiters, bartenders and admin clerks. Some were raised in foster homes, some survived on one meal a day; yet through sheer persistence and grit, they beat the odds and achieved great success.

The black race is usually first to buy the flashiest cars and most expensive watches. Black people look for that which says: 'I have arrived.' A flashy car, an expensive watch or anything that visibly demonstrates that one has money. Materialism might hold true for other races but I am more experienced with my own race. It is no secret that most black people worship at the altar of materialism. The black race spends twice as much on luxury even though the white race owns twice as much of the wealth of the world. Most of us black folks don't think of generational wealth or building anything that will outlive us. Instead, we tend to do things that keep our poverty intact and pass it on to the next generation.

I've observed the answers some people give when asked 'what would you do if you woke up the next morning ten million Rand richer?' Shockingly, 90% of people usually respond with 'I'll go on a shopping spree.' This response always makes me cringe. I can't help wondering, is our biggest problem in life lack of material possessions? Of course it isn't. So the usual answer to my question is very revealing. It indicates a sad emptiness in so many lives. If they were living for a bigger purpose, would their first response still be to go on a shopping spree if they became overnight millionaires?

Yes, I am very much aware that success means different things to different people. Different strokes for different folks, but isn't it time for the black community to realise that there are other forms of success worth glorifying that are way ahead of material luxury? When will the black community take pride in owning their own car production factories, their own retail chain stores, their own financial institutions, and their own fashion labels?

My mentor, Dr Strive Masiyiwa, founder and executive chairman of Econet Group, once told a short story about himself: 'When I left

Zimbabwe in early 2000, I had taken my local company public and it was already worth over a hundred million US dollars. Despite this wealth, I lived in a middle-income area of the capital Harare, called Vainona. It was not the wealthiest suburb by any means, as any Hararian will tell you! After leaving I directed that the house be turned into a centre to help orphans. I did not own a Mercedes Benz, even though I could have afforded an entire fleet. It is not that I have anything against luxury, but as a visionary and an entrepreneur, I was thinking beyond myself and so should you if you want to leave a legacy and build a big business in Africa.'

> The actual rich buy luxuries last while the poor buy luxury first and get stuck paying for them sometimes for the rest of their lives.

In my opinion, owning a luxurious car or house is overrated in the black community. It causes me to wonder, why are other races ahead of the black race? Why is Africa, so rich in resources, still the poorest continent in the world? The answer lies in the way we think. Our mindset is holding us back. People from other races usually build cash-generating systems first and then enjoy luxury for the rest of their lives. But most black people buy luxuries first and pay for them till they die. Sometimes, children continue to pay their parents' debts while acquiring their own. Some people take heavy loans and pour the money into acquiring luxuries. Other races pour heavy money into cash-generating assets and businesses that will run for generations to come. The actual rich buy luxuries last while the poor buy luxury first and get stuck paying for them sometimes for the rest of their lives. Real success will keep eluding us if we keep masking poverty with material possessions.

Instead of buying luxury now and spending 20 years paying for it, you can delay gratification and pour the money into a business venture or some investment portfolio that could give you great returns in 10 years. Then you can have all the luxury you want from then on. *Uber*, for example, became a $72 billion (2018 statistics) company, a household name and a global conglomerate in only 10 years. Other global conglomerates like *Microsoft*, *Dell*, *Google*, *Hewlett Packard* and *Amazon* started in a garage. The founders could never have achieved what they've achieved if they were more focused on acquiring luxury early on.

If our children see us going the extra mile just to acquire liabilities like cars, designers clothing, watches, etc., they'll do the same. We are known for slaying, looking expensive, wearing other people's names and labels and not our own. *Gucci*, *Versace*, *Givenchy*, etc. are family names, but these people decided to turn their names into cash-generating machines. Today, they are touching the four corners of the world with their fashion brands.

The next African generation is looking up to us. History is staring at us. We need to do better. We need to instil in our children the right mindset and set the right example for them to follow.

If our children see us happy only when we buy luxury brands or when we are drunk they'll think happiness comes only from wearing *Gucci* or drinking designer alcohol. Well, I really don't know if there's anything like designer alcohol but I'm sure you catch my drift. Luxury does not impact the world, vision does. Gianni Versace put his name on his passion and built *Versace*, one of the world's best clothing brands, from scratch. Here are two of my favourite Gianni quotes. 'Don't be into trends. Don't make fashion own you, but you decide what you are.' 'In the past, people were born royal. Nowadays, royalty comes from what you do.'

There are real-life scenarios of youths here in South Africa who are still living at home with their parents yet driving around in expensive cars. As soon as they get a job, purchasing a car becomes their top priority. These youths don't think of buying assets or building wealth. The relentless pursuit of looking rich has prevented many from getting rich. If there are no cash-generating assets, investment portfolios or real wealth stored up somewhere in your name, living a lavish style on the outside will only make you feel more cheap on the inside, thereby lowering your self-esteem and increasing your need to cover your inner poverty with luxury.

As the black race, we are not behind other races because of the colour of our skin but because of the colour of our minds. My audacity in saying these things is meant to make an impact, thereby changing and uplifting lives. Only the truth will set us free. My dream for Africa is a mindset revolution that will change paradigms, shift horizons and transcend time. My purpose in this world is to add value and ignite human transformation. I am passionate about Africa. I believe in the continent of Africa. I can feel the tides turning, Africa is rising and so is the black race. We will someday conquer poverty, mediocrity, conformity and our inferiority complexes.

The trap of materialism is that it celebrates the mantra, 'live for today' – but the reality is that there is a common and individual posterity to consider. What are you leaving as a footprint for the next generation? Who will di$rupt the status quo and lay a better foundation for the future generation? Children's ability to delay gratification is not a predetermined trait but rather something that's impacted by their experiences and environment. We owe it to ourselves to build a society that values making a positive impact and setting a better example for the next generation. As an anonymous writer once said, 'If the price of what you are wearing exceeds the value of your mindset then you will forever be poor.'

Visionaries are motivated by something bigger than themselves. Real success is not in 'hey, look at what I have' but in 'hey, see how many lives I've touched'. So, rather be obsessed with assets and building businesses that can create solutions for the problems in your community. Empower and add value to those around you. As educational reformer Horace Mann said, 'Be ashamed to die until you have won some victory for humanity.'

The story of Shina Peters and Jim Ovia

In 1990, Shina Peters built a magnificent house with $4 million; the same year Jim Ovia started *Zenith Bank* with the same amount. Shina Peters, in his youthful exuberance as a musician, spent his earnings on luxury, but Jim Ovia, with his youthful business acumen, had an investment mindset. Today, *Zenith Bank* is a Nigerian multinational financial service provider that employs over 7000 employees with an annual revenue of about $4.1 billion.

Shina's house was built in the heart of the largest vibey city in Nigeria, Lagos, and remains there. Jim's bank started in a small corner and now has over 500 branches in Nigeria and many international branches. Millions upon millions transact business daily in Jim's bank but Shina's house is becoming dilapidated and he is spending more money to renovate and maintain it. In 2015, he bought himself a Nissan Pathfinder worth about $28,000 to add some zest to his reputation. In the same year, Jim's bank made a profit of about $3 million.

In his book *Africa Rise and Shine: How a Nigerian Entrepreneur From Humble Beginnings Grew A Business to $16 Billion*, Ovia urged entrepreneurs to be responsive to opportunities that were lurking around unnoticed.

It is indeed time for Africa for rise and shine. Some people are living in mansions but that's all they've got. Some are driving expensive flashy cars but no investment portfolios. While people like Jim Ovia, Patrice Motsepe, Aliko Dankote and Mark Zuckerberg, among others, were navigating the business world in their youth, their peers were revelling in youthful exuberance. Nowadays, there continues to be an appalling lack of financial intelligence among the youths. But self-education and a change in mindset will always set you apart from your peers. Is your mindset wired for wealth building or wealth consuming? Don't flash money – invest it. Every penny in your hand is a seed, you can decide to eat it or sow it. Be part of the revolution happening across Africa!

Don't Judge Me by the Car I Don't Have by Merusha Govender CA(SA), MBA

Today marks my three-year anniversary of being car-less. I remember that fateful day when I handed over the keys of my shiny white BMW convertible. I remember being heart-broken as I watched the new owner rev the engine so hard that I was worried it would set off all the dogs in the neighbourhood. If that was not heart breaking enough, I realised I still had to break the news to my parents. I am sure you must be rolling your eyes thinking first world problems. But I grew up in a middle-class Indian family. The youngest child and publicly acknowledged as the blue-eyed girl of my mother.

As I told my parents, there was an awkward silence that even an atom (the particle matter and not the bomb) dropping would have been heard. My mum just replied, 'Oh,' and moved onto the next topic. But I knew this wasn't the end. Truth be told, a few days later I get a call at 6:30 on a Saturday morning. Off course it was my mother who started the conversation with 'Your father and I haven't slept in days since you told us about your situation.'

My mother usually mentioned my father to increase the impact of how upset they were. My father was a practical man and normally emotionally neutral, while my mother was our very own Indian diva. 'Your father and I haven't slept in days since you told us about your situation.' I was still a bit groggy considering it was 6:30 am and the night before had ended only three hours earlier. Nevertheless, I was sure I wasn't in a 'situation'.

Being the respectful daughter, of course I didn't mention the time or ask 'WHAT SITUATION ARE YOU TALKING ABOUT?' I let my mother go on and vent all the concern and frustration that was within her. I don't think I heard every word she said and I may have fallen asleep here and there, but I remember hearing words like 'well-educated … CA … MBA'. I had already felt my ears heating up. Generally my ears get blood red when I am about to explode like an atom bomb. So I politely told my mother my phone battery was drained and I would call her back when it was charged.

A few hours later, after a hot shower and a pot of camomile tea, I called my mother back. This time she was also calm and her disappointment changed to concern. It was heart-breaking to hear my elderly mother ask me if I needed financial help and she would give me their vehicle to get around. But this was just the beginning of concerned faces and awkward questions from family members, friends, work colleagues and even strangers. My decision not to have a car was just that: it was a decision I had made.

A few days before I sold my vehicle, I had sold my house. I decided to move from the north of Johannesburg to the east. My new apartment was 2 km from my office and the person I lived with had a vehicle. Hence paying $900 per month for a vehicle, insurance and tracker, etc., did not make sense. I did the responsible thing and saved $750 per month and spent $150 using that popular app to get me to work and back.

You know that feeling you have when you're finally out of debt. Financial freedom! The world's an oyster, and I own it! That's the feeling I have felt every day for the last three years. Okay, maybe two years and eleven months. One month more to mourn the loss of my white speed machine and handling my mothers' daily calls of 'Are you sure everything is alright?'

The idea of being able to buy ANY car I wanted but choosing not to was the most liberating feeling I have experienced since I finished my articles. Now the time I wake up is not dictated by the traffic on the road, when I get into the office I am not frustrated or overwhelmed. Generally, my ride to work is dictated by my mood, sometimes I need to make calls or reply to emails, sometimes I just want to reflect and there are days when I prefer to listen to the radio or chat to my driver. In addition, I am more productive at the office and even work longer hours more easily.

In other parts of the world not having a car is acceptable. In fact, because of the good transport infrastructure, it's considered irresponsible to the environment even to own one. In Africa, the norm is get a vehicle as soon as you earn your first pay check. That vehicle is your badge to say you made it. You have arrived. People who don't own vehicles, cannot afford them, right?

Well, in the last three years I've learnt that true happiness lies within. If you keep trying to compete with fake lives on social media and owning a vehicle so people think you have arrived, then you're never going to be happy or find financial freedom. Over these three years I've learnt to be comfortable in my own skin. Selling my car forced me to allow people not to make judgements by what I drive. It also gave me an excellent conversation topic. (If you are not a complete introvert you'll understand what a big gain this is.)

I have tried to move away from people who think not having a car is a sign of a weakness. It's not that I am intolerant of people with different views; it's just that I believe you become like the people you spend your time with. Today, I make decisions that improve my life. I wake up at 8 am because I am not an early bird. I am a Group Financial

Director and often find myself at work in a t-shirt and sneakers. I let my mind and passion for my work speak for me. All those who believe that someone in sneakers cannot add value to their business or their lives is soon to be extinct. I want to be wealthy, but not rich. Yes, there is a difference. Rich people buy things. Wealthy people buy assets that generate profit. I want to create a legacy, not just have money to buy shiny new things.

One year after selling my car, I managed to buy into that group of companies where I am now the financial director. The $750 savings a month was definitely not how I did that. It happened because I had liberated myself and was able to think creatively to reach my goal. The detail of what I did to reach my goal is a story for another day. For the moment let me say this: It's amazing what confidence does for the mind; it emboldens the imagination; and being debt-free is like a shot in the arm of the most amazing energy boost.

Understand your core values and make decisions based on those, not on what your neighbour can see. Live how other people won't, so you can live how other people can't. As for my Bollywood-inspired mum, here's the latest news. Nowadays, every time she needs a ride she uses the app! Everyone can evolve (however, I am still working on her sitting in the front seat so she can chat to the driver).

A word of advice: the next time we meet, please don't judge me by the car I don't have.

Dressing Down is a Status Symbol of the Actual Rich Elite

Some people live life as though they are permanently on an *Oscars Red Carpet*. They constantly obsess over the new fashions coming onto the market. They believe wearing designer labels is a sign of success. But the actual rich elite dress down.

If you observe carefully, you'll notice that the world's most successful people are simple dressers. People with mind boggling wealth, great success stories, inventors of extraordinary things, founders of global conglomerates, etc., don't seem to care much about material possessions, fancy cars and designer clothing like average people do. The world's richest people understand the science of simplicity. They don't have to prove anything to anyone.

The following famous examples should help explain my point:

- Mark Zuckerberg, *Facebook* founder and CEO, is known for his famous grey T-shirt. 'I refuse to spend any of my energy on things that are silly or frivolous,' he said.
- Barack Obama, former president of the United States, is known for wearing grey or blue suits. In a *Vanity Fair* interview, he said, 'I'm trying to pare down decisions.'
- Bill Gates, who was the world's richest man for 18 years, has jokingly been described as dressing like a high school maths teacher.
- Steve Jobs, founder of the most innovative tech company in the world, was famously known for wearing just a simple black polo neck jersey, blue jeans and sneakers almost every day.

A new study in the *Journal of Consumer Research* reveals that 'nonconforming behaviour can be more beneficial than simply trying to fit. In other words, when it looks deliberate, a person can appear to have a higher status than those who showed up looking like everyone else. The study showed that people attribute success, power and competence to individuals who are nonconforming. This means a T-shirt instead of a suit can actually boost your social status.'

I am in no way suggesting you come out in public looking like you were fighting a mountain lion. I am all for 'dressing nice', looking good and stuff, but the most expensive outfit or car cannot change the world, cannot impact your community and it probably won't even change your day except for couple of hours.

There is nothing inherently wrong with acquiring material possessions. The problem however is that material things are the only things most people own; they have allowed these things to define them. The subtle messages they are sending says: 'I am because of what I have; I am because of what others can see I am wearing.' This is not to say that fashion isn't important, but there is no glory in choking yourself with gold chains, diamond rings, Gucci belts and expensive designer clothes just to impress people. Simplicity and dressing down are status symbols of the actual rich elite. Real success transcends money and luxury.

Jeff Bezos is currently the world's richest man and yet there's nothing about his looks that screams 'I am the world's richest man.' He's just a simple man with a simple clean look.

Mark Zuckerberg isn't Mark Zuckerberg because he owns the most expensive car. He is Mark Zuckerberg because he built *Facebook.*

Steve Jobs wasn't Steve Jobs because he had the most expensive phone, he was Steve Jobs because he built *Apple Inc.*

The list goes on, billionaires like Warren Buffet, Elon Musk, Phil Knight, Aliko Dangote, Patrice Motsepe, Jack Ma, Strive Masiyiwa, and Larry Page are some of the wealthiest people, yet they have only a simple clean look. They understand the science of simplicity and building wealth. They understand the difference between looking rich and actually being rich. It is said that every wealthy family had that one member that broke the chains of poverty for future generations. You can be that member in your own family.

Two great world leaders, Kofi Annan and John McCain, passed on in August 2018 while I was still in the process of writing this book. Tributes poured in for them and I noticed something amazing. Not one of those tributes were about their clothes, houses or cars. No one cared to mention their material possessions, but millions of people around the world spoke of how these great men had impacted the world for the better. Their impact on humanity and their global reputations were all that mattered. Kofi Annan was remembered for negotiating global treaties and John McCain for fighting and surviving a vicious war then rising to the rank of senator and deeply respected politician. These people were not angels. They were mere mortals with weaknesses like you and me – but they did something positive for humanity.

This brings me back to the million-dollar question, what will people remember you for?

Chapter 9

SCHOOLING IS NOT EDUCATION

The world has changed but the school system has not changed with it. Students spend many years in an obsolete system studying subjects they may never use and preparing for a world which no longer exists. The school system offers a one-size-fits-all academic curriculum that doesn't work for everybody. There isn't much on offer with the school system for a curious mind or someone who yearns for something different. Schools are more about passing tests/exams and less about learning. The school system teaches different minds the same things. The school system only prepares people for jobs and not life. Schooling is more about memorisation, standardisation and conformity. Hence Albert Einstein said: 'If you judge a fish by its ability to climb a tree, it will live its whole life believing that it is stupid.'

The school system doesn't pursue tapping into pupils' natural abilities, and that's where it has missed its effective mark. The school curriculum should be honing the creative and analytical ability of young minds. Schooling prepares you for what society expects you to be. The school system programmes students not to fail. If they do fail, they are punished, criticised and even ostracised. One of the greatest disadvantages to this programming is that it leaves graduates tip-toeing around opportunities in the real world due to their fear of failure. In an effort to avoid failure, students play it safe and avoid risk – and in so doing many are sleep-walking through life.

Education is what you learn after you leave school.

No matter what you may have been told, schooling is not education. Education is about growing an ability to learn, to think, to understand, to do and to take action. Education is about preparing yourself for life and for who you wish to become. Education is not synonymous with schooling. Schooling is done in school but education can happen anywhere. Education can happen without schooling and schooling can also happen without education. School teaches you 'what' to think but education teaches you 'how' to think. Never mistake getting a certificate for getting an education. Education is what you learn after you leave school.

A lot of us assume we've been educated because we attended college or some prestigious university. There are so many uneducated graduates in our world today. The school system is obsessed with producing college graduates, perfect job candidates with impressive CVs, rather than thinking human beings. But now, more than ever before, the school system needs to be revamped to adapt to the needs of the new economic paradigm and future jobs market by focusing more on the creative skills of the young mind from an early age.

Schools need to prepare pupils for a world where humans, robots and AI will work together. Jobs of the future will use different skills and higher creativity, but the way the school system is currently structured is out of step in a world where technology is changing so rapidly. With the current education system, we might end up leaving a lot of people behind.

Since the school system is failing, parents also have the responsibility to point their children in the right direction. Graduates will have to di$rupt the status quo and upgrade their skills to battle the impact of automation. Many will have to train themselves to become entrepreneurs. We are at a point in history where we need to put the focus on self-education and tapping into students' natural abilities instead of just acquiring certificates. The world belongs to thinkers, creatives and learners. The future is more creative and self-reliant. As a graduate, don't rely only on your certificate. Now is the time to educate yourself, learn new skills, grow, improve, and reinvent yourself.

Futurist and philosopher Alvin Toffler once wrote 'The illiterate of the 21st century will not be those who cannot read and write but those who cannot learn, unlearn and relearn.'

Become the master of your own education and bring yourself up to speed with the current world order. As Mark Twain said, 'I have never let my schooling interfere with my education.' The focus should be on getting an education, not just certificates. Education happens almost every day. Education can happen as soon as you read this book or watch an iconic movie or listen to an enlightening podcast or attend some seminar, workshop or training.

There is really no formula for getting educated, but there are plenty of formulas for getting a certificate – and that's where most of the world tends to follow. So much so that those without certificates often feel like outcasts. Some even end up destroying themselves on the basis of 'I have no certificate, so am not smart.' Don't get me wrong, I'm not against schooling and acquiring certificates. Schooling is very essential. It teaches us language, facts, history, figures, grammar, and how to read and write. Schooling teaches the kind of basics that you need to exist in your everyday life as an adult. In fact, I advise everyone to have some sort of basic schooling. However, it's not a death sentence if one lacks even these basics. There is more to life than the classroom, textbooks, lectures, exams and certificates.

The mental and emotional damage done by the school system can sometimes last a lifetime, although most people do wake up at some point. Some of the mental slavery caused by the system is direct and some is indirect. Everyone is prepared for the job market. An accounting degree is offered to students with the mindset to count someone else's money, not their own. A business management degree is offered to those with the mindset to manage someone else's business, not your own. An auditing degree is for those with the mindset to audit someone else's company, not your own. Even an IT or Engineering degree is given so you can solve someone else's technical problems, not your own. You can test what am saying by typing 'benefits of a business degree' on *Google* search, or any degree that comes to your mind, and you'll discover that nearly all results are related to you having better 'job opportunities'.

Some people went to school and came back with only certificates, no education at all. If what the school system offered cannot be applied to solve societal problems or personal problems, then education did not take place. If what the school system offered cannot instigate change in your personal life, then education did not take place. If what the school system offered cannot help you stand on your own two feet, then education did not take place. If what the school system offers is only for graduates to gather certificates that can't lead anywhere other than a job, then education did not take place.

> You are yet to catch up with the real world if you've never studied any concepts outside the school syllabus or read any books beside the text books your school forced you to read.

You are not educated if all you got from school is a certificate. An academic qualification is only a piece of paper, until you can channel it and employ it (leverage it) beyond the scope of the school syllabus and societal norms. You need to be able to di$rupt the status quo and use your academic know-how for your own personal benefit. It is a criminal offence against your brain to sit on your IT or Engineering certificate only waiting for a job. Real education should help solve problems, if not your country's problems then at the very least your own. The school system should create solution finders, innovators and disruptors. The school system should create assets to society, not liabilities waiting for government, families and friends to rescue them.

Are you educated or just certificated? No matter how many degrees you have, if you cannot create value for yourself by innovating or modifying your life, aren't you the same as the illiterates, maybe even worse? What is the point of having a degree if you don't possess any added advantage in the real world over someone who never went to school? A degree is just a degree. It doesn't put food on the table just by its existence with your name on it. Don't let your brain rot simply because you have a degree or whatever higher certificate of learning you've got hanging on your wall. The world doesn't pay you for what you know; the world pays you for what you can do with what you know.

You are yet to catch up with the real world if you've never studied any concepts outside the school syllabus or read any books besides the text books school forced you to read. Most people are merely programmed, not educated. You are not qualified to address the world's problems and challenges if you have no degree from the university of life.

Academic Excellence vs Real Life

The real tragedy of the school system is that academic excellence is the only target. From childhood, we are programmed to believe that by scoring higher marks we'll have a brighter future and be more likely to succeed in life. Teachers, parents, caregivers and children alike are obsessed with high marks, thereby achieving this academic excellence. The idea of stressing creativity and nurturing growing minds is thrown out the window and the memorising of information is embraced. And then information is mistaken for knowledge. The obsession with this faulty idea of excellence goes beyond the classroom, even into the job environment, where employees are more focused on achieving results than being creative and innovative. Sadly this type of excellence is usually achieved by throwing your brains in the dustbin and following rules to the core. Many of us have experienced the rude awakening that mere academic achievement, in other words the amassing of a whole storeroom of information, or being 'employee of the week' does not necessarily guarantee success, wealth or personal fulfilment.

For those who are still in school, never limit yourself to the classroom. Continue to learn wherever you are. Practise being creative; exercise those other parts of you – other skills and talents – that the classroom doesn't touch. Life doesn't really respect certificates. Real empowerment and fulfilment lie in self-education.

> The concept of nurturing a child's natural abilities is threatened with extinction under the current school system.

While school rewards people for their caution and ability to memorise, life rewards people for their imagination, creativity and daring. Life requires much more than your ability to understand a concept, memorise it and reproduce it in an exam. Intelligence and excellence in life go beyond your ability to provide cut-and-paste answers. The concept of nurturing a child's natural abilities is threatened with extinction under the current school system.

Life's skills are vitally important. A riveting story is told of a student by the name of Devin Gaines who earned five bachelor's degrees simultaneously at the University of Connecticut (2002 to 2007). He averaged 24 credits per semester and three hours of sleep per night. He drowned in 2007 because he didn't know how to swim.

Professor Abletor Sedofia from the University of Ghana had this to say: 'Academic excellence is over-rated. Being top of your class does not necessarily guarantee that you will be top in life. You could graduate as the best student in Finance but it doesn't mean you will make more money than everybody else. Best Law students do not always become the best lawyers in the real world. School celebrates those who live by the rules. Life celebrates those who break the rules and set new ones.'

The most powerful certificate you have is your mind. Use it to create your own reality. Think less of becoming an excellent student or an excellent employee. Rather think more about becoming an excellent person. No matter what you major in at the university, there will always be lessons that can only be learned in the university of life. If you can learn new skills and try new things even while still in a formal school, you'll be more than well-prepared for the world outside of college. You'll be mentally ahead of your peers. New skills mean more earning power because money grows on skills not trees.

Don't turn the classroom into your world but turn the world into your classroom.

Am I discouraging people from achieving highest marks? Certainly not, you definitely should score with distinctions. But don't sacrifice everything on the altar of certificates or high marks. Don't limit yourself to the classroom. Do something that makes your heart tick. Do something practical. Learn new skills. Join a club or start a club. Take a leadership position. Enter a contest even if you lose. Write a book, start a blog or write articles about a subject close to your heart. Go into entrepreneurship, try something new, try arts, try politics, try agriculture, etc. Break rules, be disruptive and innovative. Doing practical things will teach you more about life and yourself than any certificate could ever teach you. Start a business even if it fails. The experience will teach you more about business than a business degree.

In an era of technological advancement, it goes without saying, you cannot survive only on what the school curriculum taught you. You have the responsibility to recreate yourself. You have the responsibility to be globally and digitally oriented with the mindset to solve global problems, contribute to the economy and create your own work. Don't turn the classroom into your world but turn the world into your classroom. Academic excellence is not everything. It is your gifts, talents and skills that will make room for you and bring you before great men.

Some of the damage done to the mind by the system is that the school system creates entitlement and promotes lazy thinking. When students are in school, they are entitled to all sorts of allowances, either from family members, the government or whatever institution is sponsoring them. This is not entirely a bad thing. Even students have to eat. But beware of the adverse results of entitlement.

Students are entitled to a textbook allowance, food allowance, clothing allowance, entertainment allowance, airtime allowance, emergency allowances, medical allowances and even dating allowance. All these are good but students need to understand there are no allowances in the real world. All too often, allowances offer comfort and shield the mind from creative thinking. When students complete their studies, they find it hard to cope in the real world without allowances. Hence the relentless pursuit of a job which replaces allowances and keeps the monthly juices flowing. Surely, as successful students, they are entitled to a job. There's that old entitlement again. That's why very few graduates attempt to get into business. There might be no allowances or even a steady monthly salary for a couple of years. That's too daunting for people who have been dependent on allowances. So employment is chosen above the risk of starting a business. As an employee, at least you have some financial reward every 30 days.

This 30-days reward is very alluring, so much so that when some graduates fail to get a job they resort to going back to university for a second, or even a third degree. Have you ever wondered why, every so often, students stage protests against the re-admissions policy of institutions which prevents students who fail from staying on campus indefinitely? They protest because they'd rather stay in school and have allowances than face the pain of the real world without a job. Since they are afraid to hustle and fend for themselves, staying in school is a perfect cover. I think I can now safely say that as a student you should check on the people around you to see if they are really in school for the purpose of gaining knowledge or for the purpose of escaping life. Pain is actually a good thing and I'll show you in chapter 10 that life isn't about avoiding the bruises but about collecting the scars to prove you showed up for it.

If the next generation of graduates is going to be entrepreneurial or adequately qualified for jobs of the future, then the school system must start preparing them now for a different kind of excellence both in academics, life, the workplace and the business world. The Department of Education, from pre-school and primary right up to the university, needs new systems of learning that include: what to learn; how to learn; how to think creatively; and how to prepare for the radical shift that is rapidly approaching in the new economic era.

But instead of waiting for the education system to change, you can upskill yourself. You can gain relevant skills and recreate yourself through platforms like the Kahn Academy, Udemy, MOOC, edX, Codecademy, Coursera, FutureLearn, and other online courses that are profoundly transforming the process of learning for all ages. These decentralised online learning platforms combined with mentors and your own self education can empower, transform, and prepare you for opportunities in tomorrow's world.

The Unconventional Success Story of Iddris Sandu

Meet Iddris Sandu, born and raised in California by his Ghanaian parents. The 21-year-old unconventional tech guru has accomplished many incredible feats, including being responsible for algorithms that have made *Uber*, *Instagram* and *Snapchat* what they are today. The award-winning innovator is the best example of the power of nurturing one's talents instead of only focusing on academic excellence and certificates.

He started learning programming at the age of 10 on his own at a public library for two years and this was where he was spotted by a designer from *Google*, who offered him an internship opportunity at *Google's* headquarters. At only age 13 he worked on many projects such as the initial *Google* blogger, Google Plus, among others. Iddris Sandu then went on to develop mobile software that gained the attention of former US President Barack Obama and landed him at the White House, where he received the honorary presidential scholar award at age 16 while still in high school. At age 18, Sandu wrote an algorithm that he would go on to sell to *Instagram* while he was already consulting for *Snapchat* before landing at *Uber*, where he created a software package for its self-driving cars.

Now at age 21, Iddris has built an impressive resume using his creativity and talent to work with prominent companies, artists and professionals implementing his 'future-proof' qualities into his projects. The Wireless Charging Table, The Smart Store collaboration with the late Nipsey Hussle, Project LiFi, Project ACDI (Uber Self-Driving Cars), Kera (a new intelligent personal assistance system), Iris Scan Technology, AIPE (Advanced Imaging Processing Experience) are a few of his personal favourites.

According to reports, Iddris has a 140 IQ that places him among the top rank with some of the world's greatest minds. He plans to change the world through design, culture, and technology.

'He's revolutionising the way technology is created and used. His position right now is so relevant because he is able to over-index both worlds to create even more of an impact,' says Gary Vaynerchuck, author and speaker.

Iddris's unique talents have given him the opportunity to sit as lead technical consultant for Kanye West, singer and rapper. He is also collaborating with Jaden Smith to create an Augmented Reality (AR) experience around music. He launched an immersive store with hip hop artist Nipsey Hussle and he has great names like NBA star Steph Curry and Tesla CEO Elon Musk on speed dial.

Iddris's story is one that speaks to young people all over the world about being disruptive, self-reliant, informed and unconventional. He recently delivered a TED Talk aimed at providing youths with the exposure they need to create their own futures; and he'll also be lecturing at Stanford University. Iddris's main focus areas are architecture and design, and cultural empowerment through technology. He has a passion for community development, and to inculcate into young people the need for invention and creativity. But above all he wants to level the playing field between Silicon Valley and young people of colour. Iddris says he was twice offered admissions to the Massachusetts Institute of Technology, but he declined in order to be a change agent for African-American culture. He is a visionary equipped with the virtual reality glasses it takes these days to see into the future.

The Parenting Story of Asim Qureshi on Home Schooling his Children

Asim Qureshi, CEO of Jibble Group & LaunchPad, blogs on www.wonderyearsschool.com about home schooling his children.

On one of his blogs, he writes 'My kids are socially fine and more confident than most average school kids. They can speak five languages and are learning more. The two older kids can understand a balance sheet. My son is learning to program to make his own app; he plays football at around state level; and is one of the fastest runners for his age over five kilometres in the country. I believe home schooling has been a key reason for all his achievements.'

'After my kids are done with their exams at 18 years, they'll spend 6 to 12 months working for tech start-ups to get some work and real life experience. From this point they will be pretty much financially independent.

'I'll invest $20,000 in any start-up they want to do. They'll probably work together on one venture. If they blow it, they have a few more rounds. It's a lot of money I know, but it's a worthwhile investment. Even if they lose it all its still way cheaper and better than university fees and degrees.

'I am hoping that they'll be millionaires before they hit 25. I'm confident they'll do well because I'm mentoring them. But if business isn't for them, it wouldn't be too late for them to take the university route. But I'm hoping things won't get to the point of them choosing a university,' Asim Qureshi says.

'Am I forcing them to do this? No, not at all. I'm simply showing them both sides of the coin. I am encouraging them in the same way 99% of parents encourage their kids to go to university and get a degree. My children have the free-will and choice to do whatever they want but as it stands they are brimming with ideas already about business and the future – and they can't wait to be let loose. The journey is theirs, not mine.

'Not having a degree will mean they can't sit back and rest on any laurels or government promises. They'll have nothing to fall back on than to get out there and fight for their future, which to me is more important than any degree. I want my kids to be fearless when it comes to entrepreneurship and risk taking, and this will be their reality from the moment they decide not to get a degree.

'I'm giving my kids what I believe to be the most valuable skills for the future. I pulled them out of mainstream school and they're learning with relevant teachers and materials from home. Instead of learning things that most likely won't be applied directly to their lives, like advanced molecular biology, chemistry, history, etc., they are acquiring creative and relevant skills that will be useful to them from the word go and into the future.'

The following are some of the things that Asim Qureshi's children are learning:

- Languages: They're learning spoken Mandarin, Hindi/Urdu, French, Malay, Arabic, and English of course.
- Numeracy: My kids have gone way too far in what's actually useful and needed in being able to do the basics well. They can work out 35% of 350 in their heads fairly quickly and so, to me, they are numerate enough.
- Coding: My two elder kids, 12 and 14, spend around two hours a day learning to code – Python. Well, I tell them two hours a day is not enough.
- Public speaking and debating: My 14-year-old regularly attends public speaking classes.
- Team skills: Through group activities or sports.
- Social skills: Being able to mix well with different people. So I ensure my kids meet other kids and people of different ages and backgrounds regularly.

- Sales: I've asked my kids to sell $10,000 worth of T-shirts which I have left over from a failed business venture. Sales is a key skill in any career. You need to sell yourself even in a job interview.
- Social media, writing and marketing: I'm lumping these together because I see them all as knowing how to get out there, relate and communicate well online. Which is why I encourage my daughter, Maryam Qureshi, to write and share her thoughts on Quora.

Invest in Your Mind – Read to Lead

Everyone is so obsessed with their physical bodies and looks. Go on a diet, get the best weight loss programme, join the gym, get a personal trainer, get the best anti-aging cream, eat healthy, eat organic food, drink lots of water, eat lots of fruit and vegetables, etc. Some keep up with the Kardashians and fashion trends. Some upgrade their phones, their computers and their apps, yet most forget to upgrade the most important thing – the mind!

The burning question is: Why don't we take our minds as seriously as we take our gadgets and physical bodies? Some people have never bought a book of any genre apart from textbooks the schools forced them to buy. We invest a lot in our physical bodies, we are on special diets, yet our minds are starving. We are in our heads all day long, every moment of every second of our lives, but we give little to no attention to our minds.

> Some people own 21st century gadgets yet have a mindset from the 17th century.

It is your responsibility to feed your mind with the right content and teach your heads how to deal with life. The right mind-set gives you the unique ability to see beyond what already exists and to handle whatever life throws at us. You can grow your success margin, experience happiness and fulfilment, expand the horizon and discover great possibilities for yourself, and some of these discoveries are to be found in books. Some people own 21st century gadgets yet have a mindset from the 17th century.

I applaud you if you've read *Disrupt Yourself Or Be Disrupted* to this point. It shows great commitment that you are on a mission to di$rupt the status quo. It is my greatest desire that you'll find jewels and nuggets in this book that will change your life and contribute greatly towards your journey and overall success.

I still remember vividly the first time I got my hands on some personal development material. It was a *YouTube* video. I was baffled, but in a good way. At that very moment I realised that my fate was not set in stone. I could become my own drill master and coach. I realised that what I watched, read and listened to could set me out on a different course than the one I was on or was familiar with. I quickly switched from sitting back and waiting on a miracle to active involvement in my own life. Until that point, I didn't really understand that I was responsible for my own success or failure. I thought someone, something, some organisation, my family, some corporate entity or even the government, were responsible for how my life turned out.

Never underestimate the impact a good book can have on your life and destiny. As Benjamin Franklin, one of the founding fathers of the United States, once said: 'An investment in knowledge pays the best interest.'

However, be careful what you invest in your mind. Some people buy porn, nude magazines, gossip magazines and newspapers. These are also investments but not the kind that can empower or position you as a leader. Watching porn, reading all the gossip in your community, watching all the propaganda on TV, reading all the abuse, killings, wars and atrocities in newspapers, will leave you feeling helpless, hopeless, angry and depressed, instead of feeling in-charge and powerful. You can transform your thinking, performance, behaviour and emotional state by changing what goes into your mind. Don't feed your mind with junk content and expect to be mentally and emotionally healthy.

I've discovered through my own personal evolution as well as studying successful people that if you want to get ahead in life, you must invest in your mind. Read as many books as you can. Never underestimate the long-term impact of compound knowledge. It's not about randomly reading anything. You have to be strategic, cautious and specific when working out your mind diet programme. Personally,

I invest time into educating myself, either via books, articles, video courses, seminars or webinars.

Successful people read books that are educational. Books on leadership, business, negotiation, love, parenting, interpersonal relationships, conflict management, technology, personal development and much more. Successful people particularly obsess over biographies and autobiographies of other successful people for guidance and inspiration. Average and poor people on the other hand read gossip magazines, fashion magazines, romance, newspapers, novels. They also listen to lots of music and watch lots of TV.

Pick books that truly interest you. Don't just read them, master them, dissect their contents and implement their wisdom into your life.

However, if you are of the latter, change is possible. You can start today. You can handpick great personal development books, autobiographies, leadership books as well as great articles online and empowering videos on *YouTube* that will accelerate your life to the next level. They will ignite fire within you and inspire you to become more than you are now.

You cannot neglect your mind if you really want to grow. Wisdom and great discoveries lie in books. Make time each day to read something that's educational, even if it's only a paragraph. Expose your mind to something different than what the media constantly feeds you. Little advances in your knowledge can lead to quantum improvements in your life over time. If you don't programme your own mind it will be programmed for you. The media has its own agenda and so should you. As a leader and pioneer of the future, be intentional with your every move.

Pick books that truly interest you. Don't just read them, master them, dissect their contents and implement their wisdom into your life. Allow the wisdom in books to transform you and you'll be amazed at how incredibly powerful the impact of just one book can be. Therefore, go on: consume everything you can about life, success, relationships, business and leadership, from great minds you admire.

News reports have revealed that Bill Gates reads about 50 books a year, which breaks down to one book per week. While some people wait for the release of the next movie, great people like Mr Gates wait for the release of the next great book. You may wonder, why would a man who held the position of world's richest man for 18 years, spend so much time leafing through pages? The answer is simple: 'a rich mind equals a rich life'. The quality of your life is determined by the quality of your thoughts.

In an interview with Katherine Rosman of the *New York Times*, Bill Gates explained that reading had always been one of the 'chief ways' that he learned things. 'These days, I also get to visit interesting places, meet with scientists, and watch a lot of lectures online, but reading is still the main way that I learn new things and test my understanding of life.'

As Charles William Eliot, an American academic who wrote a book called *The Durable Satisfactions of Life*, said, 'Books are the quietest and most constant of friends. They are the most accessible and wisest of counsellors, and the most patient of teachers.' One habit successful people have in common is that they all read a lot. Many of the greatest minds in the world today say they owe their success to reading (investing in their minds).

The following business leaders and entrepreneurs make reading a major part of their daily lifestyle:

- Warren Buffett, one of the richest men in the world, was once asked about the key to success and he pointed to a stack of nearby books and said, 'Read 500 pages like this every day. That's how knowledge works. It builds up, like compound interest.' Warren Buffett has been quoted as the undisputed king of reading.
- Elon Musk, a business magnate often referred to as the greatest entrepreneur of the 21st century, is an avid reader. When asked in an interview how he learned to build rockets, he said 'I read books.'
- Mark Zuckerberg, the undisputed king of social networking, resolved to read a book every two weeks.
- Richard Branson, founder of *Virgin Group*, a tie-loathing adventurer, thrill seeker and self-made billionaire, believes that to

nurture a healthy 'growth' mind-set it is necessary to read great leadership books.

How Reading Changed my Life: The Story of Charles Chu

It was December 2014. I'd found my dream job. Some days, I would be there, sitting at my dream job, and thinking to myself, 'My God! What if I'm still here in 40 years? I don't want to die like this.' Something wasn't right. I'd followed the prescription, 'Go to school, get good grades and get a dream job.' I was a winner. I'd finished the race. Here I was in the land of dreams. But something was terribly, terribly wrong.

Every day, from my dream job desk, I'd look into the eyes of my colleagues for answers. Most of them were empty, empty eyes. There were no answers. In January of 2015, I found Warren Buffett's quote about him reading 500 pages. I decided to read. I was going to read and read and read and never stop until I got some damn answers. I didn't quite make 500 pages a day, but in two years, I read over 400 books cover to cover. That decision to start reading was one of the most important decisions in my life.

Books gave me the courage to travel. Books gave me the conviction to quit my job. Books gave me role models and heroes and meaning in a world where I had none. Instead of relying on strength of mind, I built a fortress of habits. One game-changing idea from a good book is worth thousands of dollars. If I hadn't started reading, perhaps I'd still be at my dream job. Perhaps I'd still be at my desk, taking peeks at the clock and wondering if that was how I was going to die.

Chapter 10

PURPOSEFUL PAIN

Some of us avoid pain at all costs, even to the point of sacrificing our own growth. Personal disruption involves pain – just like those who go to the gym can testify that staying in shape involves pain. Women can testify that birthing a new life involves an indescribable amount of pain. Personal disruption cannot fully happen without pain, but understanding the purpose of the pain will help you handle the frustrations, obstacles, people, relationships and attitude that accompany disruption. It'll help you to understand why things happen the way they do and why you are who you are. Everyone experiences suffering, failures, rejection and all sorts of setbacks, but not everyone understands or accepts these as part of life or of the growth process.

You finally want to go after your dreams. You finally want to start that business you've been talking about for years. Finally, you've decided you can no longer take the abuse, or being treated like a doormat. Finally, you decide you've had it with the corporate world, the routine, the petty rules, and with being normal. You've put in that resignation letter.

Finally, finally you are ready to take on the world. You are excited. But when you make a decision to change certain things about your life, your life may actually seem, in the beginning of the process, as if it's going on a downward trajectory. You may lose friends, loved ones may judge you and you'll doubt if you actually made the right decision. It is usually an uncomfortable and painful time in one's life when all hell seems to break loose. But having the right mind-set is key to overcoming all obstacles.

Understanding why things are happening will help you complete your mission. It'll help you to find a way through failure and rejection.

The Pain of Failure

We are taught from a very young age to avoid failure at all costs. School taught us that failure is wrong and punishable. As we became adults we have to re-embrace this belief. It's strengthened in organisations where failure and mistakes are treated with the ultimate disgust, or at least with pity and disdain. We've become so afraid of failure that we don't want to try anything that could fail. Regardless of what society and schools have taught us, failure is a risk one must take to achieve success. And the risks are high.

While it is possible to study and obtain school certificates without failing any subjects, it is impossible to obtain success in the real world without some soul-wrenching failures. Maybe you are running on a smooth lane for now, but failure cannot always be avoided.

> The fear of failure does not prevent anyone from failing. Even if you don't do it - you'd still fail by default.

Life is more interesting when it is both juicy and a tad messy. Don't give up. Be willing to fumble through it until you eventually find your way. JK Rowling, novelist and film producer, said in her *Harvard University* Commencement address, 'It is impossible to live without failing at something, unless you live so cautiously that you might as well not have lived at all.'

Trying something new is inevitably risky and failure is always a real possibility. You are courting failure whenever you venture into new, uncharted territory. You wish to fulfil your ambitions and express your boundless gifts to the world, but fear does not want you to grow beyond what you are now. Lack of effort, procrastination and the dark holes of depression to which you've succumbed are all evidence of the fear of failure.

You crave achievement, but the people you hoped would support you have turned against you. Your dreams seem elusive, distant and far away from your shaky hands. That is exactly how fear wants you to see it, that it's impossible! Actually, the fear of failure doesn't prevent anyone from failing. Even if you don't do it – you'd still fail by default. The more you protect yourself from failure, the more you protect yourself from growth. Life isn't about avoiding the bruises but about collecting the scars to prove you showed up for a full dose of it.

Roll up your sleeves: before you lies an ordeal of the most grievous kind. Before you your path will be obscured by many, many long months, perhaps years, of struggle and suffering. Success and failure come in the same package. Face it! You're going to make mistakes, and lots of them. When you di$rupt yourself, you are walking into the unknown, exposing yourself to the risk of failure. But that is okay. Fail fast and fail forward. Allow people to refute and doubt you, but never allow them to dismiss you. Look at failure as education.

Disruptors rarely bring ideas that are fully formed. It is usually through a series of failures that each idea gets refined. Failures along the way are essential steps in the process of creative growth. You wouldn't know what works and what doesn't without these necessary steps. Disruptors go down first before they spin up. At the very least, failure teaches you what doesn't work.

Dealing with failure is usually a defining moment in anyone's life. But you can make it through the forest without becoming more lost. Do not be afraid of failure, it is your road to success. Something is undeniably very wrong if everything is always working out for you with no glitches. It is okay to fail from time to time. So, learn how to make your nest even in piles of broken glass.

Therefore, collapse the walls of protection you have built around yourself. Cradle your shattered ego, smile at the troubles, smile at the headshakers and the naysayers. Bring failure close to your bosom and embrace it. Never give failure the power to amplify your fears. Don't avoid failure, rather fall down seven times and get back up ten times. The person who never failed at anything will ultimately take orders from the ones who did.

> Your deepest life message will come out of your deepest pain and failures.

Failure is not an enemy, failure is a friend, failure is a teacher, and failure is part of life. When you are out there fighting to make something of yourself, you are not only building your future, your future is also building you. Nothing builds character and humbles a man better than failure. Character is revealed when pressure is applied. When the burden is beyond carrying, and the pain is beyond all description, and your dreams are twisted with confusion, don't give up! Know that the struggle is an exercise, a ritual of deepest divinity. It is preparing you for something greater. Your deepest life message will come out of your deepest pain and failures. Pain is meant to produce purpose, not kill it. Pain can give you a better perspective on things in six months than pleasure can in ten years.

Those who avoid failure are those who seek overnight success. They want to wake up one morning and – boom! – they are successful. But success is built over time, not overnight. Overnight success usually lasts for little longer than a night. Overnight success is loud, flashy, intimidating, self-seeking and usually comes with almost no pain and no failure. However, real success that will transcend generations takes time, heart-wrenching failure, persistence, and hard work to build. Success achieved over time inspires, motivates and works towards the greater good of humanity.

The Pain of Rejection

One of the biggest hang-ups for some entrepreneurs and dreamers is their innate desire to rally the troops and have everyone's permission and support before stepping out in pursuit of their dreams. They are hell-bent on getting family and friends on board before they venture out. In most cases, it's because they are trying to avoid rejection and friction. But you cannot rely on people to rally behind your vision before you take action. What if they never do? You can't bake a cake without breaking some eggs.

It might be difficult for you to do things outside the approval of your family, friends and society at large. You love your people and they obviously love you too. But this type of love scenario is like thorns that choke the seeds of greatness. Waiting on someone to grant you permission is a strategic blunder. Life become a struggle and dreams become unreachable when you focus on people's opinions and fears instead of your purpose. Being a disruptor means blazing your own trail. As Oprah Winfrey wrote in her *What I Know for Sure*: 'Understand that the right to choose your own path is a sacred privilege. Use it and dwell in possibility.' If you have an idea, go after it. There's no time to wait for others to validate your idea.

Your resolve to be different, resourceful and successful is your greatest strength. Don't hesitate on your dreams because of fear of rejection. Don't feel inferior because you are young/old. Be willing to make mistakes, break rules and overturn conventions. In so doing you'll become superior and a force to reckon with. But until then, it's war.

From the government to school systems, churches to communities, families to friends, they are all pushing everyone towards getting a job. The mantra has always been 'go to school, study hard, get a certificate and get a job'. We are all raised to be employees, and breaking away from this system doesn't go without consequences. You'll face unpleasant circumstances, rejection and mockery. You'll feel almost as if the whole universe is angry at you for not following the system. Society is softer on the unemployed than on those who are trying to create employment for themselves and others. The unemployed are an obedient bunch waiting to receive what they were promised in school. They receive a lot of attention and sympathy from society, but a disruptor tends to be perceived as a threat.

Understand that rejection is part of the process of self-disruption. Your family sent you to school so that you could get a job. Literally, you've declared war the moment you give up the idea of a job to pursue your own thing. You might be pitied, called names, misunderstood, and judged. It doesn't matter if your dreams, ambitions or start-up result in the next big thing.

> Get used to rejection: no one started from the bottom with applause or the word Yes being heard very often.

It doesn't matter if you are going to be the next Bill Gates, Mark

Zuckerberg, Aliko Dangote, Patrice Motsepe, Oprah Winfrey or anything in-between. In the past, the world would always celebrate those who got the big job better than those who started a business or followed their calling. But the tides are turning. Entrepreneurship is now becoming fashionable as young people are reading the fast-changing future and emerging as game-changers, tech gurus, innovators, thought leaders and pioneers of the future.

The exciting thing for me is that this isn't only happening in the developed countries of the world, but all across the developing south – and across the African continent as well. As a result, we need to be proud of being pioneers and a part of this very necessary revolution.

Get used to rejection: no one started from the bottom with applause or the word Yes being heard very often. Every pioneer is first ignored, or at best ridiculed, before they become respected. Even in the midst of rejection, keep going. One day it'll all make sense. Until then, cry if you have to, start all over again if you have to, but never give up.

When you pursue your dreams, your whole life wakes up, your mind wakes up and everything begins to have meaning. You'll love your life and your decisions. The more you love your decisions, the less you need others to love them.

As Mandy Hale said: 'You'll learn, as you get older, that rules are made to be broken. Be bold enough to live life on your terms, and never, ever apologise for it. Go against the grain, refuse to conform, take the road less travelled instead of the well-beaten path. Laugh in the face of adversity, and leap before you look. Dance as though everybody is watching. March to the beat of your own drummer. And stubbornly refuse to fit in.'

The beginning of anything new can be tough, and may even cause you to doubt your ability to succeed. But if you keep at it, suddenly there's an inflection point. Everything falls into place and your idea, project or career takes off almost vertically, yielding generous rewards. This is the exciting part, where all your neurons are firing and where you can feel justified in what you have attempted and achieved.

Planting and harvest don't happen in the same season.

An antidote to rejection is to understanding that if no one is cheering or booing you, it means you are not in the game. Rejection does not last forever. It is better to try something and fail or be rejected than not try at all. Getting rejected means you are trying, you're learning the market and the industry. Getting rejected means you are learning how to better run your business, write proposal emails, and query letters. Getting rejection gives you an opportunity to perfect your craft and become so good you can't be ignored. It means you are marketing yourself, networking and meeting people in the industry. And most importantly getting rejected means you are not giving up. It's not about who you are today. It's about who you want to become and the price you're willing to pay to get there. Planting and harvesting don't happen simultaneously. It takes time to get from one to the other.

The Story of Mark Victor

Mark Victor Hansen is the author of *Chicken Soup for the Soul*, a book about inspirational true life stories of ordinary people told with the purpose of awakening possibility in every soul. The book became a major bestseller and turned into a series of over 100 books selling over 100 million copies and translated into over 50 languages. It's a book that has made millions of dollars and spawned countless spin-off products. Yet this book was rejected 140 times by publishers, but Mark believed in his book, refusing to accept rejection, and kept going.

Chapter 11

MONEY CANNOT CURE POVERTY

Poverty has nothing to do with lack of money. Poverty is a state of mind. Poor people with the 'right mind-set' can pull themselves out of poverty. Poverty is the failure of the mind to think, perceive and pursue opportunities. Poverty is the nakedness of the mind. Poor people are lazy to think and hence often come up with strategies that will only help keep their poverty intact. When you are too lazy to think, you will never struggle to become poor. In fact, no one struggles to become poor. There has never been a news headline of anyone who worked their butt off or went out of their way to become poor.

Many people would probably not be poor if there were prerequisites like hard work, sleepless nights, or any form of pain one had to go through in order to achieve poverty. It really doesn't take a great deal of effort for anyone to be poor. By default we were all born naked, poor and scared. No one jumped out of their mother's womb with a bag of cash. Hence, success is a DIY process!

Many seek solutions to their problems in the wrong places. Their strategy out of poverty happens to be things that will only push them deeper into the abyss. Many have resorted to charity, gambling and black tax as their way out of poverty. But contrary to popular belief, these strategies never really rescued anyone out of poverty.

The only real strategy to beat poverty is to empower your mind. Poverty is a cankerworm whose cure must start from the mind. It is not a 'lack of money problem' as much as it is a 'poor mind-set problem'. Poverty is aggravated when money is given to a poor mind. Giving money to a poor mind is like throwing it in the dustbin. It is not money that buys one a better future. It is vision, ambition, skills, grit and sheer resilience to beat the odds and make your mark in the world. In fact, money cannot cure poverty; neither can money cure lack of ambition.

How many people do you know who have had huge sums of money, including those who once won the lottery or inherited millions, but today are broke beyond recognition? Their situation went from poverty to riches then back to poverty. As self-help guru Napoleon Hill said, 'Wealth acquired too soon is worse than poverty.'

Charity Cannot Cure Poverty

The solution to poverty is not charitable giving, but a major shift in mind-set. The mind is where the revolution begins. Transformational thinking is a key requirement to fighting poverty. Poverty can be conquered if the masses can di$rupt and re-invent their thinking. Charity is an actual hindrance to wealth creation. It's like a total blackout that is engulfing Africa. Most leaders are globetrotting, campaigning and begging for financial aid to feed and clothe their citizens instead of establishing developmental strategies that will cut off foreign aid and force Africans to fend for themselves.

If Africa could be abandoned by the West, I believe Africans will wake up and build an economy larger than the West could ever imagine. Africa has all the resources and everything it needs to rise. Giving poor people money only helps keeps them poor for longer. Charity does not cure poverty. It causes those with a poor mind-set to sink even deeper into the paralysis of being 'poor'.

If people – and communities and nations – on the charity queues suddenly received nothing, they would soon enough find a way to lift themselves out of their situation. The instinct for survival is rooted in all of us, but the fighting spirit attached to it goes on holiday as long as people are being fed freebies by charitable organisations or the government. You will never know the power of water when it is standing still. You will never know you can swim until you're thrown into an ocean of nothingness. Cutting back on charity or eliminating it completely will be considered inhumane and brutal by the masses. But such a course of action would in the short, medium and long term transform the lives of those sunk in poverty. They'd be forced to hunt for their own bread and in so doing would permanently alter their own lives – as well as the general status quo.

Helping someone in need is a kind and humane act, and I am not totally against these acts. But when this becomes a way of life, especially for the recipient, it is no longer helping a life but destroying a life. Poverty will continue to be passed down from one generation to another if we cannot slow down and rethink 'charity'. Many are drowning in the abundance of their own potential and untapped resources but fail to see it because they are blinded by charity.

The African continent as a whole is a perfect example of how people can drown in their own resources. Africa has some of the world's richest resources yet Africa is known as the poorest continent in the world. Why? This is because we are mentally blinded to see our own potential and resources. We believe the lies that other races are better than us. We believe the lie that we need 'help' from the West to survive. But developed countries often use charity as a cover-up to hide their continued looting of the continent. The illusion that charity is helping African countries has facilitated a perverse reality in which the developed world celebrates its generosity while simultaneously assisting its companies to drain African resources.

Recent reports by *Health Poverty Action* and other NGOs revealed that 'The Western world sends about $30 billion in development aid to Africa every year but more than six times that amount leaves the continent, mainly to the same countries providing that aid.'

No country or economy can be built on charity. As Mugumya Junior, founder and CEO of April Logistics Uganda, once said, 'Every country is built by entrepreneurs.' The responsibility to build Africa, her people and communities, lies with Africans themselves. The responsibility to build disadvantaged communities lies with their own people. Charity does not help the poor. Charity is a beautiful poison that kills its victims slowly. And the sooner the poor can realise this the faster they can come out of poverty. It is better to teach someone how to fish than to give them a fish. What charity does is simply distribute fishes, but real and lasting empowerment is teaching people the skills that would make it possible to own the pond and fish for themselves. When someone says they can do it for you, they usually arrive with a ready-made solution in their back pockets. Their well-meaning efforts do little more than rob you of your creative thinking.

> Charity is not a way of taking people out of poverty but a way of passing poverty from one generation to another.

Until a man sees the person he wants to become in future, the slightest help given to him is a complete waste. Charity kills creativity, encourages lazy thinking and creates dependency in the people it targets. Charity only treats the symptoms instead of the disease of poverty. Without a shift in mind-set, people depending on charity will continue to drown in their own resources. Charity is not a way of taking people out of poverty but a way of passing poverty from one generation to another.

Teach a man how to fish and in so doing you've given him an employment that will feed him for a lifetime. Poverty issues deserve a developmental strategy but not charitable giving. There is no faster way to demotivate, demoralise and disempower a person or a community than giving them freebies, providing their basic needs, and solving their problems for them.

The compassion industry is almost universally accepted as a virtuous and constructive initiative, but its outcomes are more detrimental than intended. I understand this idea may ruffle some feathers. But we need to take the gloves off and admit that much of charitable giving harms the people it is meant to help. Of course, it's an easy gift to accept, but with acceptance comes a fresh wave of lethargy and, worse still, a reinforcement of the sense of inferiority implied by the receipt of the handout.

Charitable giving has barely made a dent in reducing poverty in Africa. There are communities that have been on charity since the dawn of time, but many of these same communities have no access to electricity, no roads, no proper education, no infrastructure, no acceptable sanitation, no hospitals, no developmental platforms and no access to technology. Children born into these conditions grow up and give birth to their own children in the very same conditions. The cycle continues while millions of dollars go into feeding schemes, food parcels, and Christmas gifts every year to the same people who have no future, no hope and no infrastructure.

Charity creates dependency, kills human potential and destroys personal initiative. Charity disempowers those it is meant to empower. Charity needs a major rethink, especially in Africa. We hear heart-warming stories of lives that have been changed and how communities are being impacted by well-meaning charitable organisations but the reality is that this is usually only temporary relief. Things get out of whack in no time and the very same people sit back, cry, complain and wait for their next fix.

> What is most needed by poor communities is a long-term development plan that will build the capacity of people to own and overcome their own problems.

What creates true and lasting change is empowerment that is birthed from within a person or within the community. Transformation takes places when someone begins to ask 'how' can I change my situation instead of 'who' can change my situation. Real help and empowerment happens when each person or community is made to understand that no matter their current status, they can utilise the resources they have on hand to improve their quality of life without outside assistance.

Charity that makes a difference should focus on education, vocational training and personal development, not on handouts. Seminars, brainstorming, honing individual talents and igniting human potential should be key areas of focus in communities that depend on charities. The work of making money, providing for one's self and hunting for the next meal should be left to an individual to figure out. In so doing, there comes that moment when the light bulb goes on in their minds and they begin to realise that they have what it takes to make it on their own. They'll begin to realise that if there is going to be a shift in paradigm, it's up to them. When that moment comes, life shifts from going with the flow to taking control and making things happen. It's empowering and liberating to realise that you have the power to create your own reality.

Why stand begging for what you have the power to earn? If you are on charity and wondering if you can ever make it on your own, I'd like to assure you that it is possible. Money has not left Planet Earth. There is money out there with your name on it but it won't come and meet you. You have to go out and get it yourself. It may take years, countless nights of tossing, crying and hunger, but you'll get it eventually, only if you persist and don't give up.

Am I saying that charity shouldn't be practised at all? Of course not. Charitable giving is very much needed but should be limited mostly to emergencies like war, famine, a home burning down and natural disasters like hurricanes, flooding, mudslides and earthquakes. Charity should be given to children, elderly people, disabled people and sick people with chronic diseases who can't help themselves. Immediate crisis relief is a necessary intervention and humanity should always come first.

However, relief is no longer needed when an emergency is over and individuals have the ability to help themselves. After an emergency crisis has been averted, it is important to move quickly into a developmental strategy. A developmental strategy requires charitable organisations to move into a partnership role and allow the 'poor' to participate and plan their own recovery. But because relief is relatively easy to administer and development require much more time and effort, people often choose to just give a hand-out rather than a hand-up. Social grants are a broken system that traps too many people in a cycle of dependence. People need a 'hand-up,' not a 'hand-out.'

What is most needed by poor communities is a long-term developmental plan that will build the capacity of people to own and overcome their own problems. Charitable organisations and poor communities should work in partnership to offer education, seminars, skills training, advocacy, networking, and meaningful empowerment – building all of it on local assets (minds) is a better way to engage and help the poor than simply handing them food parcels and social grants.

Entrepreneurship, vocational training and honing individual talents should be key areas of focus. Instead of feeding schemes, coaching and mentorship for youths and adults with business ideas should be provided. Charitable organisations can also provide innovation hubs, centres where creatives, hi-tech entrepreneurs, academia and dreamers can come together. Sometimes, the poor stay poor, not because they are lazy but because they have no access to information, skill training and capital. Through partnerships and sponsorships, organisations can tap into the unique gifts of individuals and provide a strong element of ownership which allows beneficiaries to determine their own outcomes in life.

Social Grants Cannot Cure Poverty

Social grants, also known as government welfare in some countries, are income transfers paid to qualifying citizens. In South Africa, social grants are meant to improve standards of living and redistribute wealth to create a more equitable society. The grants are given to certain categories of people considered vulnerable to poverty and in need of state support. The government says that social grants remain the most effective form of poverty alleviation.

While this sounds very strategic and juicy, the reality is the complete opposite. When the government begins to throw money at poverty or to sponsor basic human needs such as food, housing, electricity, clothing, etc., this only encourages ever-growing handout queues at government offices. Government social grants have the same effect on human potential as any other charitable giving. They diminish the creativity and dignity of poor people while increasing their dependency. According to statistics, the number of people receiving social grants in South Africa increased from 2.9 million in 1994 to about 4 million in 2000. As of 2017, the number of grant recipients is sitting at a whopping 17 million out of a population of 54 million people and this number keeps rising. According to the *Institute of Race Relations (IRR)*, 'there are officially more people on grants than those with jobs in South Africa'. There are 15.5 million people with jobs and 17 million on grants.

This situation raises a question: If social grants are an effective method of alleviating poverty, as the government claims, why has the number of poor people quadrupled?

Poverty issues require a mind-set development strategy and not handouts. Social grants are not a way of taking people out of poverty but a way of passing poverty from one generation to another. The fastest way to kill creativity and human potential in any community is to keep feeding them freebies. Charity or grants cannot cure poverty. Freebies only help keep people poor for longer.

> The fastest way to kill creativity and human potential in any community is to keep feeding them freebies.

Are you on social grants? Do you really believe the government is helping you eradicate poverty? Can you really build a meaningful life on government stipends? My view is that you might remain poor forever if you are not finding new ways to cut yourself off from government grants and other charitable giving or at the very least to use the money to economically uplift yourself and help to ensure that social grants are not needed to sustain the next generation. It's up to you to demand change from yourself. Yes, you will suffer – but you will learn, grow and free yourself.

A Look at Black Tax – The Family ATM

Black tax, also known as Ubuntu tax, is a kind of pay-it-forward obligation. Black tax is an almost exclusively black experience. It is the responsibility people with jobs or businesses have to help their family members who might be struggling financially, especially their parents. Yes, helping one's aging parents is a noble cause. However, the problem comes when the context of black tax responsibility extends beyond immediate family to the clan of uncles, aunts, cousins and even children yet unborn. Those extended family members may or may not have contributed anything towards your success. Siblings usually fall under the category of those who contributed nothing to your success, yet every one demands their own share of black tax.

Once one family member gets a job or starts anything that generates an income, he/she becomes the family ATM. At this point, you begin to know family members you never knew you had, even dead aunties and uncles rise from the graveyard and queue for a withdrawal.

This is one of the heavy weights on the shoulders of most working-class black people. Sponsoring siblings in school, building a house for parents and sending money to aunties, uncles and cousins is a huge task. You become 'a one-man one-woman' type of charity organisation that's dishing out cash, food parcels, clothing, even gadgets every month to those who depend on you. Some siblings completely give up the idea of hustling for themselves just because their brother/sister, aunt/uncle has an income.

The intentions behind 'black tax', just like the intentions of social grants, are usually good. You are helping someone. But actually the opposite is usually achieved. For those people receiving 'black tax' a culture of entitlement and dependency is created.

'Black tax' should strictly be for helping one's aging parents, and sick or disabled family members. Adults who are healthy, strong and well able to earn their own income should not depend on another to take care of them every single month. The whole concept of 'black tax' should be redefined. Beliefs and practices that inflict suffering on another human being should be abolished.

Some African people travel overseas in search of better opportunities and family members at home sit back and depend on them even for the air they breathe. The entire family back home, often extending to the whole clan, look up to this one person for their daily bread. Being overseas is viewed as the promised land. Their families at home hear stories, they watch movies and base their expectations on these. Most black people overseas have to put their lives and dreams on hold to fulfil 'black tax'. Some work multiple jobs with only three hours' sleep every day or no sleep at all just to pay 'black tax' back home. Whatever the circumstances, the family commands respect from 'my brother, sister, aunt, uncle living in the UK, Canada, Japan, etc.'

This is an exploitation of human rights and an injustice in its own right. 'Black tax' is perpetuated by traditional customs that no longer apply in the modern world. It is a pernicious system which hampers those adventurous enough to go overseas, and weakens the family members who become long-distance spongers on other people's efforts to succeed. Nowadays, young people start work already burdened by student debt. They are already deep in debt before they even earn their very first salary. And on top of that come the claims of 'black tax'. Many black people are torn between this destructive tax and their own ambitions. In an attempt to meet their 'black tax' obligations, they take out more loans and end up getting stuck in a cycle of debt, thus sentencing themselves to a lifetime of financial struggle. Lack of financial education makes matters worse, often causing those who earn higher salaries to be more indebted.

You find people ranging from their early 20s to their late 40s who are stuck in the middle of supporting two generations financially and are therefore unable to pursue their own dreams. They risk sentencing their offspring to being the next 'black tax' payers due to their inability to create generational wealth through building sustainable businesses and investment portfolios. This is exactly how generational poverty is created. 'Black tax' can temporarily help and relieve symptoms of poverty but only a fundamental shift in attitude and real empowerment can lift the family out of poverty.

> Black tax payers should consider a better way to help their family members. Empowerment doesn't have to be only a university degree or monthly allowance. Entrepreneurship should be encouraged.

Yes, black tax is part of our lives and culture; it is both a blessing and a curse. However, it cannot be avoided completely. Black tax helps us take care of our parents and some other important family emergencies. But instead of being the centre of provision or the family's ATM, it's better to empower other family members to earn their own income, thereby increasing the collective earning ability of the family.

Black tax payers should consider a better way to help their family members. Sponsoring your siblings to get a degree is no guarantee they'll get a job and a job is not the only way of making an income. Entrepreneurship should be encouraged. There are vocational training facilities and practical skills that can be learnt to help individuals become self-employed. Pay for your siblings to have some vocational training. If they have a business idea, support them to start a business even if it's to sell vegetables on the street. Empower them to stand on their own two feet. If this is accomplished, then black tax has been put to good use – but until then it is just another form of charitable giving that disempowers those it is meant to empower. Radical economic disempowerment is when you are paying black tax to siblings (mature healthy adults) who wear Gucci shoes, Brazilian weaves, and own iPhones and party every weekend.

Gambling Cannot Cure Poverty

Gambling should actually top the list of things that cannot cure poverty. Gambling has been part of the world system almost since the creation of the world. As the human race advanced, so has gambling. Gambling comes in different forms – slot machines, horse racing, dog fights, the poker table, roulette, bingo, lotteries, etc. With the growth of the internet throughout the world, more and more online games are emerging. According to data published by one of the European universities, 40% of all internet users play online gambling games, spending from three to five hours every day. Soccer betting has become the norm in Africa. Young people carry files/papers around hoping to become overnight millionaires. One could easily mistake this as a generation that's actually interested in reading, but they are simply scheming their luck on numbers. Dreams, ambitions and business ideas are being slaughtered every day on soccer-betting tables in exchange for illusory overnight riches.

People are looking for the easy way out but there is no easy way out. Many see gambling as an option to cure their poverty and in doing so have compounded their misery. People most addicted to gambling are the poor who are looking for a get-rich-quick way to taste a better life. But instead of getting rich, they end up getting poorer and poorer because any little earnings they have are squandered on gambling tables in hopes of more.

While there may be valid claims that some people built houses, bought cars or even started businesses because of their gambling winnings, there are more numerous claims, all equally valid, of people who became bankrupt and lost everything as a result of their gambling addiction. Gambling has produced more penniless people than rich people. Gambling creates dependency on a system that is highly structured, organised and calculated to work against you.

Occasionally, the system will throw some cash at you to keep you from trying to escape, but a gambler's life is dependent on luck and high blood pressure rather than a well-designed plan he or she can control. The odds are always against you and the results are out of your control. The pattern of gambling is the same for everyone. Win-lose-win-lose and so the cycle continues and the addiction deepens. You win today, you lose tomorrow. Maybe not tomorrow, but the next day or another day.

> Gambling reduces creativity and sends one away to a fantasy world, making dreams and aspirations rely heavily on luck.

The biggest evil with gambling is that people think they can become successful without work. Imagine betting your whole future on numbers! The promise to make you rich overnight is an illusion and a marketing strategy to make more money off people who are too lazy to work or to think for themselves.

Overnight riches usually last only for the night. Success rarely happens without a planned process and with hard work involved. Gambling has the same effect as a charity handout or a social grant. It creates dependency, entitlement and lazy thinking. Gambling reduces creativity and entices its victims away to a fantasy world, making dreams and aspirations rely on nothing but luck.

Gamblers believe they can become rich by winning those millions promised but one does not become rich simply by having access to money – just as one does not become poor simply by not having access to money. Rich people became rich because they had a wealth-building mentality.

There are billionaires who have been bankrupt three to five times in their life-time. How did they rise back up? The answer is simple – they had a wealth-building mind-set. It was never about the money in their bank accounts but about the money in their mind accounts. The money in your bank account can get finished but the money in your mind account is infinite. A gambler can win millions, lose it all and go back to abject poverty. But a person with a wealth-building mindset can lose billions and still won't taste poverty. It's all about your mind-set.

Meet the man who holds the title of losing the most money in history

His name is Masayoshi Son, a Japanese business mogul, Founder/CEO of *SoftBank Mobile* and the richest man in Japan, according to the 2018 *Forbes* list. What sets Masayoshi Son apart from other billionaires is the fact that he holds the distinction of losing the largest stash of personal wealth anyone has ever lost in the history of humankind. He lost approximately $70 billion during the dot-com crash of 2000. Now, less than two decades later, he's the richest person around.

Most people on gambling tables don't have a wealth-building mind-set. They wouldn't be there to begin with if they did. Show me a man with access to money but with a poor mind-set and I'll show you a poor man tomorrow. Show me a poor man today who has a wealth-building mind-set and I'll show you a wealthy man tomorrow. It is never about having access to money or not having access to money. It is how your thinking is wired.

How many people do you know who inherited great fortune but squandered everything? The same goes for people who won millions on gambling tables and became notably worse off than before. Overnight riches won't help anybody if that person is not mentality wired to handle wealth. One who won a jackpot does not become poor later on in life simply because the money came easy, but mostly because he/she has a poor mind-set.

Success is built over time not overnight.

That said, asking if you have ever seen any lottery winner who remained successful afterwards is the equivalent of asking if you have ever seen any criminal who became successful through the money from his crimes. Money usually takes on the character of the immediate holder, not that of the source it came from.

Money has its principle and we must put the plough to the ground to reap. To become rich or poor doesn't lie in the source of money or the amount of money. Success or failure lies in the content of the individual. What is the content of your mind? Are you wired for wealth building? Success is built over time, not overnight.

15 Lottery Winners Who Lost It All

While it may be tempting to buy a lottery ticket that could turn you into an overnight millionaire, it is certainly not worth it. History has shown us countless examples of lottery winners whose lives took a turn for the worse after hitting the jackpot. You'd think that winning the lottery should be the first step towards financial freedom, but the stories you are about to read prove that good luck can actually be the beginning of deeper poverty. There's hardly anyone on the list of world's richest people on *Forbes Magazine* whose source of wealth can be traced back to winning a jackpot. Why? This is mainly because people who play the lottery are not mentally wired for wealth creation, wealth building or wealth management. They lack financial intelligence; and financial catastrophes are usually created from financial ignorance.

It does seem Napoleon Hill was right when he said: 'Wealth acquired too soon is more dangerous than poverty.'

Here are 15 lottery winners who lost it all, and whose lives became notably worse than before.

1. A former police officer, from Pietermaritzburg in KwaZulu-Natal, won $750,000 in 2009. He resigned from the police service, divorced his wife, bought five vehicles, put a deposit on a house, and gave some to charity. He also threw lavish parties for friends and squandered everything in less than four years. He did invest in a chicken soup franchise, but lost it when he didn't abide by the rules of the franchise. In 2014, the ex-cop was arrest for impersonating a police officer with a fake badge and stealing $15. He is now penniless and shares a tiny flat with his two siblings.
2. In 2015, a Bloemfontein man won $7.1 million in the Lotto. Three years later it was all gone. He squandered it on fast cars, gambling tables, sex, designer alcohol and drugs.

3. William Bud won $16.2 million in the Pennsylvania lottery, but he was $1 million in debt within a year. 'I wish it never happened,' Mr Bud said. 'It was totally a nightmare.'
4. Sharon Tirabassi, a Canadian single mother who had been on welfare, won the jackpot for more than $10 million. She spent her winnings on a mansion, fancy cars, designer clothes, lavish parties, exotic trips, handouts to family, loans to friends, and in less than a decade she was back to riding the bus, working part-time, and living in a rented house.
5. Gerald Muswagon won $10 million in the super 7 jackpot in Canada. He bought many cars for himself and his friends, purchased a house that turned into a mini-night club and often celebrated his new lifestyle with copious amounts of drugs and alcohol. In a single day, he bought eight big-screen televisions for friends. He blew all his money and was eventually forced to take a job doing heavy lifting on a friend's farm just to make ends meet. Filled with regret and shame, Muswagon hanged himself in his parents' garage in 2005.
6. Michael Carroll was a garbage collector when he won the $15 million jackpot. He was only 19 years old but a penchant for crack, parties, prostitutes, and fast cars put him back at square one in just five years. According to a report from his own mouth, he slept with over 2000 prostitutes in an eight-year period. He ended up living on government welfare and begging to get his old job back as a garbage collector after spending years living a rock star life of sex, drugs, rock 'n' roll and fast cars.
7. In 2002, West Virginia building contractor Andrew Jackson Whittaker Jr. walked away with $114 million jackpot after taxes. But within five years, Whittaker had squandered every cent on bad investments and luxury and was being sued by Caesar's Atlantic City for bouncing checks.
8. Billy Bob Harrell Jr, a Pentecostal preacher, working as a stock boy at Home Depot, got his prayers answered when he hit the $31 million Texas jackpot in 1997. At first life was good; Billy quit his job, travelled to Hawaii, bought a ranch, six other homes, new cars and donated some to the poor. The money brought trouble to his

marriage, he divorced and two years later the money was all gone. He ended up committing suicide. Shortly before his death, he told a financial adviser that 'winning the lottery is the worst thing that ever happened to me'.

9. Willie Hurt won $3.1 million in the Michigan Lottery in 1989. He picked up a crack cocaine addiction. The habit sucked away his entire fortune in just two years. Hurt was divorced, lost custody of his children, and was charged with attempted murder.
10. Janite Lee won $18 million lottery jackpot in 1993 and her winnings were gone within a decade. She blew it all on charity.
11. Luke Pittard of Wales won $1.9 million in 2006, but spent it on an exotic trip to the Canary Islands, a lavish wedding and a mega house. A year and a half later, Pittard was forced by poverty to return to his job at McDonald's.
12. Callie Rogers was just 16 years old when she won $3 million in the UK's lottery in 2003. She spent millions on exotic vacations, designer clothing, fast cars, cosmetics, breast implants, and according to British tabloid, *The Sun*, she spent more than $300,000 on cocaine. She was back to poverty before her 23rd birthday.
13. Evelyn Adams won a total of $5.4 million in the USA. Many people are lucky to win the lotto once. Evelyn won it twice – once in 1985 and again in 1986. She blew it all away mainly on gambling hoping to get more and giving it away to whoever asked. She now lives in a trailer park, barely scraping by, at age 64.
14. David Lee Edwards won a $27 million Powerball jackpot in 2001, a win that came while he was unemployed and living in his parents' basement. He bought a $600,000 house, a $1 million fleet of cars, a $78,000 watch, a $1.9 million private jet, 200 swords and other medieval weapons, and a $4.5 million fibre-optics installation company. Within a year, he had spent over $12 million. The house was soon lost to foreclosure and he died in 2013 a penniless man.
15. In March 2000, a Durban man won $150,000. He dined at some of Durban's finest restaurants and hotels. He drove luxury vehicles, blew thousands on drugs, alcohol and sex. He was back

to nothing in no time. Today, the former taxi driver has nothing to show for his winnings but regret. He became the laughing stock of his community, with accounting teachers using him as a case study when teaching pupils about the culture of money.

PART THREE

Youth unemployment is on the rise globally. According to 2018 ILO statistics, the global youth unemployment rate stands at 13%, which is three times higher than the figure for adults.

This part of the book offers 21st century business nuggets, business lessons and innovative business ideas as more and more young people on the African continent and around the world are rising as entrepreneurs, inventors, risk takers, tech gurus, disruptors, innovators, visionaries, thought leaders and pioneers of the future.

Isn't it time you jump on the entrepreneurial wagon?

Chapter 12

BUSINESS NUGGETS FOR THE NEW ECONOMIC ERA

The world today is wildly different from the world our parents grew up in. We are in a completely new economic era with different rules for the game. The world's largest taxi chain, *Uber,* owns no cars. The world's largest media company, *Facebook,* creates no content. The world's largest hotel chain, *Airbnb,* owns no hotels and the world's largest online retailer, *Alibaba,* holds no inventory and owns no warehouses. We are now living and working in a new world and within an economy that is more sophisticated than ever. The rules have changed and will continue to change. To compete and survive in this new era requires a disruptive approach.

It is time for us to shed myths of the past, question conventional wisdom and rethink our views on life, work, business and success. The Fourth Industrial Revolution is blurring the lines between the physical and the digital, between formal education and informal education, as well as between success and failure. In this developing environment disruptive technologies and trends such as robotics, IoT, VR, blockchain, AI and AR are changing the fabric of our lives, businesses and work.

In the past, businesses were built on the brick and mortar model, transactions were done in triplicate, using carbon paper, and success was based on educational background and certificates. Sending money to family took weeks if not months internationally and days locally.

Fast forward to today. The internet, connectivity and emerging technologies have completely changed the game. Thanks to the power of the internet, mobile connectivity and apps, we are now able to transact between cities and villages in an instant. A nine-year-old kid can easily build an online system that can topple other businesses. Farmers can check on the latest data available about crops, the weather, animals and market prices. Thousands of educational tools are being built to assist teachers, students and parents. Transactions are happening at the speed of light and at the touch of a button. Entrepreneurs are launching businesses overnight. And things are only going to get better and more interesting. In the next decade or so, we are going to witness businesses we have never dreamed of, let alone knew they existed.

According to Whitney Johnson, a leading business thinker and innovation theorist, 'Companies don't di$rupt, people do. Businesses require disruptive people to be disruptive. A business consists of holdings – office buildings, warehouses, desks and chairs, sophisticated machinery, and electronics. They're shells: inanimate, creating nothing. Like a beehive, minus the bees. It's pretty difficult to get honey that way. People are required to breathe life into a company to achieve innovation, growth, and productivity. It requires people who think, move, work and do.'

The Fourth Industrial Revolution is not about new Apps or new technologies. It is about a new era, new ways of thinking and new ways of doing business.

Africa's hopeful transformation lies in innovation, entrepreneurship and a big shift in mind-set. Hence, staying abreast with changes and rules for the new economic era will keep you relevant in your industry, thereby giving you a competitive advantage. Businesses will most likely go stale without disruptive people who are evolving and reinventing. The Fourth Industrial Revolution is not about new Apps or new technologies. It is about a new era, new ways of thinking and new ways of doing business.

Below are 13 nuggets for savvy individuals to forward their growth. I believe you'll find these nuggets and rules valuable, whether you are still thinking of getting your feet into business waters or you are already swimming with the sharks.

14 Business Nuggets for Competing and Thriving in the New Economic Era

1. Stop Consuming and Start Producing

You might think this point is irrelevant but our generation needs to wake up. We are conditioned to consume from an early age. As children, our parents gave us milk, food, snacks, toys, clothing, etc. As adults some of us sink deeper into the culture of consumerism without ever wondering, 'But wait! How are these things produced, who produces them and can I also produce?' If we really want to make an impact in the world, we need to switch off the consuming mind-set and be curious about the world of producing and the creative process.

Don't throw money at another pair of shoes, wristwatch, designer clothes, cosmetics or car you really don't need. Start switching from consumer into producer mode. Look at the packaging of products/brands you're addicted to. Ask yourself: how does it feel? What is it about this product that makes me love it so much? Check out what words they are using in their commercials. Where do they produce? What if you could switch from buyer to seller of that product? Can you find out how much profit they make off you? How is their business structured?

You are ready to change the world when you start asking these types of questions instead of your usual one: where can I get money to buy the new release?

You'll be well prepared to start and run your own business when you start thinking like a producer. You should be able to think on a higher level, instead of being strictly a consumer. And people of colour in particular are more likely to be consumers than creators. It's really hard to get out of poverty or to change the structure of economic power if you're always going to be a consumer rather than creating something.

2. Be Relevant

The world we live in is constantly evolving. Businesses, jobs and social norms are changing. Old business models don't stand a chance in the face of emerging technologies. See what *Uber* is doing to the taxi industry. Since *WhatsApp* came into existence, traditional text messaging is no longer popular. *Netflix* killed renting of DVDs.

Our world is rapidly changing. Things are moving so fast your business model could become outdated before you even implement it. What got you here won't get you there. Everything is evolving and so should your business model. No business can survive a brick and mortar mind-set in the new economic era. As an entrepreneur, you have to constantly evolve to stay relevant and keep up with disruptive innovations. The world will never again be as slow as it is right now. As a result, study your industry, study your business idea and be sure that what you are offering is relevant.

3. Don't Just Start a Business, Solve a Problem

Your business model can be very lucrative if you do a proper background study and find out what people's needs are first. It is necessary to identify a gap in the market as well as the market in the gap. Don't just start a business, solve a problem. Look for problems and create innovative solutions for which people will be willing to pay. Success is an exchange for adding value to people's lives. Hence, solve a problem and money will come running after you. Don't start a business with only the mindset to make money. Start a business to make a difference, and the money will flow in your direction.

Every business is a solution to a problem. Problems in your life or in society at large are businesses waiting to be discovered. The more problems you can solve in your life and the life of others, the more money you'll make. A perfect life and a perfect society are no place for an entrepreneur to be. Entrepreneurship is all about solving problems and adding value. Do not curse a problem – use it. Develop the capacity to identify problems and solutions and you will become a successful entrepreneur. The more value you add to people, the more they will see you as their life-cover: eventually you will become the person they make important decisions with.

Travis and Garrett set out to solve a problem of inconvenience in transportation. 'How do you get a ride at the push of a button?' they wondered in the cold of the night. Consequently 'tap a button and get a ride' was born. Today *Uber* is a household name. What started as a simple desire to solve a problem quickly become a global logistics conglomerate operating in 78 countries and 600 cities, with 16,000 employees, 7 million of them drivers, averaging 10 million daily trips, and a total valuation of $72 billion, according to 2018 *Uber* Statistics. You really don't have to invent anything new, you only need to identify loopholes in what already exists, then develop new improved and innovative solutions.

4. Brand Yourself

Don't be scared to present the real you to the world: authenticity is at the heart of success. You can't find real success while pretending to be someone else. You are an entrepreneur, a consultant, singer, graphics designer, speaker, writer, etc., but we only see images of cats or your favourite celebrities on your social media platform. In this new economic era, your social media is your business card. To avoid branding yourself is like shooting yourself in the wallet.

People don't buy products. They buy people; they buy the story. Being a person of quality attracts clients of similar mark to your business. How you look, how you speak, how you smell and even what you write on your social media platforms are all important factors that contribute to how people see you. Not just your personal appearance, of course, but your overall branding: business cards, logos, website, etc. Your employees, business associates, representatives and even friends are seen as an extension of you. Therefore, promote a culture that deeply reflects who you are in your organisation – and be careful who you hang out with. Hanging with the wrong crew can hurt your brand and vice versa.

5. Find your WHY

Simon Sinek, a business consultant and author, said: 'Customers don't buy what you do or how you do it, they buy WHY you do it, especially if those values are aligned with their own.'

Everyone has a WHY. Your WHY is the purpose, cause or belief that inspires you. Knowing your WHY gives you a filter to make choices that will help you find greater fulfilment in all that you do. Everything around you may change, but your WHY won't. Your WHY is what keeps you going when you feel like you're at your absolute limit and in the depths of despair. Your WHY propels you forwards in times of failure and rejection and in times of success and happiness. As German philosopher Friedrich Nietzsche said: 'He or she who has a WHY, can endure any HOW.'

Once you've discovered your WHY, The HOW looks after itself. Knowing your WHY will help you compete and thrive under any circumstances.

6. Eliminate Friction Points and Improve Customer Experience

No matter what business you're into, ensure you challenge basic assumptions and rethink how you can make the experience better for your clients. Businesses that will win in the new economic era are businesses that add value to their clients. Clients expect convenience, speed and efficiency. Sell access to these things. Identify friction points in the consumer's day and solve those problems for them. Maybe they don't want to stand in the queue. This is the *Uber* economy, a world where you touch a button and magic happens. Therefore, make it easy for your clients to interact with your business on their phones by making sure your website is mobile friendly. Can certain processes be completed online or on the phone instead of coming to your business premises? Is there perhaps an app they can use to engage deeper with your company?

Be different, adore your clients and shower them with convenience, efficiency and speed. Taking friction out of the way will encourage your clients to become addicted to you. Your clients are used to using apps. *Uber* has minimised as much friction as possible, so much so that all you need is a smartphone. All your personal information, right down to credit card details, is captured at the sign-up stage. Then all you need is to tap a button, a car arrives, and when you get to your destination, you just step out and go without having to pay for anything. All friction points are taken care of at the sign-up stage. So, know your business, know your clients and their challenges, because you cannot solve problems or eliminate frictions you're not aware of.

7. Network and Collaborate

In the industrial economy, value was mostly created through massive capital spending on plants and equipment, but in a world of exponentially increasing complexity, value is being created through relationships. The value of business relationships cannot be overstated. Where would the economic world be if not for relationships! Those who can network and collaborate well with others have a distinct advantage in the new economic era. Networking is now possible in many different ways, through the online atmosphere of forging business relationships on *LinkedIn*, to the old-school method of meeting at conferences or seminars. Things have changed and competitive advantage is no longer driven by the resources you control, but those you can access.

The path to success no longer lies in clawing your way to the top of the heap, but in nudging your way to the centre of the network. Rather than owning resources and capabilities absolutely, you can use collaborative platforms to access ecosystems of technology, talent and information. Smart leaders are putting aside self-interests and collaborating to build a better civic business environment that can advance their shared objectives. Problems that have been written off as unsolvable are resolved when people come together to collaborate and challenge conventional thinking.

8. Rethink your Business Model

Today's world is feeling the economic upheaval brought about by the latest generation of internet superpowers and start-up superheroes that are toppling giant industries and bringing them to their knees. The creation of some billion-dollar global companies and the ruthless murder of traditional businesses happened in the last ten years. *Uber is* one of these global giants. As you might have noticed, *Uber* is my favourite example. Millions of people around the world today cannot imagine their lives without *Uber*. Yet *Uber* was founded only in 2009.

Ten years ago, the idea of getting into a stranger's car would have seemed weird and dangerous, but today it's as common as tuning to your favourite radio station. From only a mere idea, *Uber* has turned into a merciless machine for disruptive innovation. It is a household name that's challenging old business models, redefining neighbourhoods and challenging the conventional system of moving from point A to B. In nearly every country where *Uber* operates it's been attacked by the traditional taxi industry. Why? Because people prefer the convenience *Uber* offers, and which traditional taxis can't match.

You don't need to mimic *Uber* or any other business. You only have to ensure your business model is built for the current economic atmosphere and not the seventeenth century. Resist the urge to keep digging in the same old bricks-and-mortar graveyard. The new economic era heavily demands that your business model be technologically friendly. So, whatever you are doing, make sure it is mobile friendly.

9. Be on the Lookout for Untapped Markets

My mentor, Dr Strive Masiyiwa, Founder of *Econet Group,* said: 'Rural areas remain some of the most untapped markets in the African continent. Most people in Africa live in rural areas and hence we'll never truly be able to develop Africa without developing rural areas.' Entrepreneurship is the main vehicle through which this development can travel. Bringing innovative ideas to rural areas should be one of the key frontiers of African entrepreneurs tackling problems that have long been ignored by policy makers. According to Dr Strive Masiyiwa, 'China and India are beginning to take the bull by the horns and getting smart entrepreneurs to focus on rural businesses, with Israel being the world leader when it comes to using entrepreneurship in rural areas as a platform for national development. … Rural water, rural banking, rural education, rural agriculture, rural sanitation, rural real estate, rural healthcare, rural nutrition and much more are many areas of untapped markets African entrepreneurs should be looking into.'

As pioneers of Africa's transformation, we should challenge ourselves to find solutions to improve the lives of people in rural areas and empower them to generate their own income. It'd be virtually impossible to tackle unemployment without focusing on rural entrepreneurship. We'll only end up with ever-growing urban slums as despairing youths flee to the city in search of non-existent jobs.

Even in the suburbs, you can still think of processes that will help improve or transform sectors like agriculture, healthcare, education, nutrition, etc. If there's one area where resource optimisation is needed more urgently than any other in the world, it's in agriculture. According to the *United Nations Food and Agriculture Organisation*, projections indicate that Earth's population will exceed nine billion by 2050, that's about two billion more than at present (2019). Feeding all those people will require an increase in food production by 70%. But, of course, the world is running out of new land for farming. We cannot expand land but we can expand on more efficient ways to use it.

The solution lies in innovative thinking. The potential for harnessing technology to Africa's benefit is enormous. You don't have to be an engineer or a tech guru to be part of the solution. You just need to be open minded and ready to spot opportunities.

Technology can bridge the gap between physical infrastructure inadequacies and consumer demands. Artificial Intelligence devices and drone technology can be of tremendous use in the agriculture and healthcare sectors. Basic services could be revolutionised. Education and banking could be made much more accessible with digitalisation. Your responsibility as an entrepreneur is to identify the gaps and bridge them. You don't necessarily need a degree or some special certificate. Visionaries identify opportunities and problems, then look for competent people to exploit the former and solve the latter.

Steve Jobs built the greatest innovative tech company in the world without writing a line of code himself. He had the ideas and he got the right people to bring his ideas to life. If you've identified a gap in the market or discovered an untapped market in the rural area, don't hold back. Don't wait until someone else does it and then you say, 'I had that idea five years ago.'

10. Adopt a New Marketing Approach

Since the rise of digital marketing, traditional marketing is declining. Traditional marketing techniques cannot challenge the requirements set out in the new economy. Marketing is now moving from product centred to customer centred. Marketing in the new economic era does not solely rely on building brands through advertising but rather on building brands through performance. A good brand is built by the customer's experience with the brand. The old system of marketing is dead. Marketing now is about adding value. Consumers are smart and want value for their money.

Learn how to sell through education and storytelling. Tell powerful, creative and authentic stories to breathe life and emotions into your brand. Educate your clients through content marketing. Add as much value as you can to your target market. This means, instead of first asking for money, take the time to understand their needs and show them the value your product or service can add to their lives.

11. Be a Disruptor

Innovative organisations require innovative thinkers, and in order to be an innovative thinker you need to di$rupt your thinking and embrace technology. With the right mind-set, you can use little or no resources to enter a certain market and even displace established systems. Disruptors play where no one else is playing. They can create a market where none existed before. Statistics shows that, ten years ago, people spent only about three hours every day on their screens but today this number has moved up to about seven hours a day. Laptops, tablets and mobile phones are where the people are spending their time. This trend is changing how business is conducted in the new economic era. Smart entrepreneurs have to think of novel ways to put their products or services in front of these people. As Jay Samit said, 'Each and every one of us carries a device that connects us to 6 billion people – a mobile phone.'

No one knows the full weight of Artificial Intelligence as it rolls more and more into businesses but you can pivot this change – think ahead, think how to compete, think how to leverage this technology to save cost and improve efficiency in your business. In this era, your mind-set as well as your business should reflect global thinking. Think e-commerce, innovation and technology. Think beyond where you are and what you see. Businesses that will succeed in the new economic era will be the ones prepared to think innovatively and expansively. Don't be a tech laggard, move fast, disrupt, and use technology as a strategic asset for your business.

12. Leverage on the Internet

The evolution of the internet has changed the game. With just a click, you can reach millions of people online. Never before have we had at our fingertips access to so much information that can help us run our businesses more successfully. Thanks to the internet and mobile connectivity, it now takes less capital to launch a business than it did a decade ago. There are no gatekeepers blocking your way to success. Whether your idea is a product/service, magazine, blog, an app, an online store, etc., testing and launching it is faster and more cost-effective today than it would have been ten years ago.

You can run your business campaign on crowdfunding websites to raise capital or get in contact directly with an angel investor or venture capitalist. It doesn't matter whether you are in your room, in the village or in the biggest city in the world. You still have access to millions of people. You can create systems that will solve problems and di$rupt industries even from the comfort of your home. The number of digital start-ups has exploded in recent years. Just as Mark Zuckerberg invented a platform that humanity never knew it needed but now cannot do without, so can you create a new product or service we don't even know we need yet.

The internet is an equal opportunity for everyone and smart entrepreneurs are using it to create a spotlight for themselves. Social media platforms are global platforms with access to billions of people. Why aren't you making good use of it? Gone are the days when people logged onto social media only to see who's wearing what or who's dating who.

As an entrepreneur, you can leverage the power of the internet and social platforms to make your voice heard and your business seen. We live in an era where you have to visually showcase what you've got. If you have even a smattering of some talent, a hobby or a business, don't be invisible – bring it online. You might just be a hashtag away from being the next big thing.

Many great businesses and talents have been discovered on the internet. *YouTube, Facebook, Twitter, Instagram* and other social platforms are tools you can use to fast-forward your growth. All it took was one video on *YouTube* and Justin Bieber became a global sensation. Be strategic online and give your talent, start-up or whatever you are doing a face and a voice.

13. Leverage on Existing Customers

Apple recently announced plans to launch their own credit card. The card will heavily integrate with the iPhone and the company has named it the Apple Card. The actual card is minimalist and sleek in the most Apple kind of way. No late fee, no annual fee, no over the limit fee, no card number, no signature, no expiration date, no CVC number, no barcode. This is innovation at its best and people are literally falling over themselves in anticipation to sign-up for this historical credit card.

Here is the catch. Apple already has a more than 1.3 billion active users worldwide, most of whom can be considered affluent due to the price of the products. From a business point of view, it's cheaper to grow an existing customer than to acquire a new one. Hence it is better to leverage on existing customer base than to start a brand new company with zero customers, spend billions of dollars to establish the brand locally and internationally, spend billions more to acquire customers and spend still more every year maintaining that customer base. What Apple is doing by collaborating and branching into the financial segment makes perfect sense. They already have a billion qualified leads, iPhone users to be specific. This is an already warm market and only needs a few marketing tweaks and direct communication to sell the credit card. Initially Apple took a small cut with Apple Pay Cash, now it's trying to take the whole pie by offering a credit card. This in turn will attract new customers. If you want the card, you will need an iPhone. So, like Apple, think of new ways to leverage on your existing customers.

14. Find a Mentor

Last but not the least, find a mentor. Mentorship is an integral part of success in life, and more so in business. Whatever you do, find someone you can confide in and talk to. Good things are rarely accomplished alone. Success often hinges on getting the right advice or support from the right people. Don't only look for someone with the right connections but someone with the right principles, character and expertise. You need someone who can listen to you, push you, teach you and offer advice in your specific field or life in general. Depending on what you do and where you are in life, you can find mentorship in a parent, a teacher, a friend or a complete stranger.

However, when it comes to serious business, look for people who have walked the talk. Good mentors will share their own experiences with you and help you apply what they have learned. There is always that numbing fear and a mountain of self-doubt involved whenever you step out to try something new. You might be tenacious enough to overcome some of these uncertainties on your own, but it's a lot easier if you get support from someone you look up to. An encouraging email from someone who believes in you can make all the difference.

Studies have shown that most new businesses don't last longer than five years, but other studies show that 70% of mentored businesses survive longer than five years. A mentor can have a tremendous impact on your self-confidence. Sites like *LinkedIn* or *Twitter* are more business savvy, and you can probably find someone in your industry on these platforms to mentor you. You can also hire a business coach/consultant to be more hands-on and hold your hand every step of the way.

When you do find a mentor, be respectful of their time. It is one thing to ask one question a month that requires a quick email to solve and another thing to ask ten questions a week that require hours to solve. And when a mentor does something really helpful for you, always remember to send a thank you note, gift or bottle of wine to show how much you appreciate his/her help.

Chapter 13

DECODING GREATNESS

Some people feel stuck in life because they are waiting for someone, who isn't forthcoming, to help them. As the stuck feeling intensifies, some choose to give up and settle. But feeling stuck is a sign that something needs to change in your life. Decoding greatness is about waking yourself up from sleeping on your own resources and overlooking opportunities around you. Your power comes from who you are and what you have, not what someone else can give you. You are enough!

Decoding greatness is about the way you interact with your world, about having a deeper understanding of your core values, resources, characteristics, and what makes you unique. This understanding creates a mind-set revolution that is open to new perspectives. Knowing more about yourself can help you accomplish more with what you already have and move forward with a greater sense of purpose and vigour. Awareness of certain behaviours allows you to grow on your own resources and move beyond your current capacity and circumstances. Sometimes you may get help from others, there's nothing wrong with that, but fostering a mind-set and culture of 'I can do it myself' will take you further in life than depending and waiting on someone, some 'funding', or on the government.

Are You Funding Your Dreams or Your Lifestyle?

Many are drowning in their own resources while they wait for someone to help them. One of the biggest obstacles to people with dreams is lack of funding. As much as this is truly an obstacle for many dreamers, I believe it is just a well-designed excuse for others.

Some people are working at full time jobs while dreaming of starting something of their own some day, and this is really commendable. I have deep respect for those who hold the job in one hand and their dreams in the other. But then someone with a job and a dream shouldn't really have the same funding problems as someone with no job. If you have a job and a dream, then your job is your first investor. As Eric Thomas, author and speaker, asked: 'Are you ready to sacrifice who you are, for what you will become?'

> Salary should be your number one source of capital if you have a dream and a job.

Sadly, most people are just earning and burning with no end in sight. They use their salary to fund their lifestyle and then look for people to fund their dreams. Using your salary to fund your lavish lifestyle and expecting someone else to fund your dream is a strategic blunder in a category of its own. Some dreamers have bought themselves a superlative car, a fancy apartment, full package DSTV. They wear *Gucci* and *Versace*. They are out every weekend celebrating false symbols of success, spending huge amounts of money on parties and expensive alcohol. If you are not where you want to be in life, if you are not able to fund that dream you've been carrying in your heart for years, what exactly are you celebrating every weekend? Shouldn't extravagant parties, designer labels and luxury living be reserved for those who have made it in life? All the same, when the dust settles, the same individuals pull out their shiny business plans and start looking for someone to fund their big dreams.

Dreamers are willing to spend a few years of their lives like most people won't so that they can live the rest of their lives like most people can't. Why do you think the rest of the world mocks dreamers? It's because we don't try to fit in or be like everyone else. We are okay being the misfits, the oddballs, the square pegs in round holes. We are okay being different and losing friends in the process. There are still many causes worth sacrificing for, so much history yet to be made.

Instead of buying that fancy car and paying car instalments every month, you can buy a second-hand car or use public transport while building and investing towards your dreams. Instead of renting a fancy apartment, you can stay in a tiny room or share with friends while building your empire. This might be too great a price to pay for those who want to fit in. But happy are those who dream dreams and are willing to pay the price to make them come true. A wise man said, 'A dream costs nothing unless you want it to come true.' A salary should be your number one source of capital if you have a dream and a job.

The sooner you realise you can never get rich off a salary, the quicker you can start doing things differently. How many rich employees do you know? I am not asking how many fancy, luxurious employees you know. Looking rich and being rich are sold separately.

Most employees are trapped in debt because they want to impress people. But the wise ones can escape a debt trap by not going for the car or house first as soon as they get a job. Wise people buy cash-generating assets first and luxury last. Most people buy a rich lifestyle and luxuries first, then get stuck in a lifetime of paying for it. Owning things that visibly demonstrate that you have money and that shout out across the rooftops 'I have arrived' will more than likely prevent you from ever actually arriving. The rich buy assets first and luxury last, while the poor buy luxury first.

Decode your greatness, grow on your own resources and chase your dreams ridiculously even if your family, friends, or even the entire world laughs at your guts. Go after your dreams first. Sow, even in tears; plant the seeds of greatness so that it will be easier for you to get out of debt and the corporate world once it's time to focus on building your dreams full-time. There are many people in our world today who sincerely want to get out of corporate jobs but are trapped because they funded their lifestyle first. Now that they are stuck between a rock and a hard place, they keep wondering to themselves, 'If I quit my job, who will pay for the car, the house and all the lifestyle add-ons?'

And so, they are obliged to keep going to work every single day even though their hearts are no longer at work. They now live for one purpose and one purpose only: to pay debts and maintain the status quo. Their hearts are no longer in what they do. They are miserable and angry at the world but they keep a brave face because there's no way out.

This is the price of conformity and ignorance of how money

works, but a new generation of dreamers is doing things differently. The knowledge contained in this book will save many from going down the same path of nothingness, barely reaching the speed limit on their journey to nowhere. The new mantra is: 'Fund the dream first, suffer now and shine later.' Great success requires greater sacrifice. If we don't di$rupt and break the cycle of relentless luxury now, mediocrity and poverty will be inherited by the next generation.

As Nathan W Morris, an author and personal finance coach, once said: 'The speed of your success is limited only by your dedication and what you're willing to sacrifice.' Of course, not everyone's salary can fund their dreams but if you can fund a comfortable and fancy lifestyle then you can fund your dreams. If you truly want this entrepreneurial life, you'd have to make sacrifices and eliminate things holding you back from stepping up to the new levels.

Dream big and start small. The greatest power on earth is the cumulative potential of little steps. As Grant Cardone, author and sales coach, said: 'Let the rest do whatever, while you do whatever it takes.'

Bootstrap Your Way to Success

You may be asking: But what about those who don't have a job? Well, whether you have a job or not, so long as you have a dream, responsibility lies with you to make your dreams a reality. You have to look to your own hands for capital. You have to grow on your own resources. There is always something in our hand, but we often look to external resources so much we fail to see our own resources. If you truly believe in the dream, you'll find a way to kick start it off the ground. People are more likely to lend support only when you are in motion. Imagine a scenario where two cars broke down in the middle of the road, one driver got out and started trying to push the car while the other sat in his car lamenting, complaining and cursing the world. Who do you think other motorists will stop to help? Yes, that's exactly my point. It is up to you to get your dreams moving.

> If you don't have capital, you still must find capital. Bootstrap your way to success.

Money is not the sole currency when it comes to starting a business. Money can only get you so far. Passion, sheer determination, and hard work are all free and are more valuable than a pot of cash. Besides the funding issue, what have you done regarding your dreams? Some people cannot even conduct simple research on their business model and target market; cannot even endeavour to come up with a marketing plan or business plan on their own. There's so much you can do about your dreams at the initial stage that doesn't really require money. It is important for you to learn and understand concepts like sales, customer relations, target market, market segment, content marketing, leadership, financial intelligence, etc.

Don't focus only on looking for funding when you don't even know who your customers are yet, what their needs are or how you can meet those needs. Start small, study your market. As a new entrepreneur launching your first start-up, a big pot of money may only mask problems that will eventually catch up with you later on.

If you don't have capital, you still must find capital. Look to your own hands, sell something to raise initial capital. Think big and start small. Anyone with a wealth creation mind-set will always find a way to make it work. Paulo Coelho, a prolific novelist, said, 'When you want something, all the universe conspires in helping you achieve it.'

Bootstrapping is the only way for most dreamers to start their business. What is bootstrapping? In the context of entrepreneurship, bootstrapping is the act of starting a business with no money or, at least, very little money. It means building a business out of virtually nothing. Bootstrappers rely usually on personal income and savings, sweat equity and lowest possible operating costs. It certainly means starting a business without the help of venture capitalists or significant investors. It means ploughing back into the business the profit earned from customers. 'Bootstrapping' comes from the term 'pulling yourself up by your own bootstraps'. That is to say, doing something difficult all on your own. So, pull yourself up and get going. If it were easy, everyone would do it.

As the Rwandan President, Paul Kagame, said at the 2018 African Leadership Forum, 'I would rather argue that we need to mobilise the right mind-sets, rather than more funding. After all, in Africa, we have everything we need. Whatever is lacking, we have within us the means to acquire. And yet we remain mentally married to the idea that nothing can get moving without external resources. We are even begging for things we already have. That is absolutely a failure of mind-set.'

The Government and the Paradox of Job Creation

It's only natural for people to think the government creates jobs because that's what politicians always say. Politicians have a self-interested motive to move in that direction because it increases their power and influence over people. No one will vote for them without any lavish promises of job creation. So politicians continue to perpetuate this fallacy simply to foster their own agenda. The tragedy though is that many young people sit back on their brains, waiting and hoping the government will shower them with jobs. The stark truth of the matter is that governments are never an efficient way to build an economic growth objective.

The theory that the government creates jobs sounds good, and it would be nice if it were true in real life, but it has a glaring logical incongruity. It overlooks the fact that, in the real world, the government can't inject money into the economy without first taking money out of the economy. You may argue that the government does create jobs, including teachers, police officers, firefighters, soldiers, sailors, astronauts, antiterrorism agents, park rangers, diplomats, etc. And this is technically true. In a smoothly functioning market economy, the process feeds on itself.

What most people fail to see is that the money to pay government employees must come from somewhere, generally, taxes and loans. But if the people whose money is taken via taxation had kept the money, they would have spent most or all of it on something and that would have boosted the economy and the employment market. Taxes and complex government regulations actually slow job creation. The government spends millions of taxpayers' money on job summits annually that actually marginalises start-ups and entrepreneurial endeavours. And at the end of each job summit, the unemployment statistics remain the same or, as is more likely, increase.

Economic growth and job creation only happens if government

empowers people (entrepreneurs), removes obstacles and gives them freedom to explore, di$rupt, create, innovate and profit. The focal point for all government leaders across Africa should be to create an environment where the entrepreneurial spirit in Africa can prosper. Humans have needs and entrepreneurs see these needs as opportunities. Entrepreneurs are the life blood of any economy. They expand the size of the economic pie for everyone. They are the people shaping the world for the better. They are the best among the rest and are legends as the continent struggles for a greater future. Economic growth and job creation come from the government getting out of the way and letting entrepreneurs and the private sector do what they do best – producing goods and services. As Mugumya Junior, founder/CEO of April Group, said, 'Every country is built by entrepreneurs not by politicians.'

How long are the youth going to wait or blame the government for where they are in life? The mind-set that the government creates jobs has turned youths into liabilities waiting on the fulfilment of the promises of election after election. But instead of results, every election brings even more promises.

But the hard truth is that as soon as you become an adult or complete school, responsibility lies with you to create something. As John F Kennedy said, 'Ask not what your country can do for you, but ask what you can do for your country.'

Don't be a spectator in your own economy.

The responsibility to change things, create jobs and boost any country's economy lies with the people and not the government. Africa has an overwhelming supply of talented youth who need to wake up from slumber and heavy reliance on government for jobs. The work of government is not to create jobs, but to create an environment for you to develop your own work. This process is what will foster economic empowerment, creativity and entrepreneurship, thereby creating jobs we haven't even imagined yet.

The government does not create jobs. Therefore, don't be a spectator in your own economy. Be part of those working to balance the socio-economic status quo. As a matter of fact, the government is looking to you to use your mind, your academic qualifications, and come up with novel ideas that'll change the economy. As we boldly enter the future, we need to make sure that we do so in a way that discourages a dependency mind-set, that promotes self-reliance and stimulates the entrepreneurial spirit in Africa. Young people are rising as risk takers, inventors, disruptors, thought leaders and pioneers of the future. But we need a great many more of them. In 2018, there were at least 700 million Africans under 25 years old. If this vast army of energy and talent can only enter the economy with the sort of mind-set changes we have been discussing, Africa will become a leading voice in shaping the world. With a new perspective and an unconventional approach to our problems, we can and we will make Africa great.

Caught Between Greatness and Mediocrity: The Enthralling Story of Ronald Wayne

Since *Apple Inc* became the first company to reach a whopping record-breaking market cap of $1 trillion valuation in August 2018, the riveting story of Ronald Wayne, *Apple Inc's* third co-founder, has resurfaced. Nevertheless, it's a story that is truly worth telling over and over again. A great deal of lessons can be learned from the mistakes of others as we can't live long enough to make them all ourselves.

When *Apple* was incorporated on April 1st, 1976, Wayne was named alongside Steve Jobs and Steve Wozniak as one of three founders. Mr Wayne drew the first *Apple* logo, drafted the first original agreement between the founders and wrote the first manual for their first computer. He held a 10% share in the company but soon decided to relinquish it for $800 and was given an additional $1500 to forfeit all right of ownership two weeks after the company was officially registered.

Wayne threw in the towel and sold his shares back to his co-founders for just $800 because he was worried he'd lose the most if things didn't go well. Jobs and Wozniak's general lack of funds at the beginning of their journey made Wayne, a homeowner, very concerned he'd end up having to bail out the company from financial crises. His reason for the decision to leave *Apple* was that the company was financially demanding and he didn't want to lose his home should things fall apart. He looked into the immediate future and then decided it was not worth the risk. He was caught between greatness and mediocrity. But he chose mediocrity, security and comfort. This is an everyday reality in our world today as there are many people who won't risk losing their house or car for a dream or business venture.

Owning a tenth of *Apple* today would eventually have given Mr Wayne a net worth of about $100 billion but he sold those same shares for just $800. Shares that would have made him the richest or second richest man in the world. But he gave it all up in order to secure his comfortable little life he had at the time. Nobody could have anticipated *Apple* would balloon 40 years later as the world's most valuable company, the first to hit $1 trillion market cap valuation.

Wayne was feeling out of place and intimidated by the youthful vigour of his co-founders. He described his time working with Jobs and Wozniak in a Bloomberg interview as 'standing in the shadow of intellectual giants'. 'I was 40 and these kids were in their 20s … They were whirlwinds; it was like having a tiger by the tail. If I had stayed with *Apple* I probably would have wound up the richest man in the cemetery,' he said. Well, we really don't know that for sure, do we? From my own vantage point, it seems like Mr Wayne is the type of person who'll do just about anything to avoid risk and discomfort.

Another of Wayne's financial catastrophe that he sold his original *Apple* contract in the early '90s. 'I had this *Apple* contract sitting in my filing cabinet, covered in dust and cobwebs, and I thought, 'What do I need to hold on to that for?" he said in an interview. And so, he sold the contract to the autograph collector for $500. But this same contract was sold at an auction in 2011 for $1.6 million. Talk of bad luck or bad decision making. The latter seems to be in sync with Mr Wayne.

Unlike Jobs and Wozniak, who became multimillionaires at a young age, Wayne's finances have been 'in a deep hole for the last 40 years'. Today, Wayne resides in a small house in Pahrump, Nevada, USA. At age 80, he lives on Social Security checks and money made selling rare coins and stamps on the internet. His financial crises are so bad he decided to sell off what's left of his *Apple* archives which includes original proofs of the Apple-1 manual he created and unused designs for a proposed *Apple II* case, among other documents — in a

Christie's auction at about $30,000. The archives gave its new owner a tangible piece of Apple's early existence.

Ronald Wayne said *Apple Inc* was demanding on him financially. Are you perhaps letting something of value slip through your fingers because it's demanding on your finances, time and or emotions? If only Ronald Wayne had the ability to see into the future, his decision of 1976 would have been different.

You cannot feature in a future that you cannot picture. Everything of lasting value is highly demanding. The greatness of tomorrow begins with the sacrifices of today. Don't protect your house or car at the cost of your future. The pain of knowing you had the opportunity at your fingertips to change the course of your life is the greatest pain of regret any human can ever live with. Therefore:

- If you need to sell your house or car to start a business or save a dying one, do so!
- If you need to live in one room or share with friends today to own mansions tomorrow, do so!
- If you need to walk or use taxis today in order to own a Rolls-Royce tomorrow, do so!
- If you need to buy cheap or second-hand clothes today to own a boutique tomorrow, do so!
- If you need to hustle on street corners, sell stuff or join a marketing network for a future only you can see, do so!

> Greatness is not a product of convenience.

The news of *Apple* hitting the trillion dollars mark must have sent shock waves through Ronald Wayne's mind. Imagine the pain, frustration and disappointment his family, relatives and children might be feeling. 'If only ...' are the saddest words in the English language.

Sometimes, it is not about you. There is posterity to consider. The future belongs to those who can foresee it and sacrifice the pleasures of the present to gain it. Greatness is not the product of convenience. As JA Shedd, author and professor, observed, 'A ship in the harbour is safe, but that's not what ships are built for.'

Chapter 14

WEALTH CREATION PARABLES

Parables use human characters in believable situations so that readers can relate to the story. The world is mostly familiar with biblical parables as told by Jesus but there are also other stories told as parables to give us a deeper meaning on love, business or life in general. A parable is a story that is told to illustrate hidden mysteries of truth that can be understood and applied in any generation. A parable by dictionary definition is a 'short, didactic story that is meant to teach a moral or principle'.

The following are some of my favourite parables on wealth creation and success. They contain ancient wisdom which you can apply to your life immediately. They also contain unparalleled financial lessons that could shift your mind-set, set you free and fast-forward your success. In a nutshell, you are about to uncover the secret to wealth creation and escape blind ambition once and for all.

In his book, *The Millionaire Fastlane,* MJ DeMarco told the fascinating parable of the Fastlane Wealth.

The two parables that follow, the parable of *The Pipeline* and *The Mexican Fisherman* are written by Burke Hedges and Heinrich Böll respectively.

The Parable of Fastlane Wealth (Building a System)

A great Egyptian pharaoh summons his two young nephews, Chuma and Azur, and he commissions them to a majestic task: Build two monumental pyramids as a tribute to Egypt. Upon completion, Pharaoh promises each an immediate reward of kingship, retirement amidst riches, and lavish luxury for the rest of their natural lives. But each nephew must construct his pyramid alone. Chuma and Azur, both 18, know their daunting task will take years to complete.

Nonetheless, each is primed for the challenge and honoured by Pharaoh's directive. They exit Pharaoh's chambers ready to begin the long pyramid-building process. Azur begins work immediately. He slowly drags large heavy stones into a square formation. After a few months, the base of Azur's pyramid takes shape. Town folks gather around Azur's constructive efforts and praise his handiwork. The stones are heavy and difficult to move, and after one year of heavy labour, Azur's perfect square foundation to the pyramid is nearly finished.

But Azur is perplexed. The plot of land that should bear Chuma's pyramid is empty. Not one stone has been laid. No foundation. No dirt engravings. Nothing! It's as barren as it was a year ago when Pharaoh commissioned the job. Confused, Azur visits Chuma's home and finds him in his barn diligently working on a twisted apparatus that resembles some kind of human torture device. Azur interrupts, 'Chuma! What the hell are you doing!? You're supposed to be building Pharaoh a pyramid and you spend your days locked in this barn fiddling with that crazy machine?' Chuma cracks a smile and says, 'I am building a pyramid, leave me alone.' Azur scoffs, 'Yeah, sure you are. You haven't laid one stone in over a year!' Chuma, engrossed and unfazed by his brother's accusation retorts, 'Azur, your short-sightedness and thirst for wealth have clouded your vision. You build your pyramid and I will build mine.'

As Azur walks away, he chides, 'You fool! Pharaoh will hang you on the gallows when he discovers your treason.' Another year passes and Azur solidifies the base of his pyramid and begins the second level. But a problem arises and Azur struggles in his progress. The stones are heavy and he cannot raise them to the pyramid's second level. Challenged by his physical limitations, Azur recognizes his weakness: he needs more strength to move heavier stones, and to do so, seeks the counsel of Bennu, Egypt's strongest man. For a fee, Bennu trains Azur to build bigger and stronger muscles. With great strength, Azur anticipates the heavier stones will be easier to lift onto the higher levels.

Meanwhile, Chuma's pyramid plot of land is still barren. Azur assumes his brother has a death wish since, by all appearances, Chuma is violating Pharaoh's mandate. And so Azur forgot about his brother and his non-existent pyramid. Another year passes and Azur's pyramid construction slows to a disheartening crawl. It often takes one month just to place one stone. Moving stones to the upper levels require great strength and Azur spends much of his time working with Bennu (his personal trainer) to build greater strength.

But Azur is spending most of his money on counselling fees and the exotic diet required for the training. Azur estimates that at his current construction pace, his pyramid will be completed in another 30 years. Unfazed, Azur allows himself to boast a little. 'After three years, I've far surpassed my brother. He hasn't placed one stone yet! That fool!'

Then, suddenly, one day while hauling a heavy stone up his pyramid, Azur hears a commotion erupting from the town square. The townsfolk, regular observers of his work, abruptly abandon his plot to examine the celebratory fuss. Curious himself, Azur takes a break and leaves to investigate.

Surrounded by a cheering crowd, Chuma has entered the town square with a 25-foot high contraption built from a maze of gantries, wheels, levers, and ropes.

As Chuma slowly moves up the village street amidst the buoyant crowd, Azur fears the explanation. After a short walk to Chuma's barren pyramid plot, Azur's suspicions are confirmed. Within minutes, Chuma's strange machine starts moving heavy stones and begins to lay the foundation to his pyramid. One after another, the machine effortlessly lifts the stones and softly places them side-by-side in their correct place. Miraculously, the machine requires little effort for Chuma's operation. Crank a wheel attached to a rope which engages a system of gears and levers – and bingo! Heavy stones are moved quickly and magically.

While Azur's pyramid foundation took over a year to build, Chuma lines up the foundation to his pyramid within one week. The second level that Azur so arduously struggled with is even more shocking: Chuma's machine does the work 30 times quicker. What took Azur two months takes Chuma's machine two days. After 40 days, Chuma and his machine accomplish as much as Azur's three years of toilsome work.

Azur was destroyed. He had spent years doing the heavy lifting while Chuma built a machine to do it for him. Instead of honouring the machine, Azur vows, 'I must get stronger! I will lift heavier stones!'

Azur continues the hard labour of pyramid building while Chuma continues to work the crank of his machine.

After eight years, Chuma finishes his pyramid at age 26: three years to build the system and five years to reap the benefits of the system. The great pharaoh is pleased and does as promised. He rewards Chuma with kingship and endows him with great riches. Chuma never has to work another day in his life. Meanwhile, Azur continues to dredge away at the same old routine. Lift rocks, waste time and money to get stronger.

Sadly, Azur refuses to acknowledge his flawed strategy and continues to endure the same old process: Lift rocks, and get stronger. Carry heavy stones until he could carry no more, then go back to his personal trainer, get stronger so he could lift even heavier stones.

This mindless prescription leads Azur to a lifetime of toil. He never finishes his pyramid promised to Pharaoh, simply because he decided to do the heavy lifting himself when he should have focused on a system to do it for him. Tragically, Azur has a heart attack and dies while on the 12th level of his pyramid, just two levels from finishing. He never experiences the great riches promised by Pharaoh. Meanwhile, Chuma retires 40 years early in a crown of luxury. Sloshing in free time, Chuma goes on to become Egypt's greatest scholar and an accomplished inventor of the machine that helped to complete his pyramid faster. He is entombed alongside Pharaoh in the same pyramid he built.

The fast-lane in this parable is the machine that Chuma built, which is an analogy for a business system; the slow-lane is a job where your hard work and time are traded for your employer's cash. Azur's struggles resemble those of an employee, one slaving away at a job for 40 years. To get rich, you're told to get stronger so you can lift heavier stones (go to school, get more certificates, settle into a job, spend money, get into debt, return to school again to earn more in the job market). The Fastlane is about identifying opportunities and about building a better system, a better contraption, a better product, a better service, or a better 'something' that will leverage your work.

In the slow-lane, you are the source of heavy lifting, while in the fastlane you construct a system that does it for you. On your wealth road trip, the slow-lane roadmap asks that you endure a long and tiresome walk to wealth. In the Fastlane, wealth is driven by a business system you create – the toil is the creation and management of the system itself.

> 'If you put bananas and money in front of monkeys, monkeys will choose bananas because monkeys do not know that money can buy a lot of bananas. In reality, if you offer a job and a business to people, most people will choose a job because they don't know that business can bring them more money than a job.'

This ancient parable points out the major flaws with the old system of 'go to school, get a degree, get a job, work hard and retire rich'. But the parable defines success and wealth in a new way, showing you a better way to work smart and achieve success in life without a job. Don't believe it if anyone tells you that success and wealth can only be achieved through a job. You can work hard or you can work smart.

As Jack Ma, Chinese business magnate and Chairman of Alibaba Group said, 'If you put bananas and money in front of monkeys, monkeys will choose bananas because monkeys do not know that money can buy a lot of bananas. In reality, if you offer a job and a business opportunity to people, most people will choose a job because they don't know that business can bring them more money than a job.'

The Parable of the Bucket Carrier and the Pipeline Builder

Once upon a time long, long ago, two ambitious young friends named Pablo and Bruno lived side by side in a small Italian village. The young men were best buddies, and big dreamers. They would talk endlessly about how some day, some way, they would become the richest men in the village. They were both bright and hard working. All they needed was an opportunity. One day that opportunity arrived. The village decided to hire two men to carry water from a nearby river to a cistern in the town square. The job went to Pablo and Bruno. Each man grabbed two buckets and headed to the river. By the end of the day, they had filled the town cistern to the brim. The village elder paid them one penny for each bucket of water. 'This is our dream come true,' shouted Bruno, 'I can't believe our good fortune.' But Pablo wasn't so sure. His back ached and his hands were blistered from carrying the heavy buckets. He dreaded getting up and going to work the next morning. He vowed to think of a better way to get the water from the river to the village.

'Bruno, I have a plan,' Pablo said the next morning as they grabbed their buckets and headed for the river. 'Instead of lugging buckets back and forth for pennies a day, let's build a pipeline from the village to the river.' Bruno stopped dead in his tracks. 'A pipeline! Whoever heard of such a thing?' he shouted. 'We've got a great job, Pablo. I can carry 100 buckets a day. At a penny a bucket that's a dollar a day! I'm rich! By the end of the week, I can buy a new pair of shoes. By the end of the month a cow. By the end of six months I can buy a new hut. We have the best job in town. We have weekends off and two weeks paid vacation every year. We're set for life! Get out of here with your pipeline.'

But Pablo was not easily discouraged. He patiently explained the pipeline plan to his best friend. Pablo would work part of the day carrying buckets, and part of the day and weekends building his pipeline. He knew it would be hard work digging a ditch in the rocky soil. Because he was paid by the bucket he knew his income would drop. He also knew it might take a year or two before his pipeline would pay off. But Pablo believed in his dream and he went to work.

Bruno and the rest of the villagers began mocking Pablo, calling him Pablo the Pipeline Man. Bruno, who was earning almost twice the money that Pablo earned, flaunted his new purchases. He bought a donkey outfitted with a new leather saddle, which he kept parked outside his new two-storey hut. He bought flashy clothes and fancy meals at the inn. The villagers called him Mr Bruno, and they cheered when he bought rounds at the tavern and laughed loudly at his jokes.

While Bruno lay comfortably in his hammock on evenings and weekends, Pablo kept digging his pipeline. The first few months Pablo didn't have much to show for his efforts. The work was hard, even harder than Bruno's because Pablo was working evenings and weekends too.

But Pablo kept reminding himself that tomorrow's dreams are built on today's sacrifices. Day by day, inch by inch, he dug. Inches turned into a foot, then 10 feet, then 20, then 100. 'Short-term pain equals long-term gain,' he reminded himself as he stumbled into his hut after another exhausting day of work and digging. 'In time my reward will exceed my efforts,' he thought to himself. 'Keep your eyes on the prize,' he kept thinking as he drifted off to sleep with the sounds of laughter and enjoyment from the village tavern in the background.

Days turned into weeks and weeks into months. One day Pablo realized his pipeline was half-way finished, which meant he only had to walk half as far to fill his buckets! Pablo used the extra time to work even more on his pipeline. During his rest breaks, Pablo would watch his old friend Bruno lug buckets. Bruno' shoulders were more stooped than ever. He was hunched in pain, his steps slowed by the daily grind of carrying buckets. Bruno was angry and sullen, resenting the fact that he was doomed to carry buckets, day in, day out, for the rest of his life. He began to spend less time in his hammock and more time in the tavern. When the tavern's patrons saw Bruno coming they'd whisper, 'Here comes Bruno the Bucket Man,' and they giggled when the town drunk mimicked Bruno's stooped posture and shuffling gait. Bruno didn't buy rounds or tell jokes anymore, preferring to sit alone in a dark corner surrounded by empty bottles.

Finally, Pablo's big day arrived: his pipeline was complete! The villagers crowded around as the water gushed from the pipeline into the village cistern. Now that the village had a steady supply of fresh water, people from around the countryside moved into the village and the village prospered. Once the pipeline was complete, Pablo didn't have to carry buckets anymore. He had a system to manage. The water flowed whether he worked or not. It flowed while he ate. It flowed while he slept. It flowed on weekends while he played. The more the water flowed into the village, the more money flowed into Pablo's pockets. Pablo the Pipeline Man became known as Pablo the Miracle Maker. But Pablo understood what he did wasn't a miracle. It was merely the first stage of a big, big dream. You see, Pablo had bigger plans. Instead of carrying buckets, Pablo planned on building his pipelines all over the world!

The pipeline drove Bruno the Bucket Man out of employment. He was now jobless, back to where he began, and it pained Pablo to see his old friend begging for drinks at the tavern. So, Pablo arranged a meeting with his old friend. 'Bruno, I've come here to ask you for your help.' Bruno straightened his stooped shoulders, and his dark eyes narrowed to a squint. 'Don't mock me,' Bruno hissed. 'I haven't come here to gloat,' said Pablo. 'I've come here to offer you a great business opportunity. It took me more than two years before my first pipeline was complete. But I learned a lot during those two years. I know what tools to use now, and where to dig. I know where to lay the pipe. I kept notes as I went along so now I have a system that will allow me to build another pipeline in less time, then another, then another. I could build a pipeline a year by myself, but what I plan on doing is to teach you how to build a pipeline, then have you teach others and have them teach others. Just think, we could make a small percentage from every gallon of water that goes through those pipelines.' Bruno finally saw the big picture. They shook hands and hugged like old friends.

Now they had a pipeline dream in a bucket-carrying world. Years passed and their pipelines were pumping millions of dollars into their bank accounts. Sometimes on their trips through the countryside, Pablo and Bruno would pass villagers from other villages carrying buckets. The friends would pull over and tell them their story and offer to help them build a pipeline. But sadly, most bucket carriers would hastily dismiss the notion. 'I don't have the time.' 'My friend told me he knew a friend whose uncle's best friend tried to build a pipeline and failed.' 'I've carried buckets my whole life, I'll stick to what I know.' 'I know people who lost money in a pipeline scam.'

Finally, both men resigned themselves to the fact they lived in a world with a bucket-carrying mentality and only a very small percentage of people would ever see the vision.

So, it's back to you... Are you on a bucket-carrying plan or the pipeline building plan? The problem with bucket carrying is that the money stops when the bucket carrying stops. Which means the concept of a secure job or permanent employment is an illusion. The inherent danger of carrying buckets is that the income is temporary instead of ongoing. If Bruno woke up one morning with a stiff back and couldn't get out of bed, how much money would he earn that day? Zero! Nothing!

Most people mistake bucket-carrying for pipeline building. We observe that 90% of people in the world are buckets carriers and so we assume bucket carrying is the only way to get what we want in life. We grow up surrounded by bucket-carriers, so we figure that's the way life should be. It reminds me of a bumper sticker I once saw which read '100 lemmings can't be wrong'.

People think the same way about bucket-carrying. 100 million bucket-carriers can't be wrong. Well, they can! Let's face it. There are a lot more bucket-carriers in this world than pipeline builders. Why? The answer is straightforward: because bucket-carrying is the model that our parents followed and the one that they taught us to follow. The bucket-carrying model tells you Here's what you do to get ahead: go to school and learn how to carry buckets. Work really hard. Earn the right to carry bigger buckets, get promoted.

Resign from Bucket Company A to carry buckets for Bucket Company B. Work longer hours so you can carry more buckets. But bucket carrying money is not always enough for one to live on. So, what do bucket-carriers do when they need more money? Because they have a bucket-carrying mentality, they come up with a bucket carrying strategy. If you need more money you've got to carry more buckets! 'I'll get a second job carrying buckets in the evenings and on weekends' or 'I'll go back to school to learn how to carry bigger, heavier buckets.'

What's wrong with this strategy? It's the fallacy of carrying bigger buckets. Bucket carriers tell themselves everything would be okay if they could just carry bigger buckets, but a bigger bucket won't solve the problem. Yes, the doctor's bucket is a lot bigger than the waiter's, about ten times bigger! But that doesn't mean the doctor is financially independent. He's just as dependent on his bucket-carrying job as the waiter. He's trapped in the system as much as the waiter. This is because big bucket carriers spend more! They have a reputation to protect. A doctor or lawyer making six-figures spends most of his or her income to maintain lifestyle. The average worker is maybe using public transport or driving a second-hand car, but the doctor or lawyer will drive the latest model *BMW*, *Lexus* or whatever depicts status. The average worker may send kids to a public school, but the doctor sends kids to a private school and so the circle continues. At the end of the day, everyone from the top of the pyramid right down to the bottom is living paycheck to paycheck. The system is designed to work against everyone, including the middle class.

All buckets eventually dry up. Buckets dry up according to different situations: retirement, retrenchment, being fired, terminal ill health, etc. But pipelines continue to run irrespective of what happens to the builder. Pipelines can go from one generation to the next if properly structured and managed.

When bucket carriers get a salary increment, instead of investing in a pipeline, they increase their expenses. They upgrade their houses, cars, gadgets, fashion style and even holiday destinations. And then it's back to the beginning, just one dismissal letter away from bankruptcy.

Some people live in circles and put off preparing for the future or building their pipelines because the time is not right. Guess what? The time is never right for any of us! We're all stressed. We're all busy. We're all putting out fires and dealing with unexpected emergencies.

The Story of Darryl Strawberry

He was perhaps one of the most electrifying players in *Major League Baseball* history. During his 17-year career, Darryl Strawberry made eight consecutive *All-Star Game* appearances and captured four *World Series Championships*. This great outfielder broke into the Majors as a teenager and was hailed as the next Ted Williams! Strawberry made a fortune in his career, about $2 to $5 million every year. That was just from his baseball contract. Add a couple of million more from endorsements, speeches, autographs and he's earned $50 to $100 million before his 40th birthday! A guy like that has to be set for life, right? Wrong!

According to a local newspaper report, 'Strawberry had no income or savings to support his wife and their three children after he ended his playing career.' What happened? Strawberry bought expensive everything, including fast cars, drugs and alcohol. Strawberry didn't build a pipeline because he thought he had enough money to last forever. He couldn't continue to play baseball anymore because of his drug addiction problem. Just like many people today, Mr Strawberry had no pipeline to fall back on when his bucket finally dried up.

The Parable of the Mexican Fisherman and the Banker

An American investment banker was taking a much-needed vacation in a small coastal Mexican village when a small boat with just one fisherman docked. The boat had several large, fresh fish in it. The investment banker was impressed by the quality of the fish and asked the Mexican how long it took to catch them.

The Mexican replied, 'Only a little while.'

The banker then asked why he didn't stay out longer so he could catch more fish.

The Mexican fisherman replied he had enough to support his family's immediate needs.

The American then asked 'But what do you do with the rest of your time?'

The Mexican fisherman replied, 'I sleep late, fish a little, play with my children, take siesta with my wife, stroll into the village each evening where I sip wine and play guitar with my amigos: I have a full and busy life, señor.'

The investment banker scoffed, 'I am an Ivy League MBA, and I could help you. You could spend more time fishing and with the proceeds buy a bigger boat, and with the proceeds from the bigger boat you could buy several boats until eventually you would have a whole fleet of fishing boats. Instead of selling your catch to the middleman you could sell directly to the processor, eventually opening your own cannery. You could control the product, processing and distribution.' Then he added, 'Of course, you would need to leave this small coastal fishing village and move to Mexico City where you would run your growing enterprise.'

The Mexican fisherman asked, 'But señor, how long will this all take?'

To which the American replied, '15-20 years.'

'But what then?' asked the Mexican.

The American laughed and said, 'That's the best part. When the time is right you would announce an IPO and sell your company stock to the public and become very rich. You could make millions.'

'Millions, señor? Then what?'

To which the investment banker replied, 'Then you would retire. You could move to a small coastal fishing village where you would sleep late, fish a little, play with your kids, take siesta with your wife, stroll to the village in the evenings where you could sip wine and play your guitar with your amigos.'

Soon after the American left after his holiday, things changed in the little coastal village. The government, desperate for tax dollars, levied a series of boating, gaming and licence fees. To continue fishing, the Mexican must pay $400 for a fishing licence, $200 for environmental fees, a $350 game endorsement and $1800 a year in mooring fees. If he can't pay, he'll be barred from fishing.

After paying all the fees, the Mexican has little money to insure and licence his boat. Unable to legally operate at his favourite fishing town, he drives three hours to another location for fishing. The long drives starts to take a toll on his car, which ultimately breaks down.

Things get worse and the Mexican eventually loses his boat when he fails to pay mooring fees to the harbourmaster. The fisherman who had spent his early life in a state of unpreparedness and merriment, strumming around with his amigos and sipping wine, is now unable to take care of his family. His wife divorces him. He is left broke and broken with regret, wishing he had done things differently.

Chapter 15

25 INNOVATIVE BUSINESS IDEAS TO CREATE YOUR OWN ECONOMY

The Fourth Industrial Revolution has democratized entrepreneurship. The old entrepreneurial model was capital intensive – premises, equipment, brick and mortar stuff. But now there's opportunity for businesses that can even be run from a smart phone or Internet cafe. Some businesses can be set up in a day or two and with minimum risk and capital. As I mentioned in part one of this book. "You can do more today with your life having just an internet connection; and that's an opportunity our parents and grandparents never had."

Opportunities don't happen: you create them. You cannot live in the midst of millions of people and not find a problem you can solve for them for a fee. Business is all about solving problems. Your financial breakthrough is determined by the number of problems you can solve. Every day you are making someone somewhere rich. From the fuel you put in your car, to electricity, airtime you buy, to clothing, to food, to taxis, right down to the sweets and fruits you buy on street corners. Every cent you spend ends up in someone's wallet.

The question is who is putting money into your own wallet? Your wealth is tied to the problems you can solve. Put commercial value on the problems in your community, country, the entire continent of Africa, and on your own personal life. Find solutions and leverage on these problems. Find a solution you can offer in exchange for the money you need. Wealth is directly proportional to value addition. In other words, you can only make as much wealth as the amount of value you add to the society. Create tools to fundamentally transform people's lives, and you will be financially compensated in exchange. If there is no need in your community, create one! We never knew we needed

Facebook, *WhatsApp*, *YouTube*, *Uber*, *Bolt*, but the founders created the need and now we can't imagine life without these platforms. Instead of constantly complaining how bad the economy is, you can create your own economy. As a wise man once said, 'Every wealthy family had that one member who broke the chains of poverty for future generations.'

As seen in Part One of this book, the future will demand from everyone a more self-reliant spirit and a greater emphasis on entrepreneurial thinking. The impact of cutting-edge technology and robotics on the job market is going to be disastrous, which in turn will demand that you start depending more on yourself than on the system. Most of the problems that face us will only be solved through entrepreneurship. And, thanks to the evolution of the internet, it is now easier for people to quickly and cheaply launch and promote their business ventures and ideas, regardless of their backgrounds or capital capacities.

> 'Ideas don't come out fully formed, they only become better as you work on them.'
> - Mark Zuckerberg

Businesses and even jobs that existed in the time of our grandparents and parents are slowly fading away. Uber only became a thing 10 years ago. Several incredible products and services have been invented only in the last 10 years and some in the last five or eight. Statistics show that by 2035, up to 85% of jobs will be in companies that have not yet started. All of them are still ideas. And so your business idea could be the next big. How amazing is that!

Put your thinking cap on. Poverty is not lack of money but lack of ideas and lack of action. You can fast and pray for success, but God will never give you a pot of cash. God gives ideas on how you can create wealth.

The business ideas I'm sharing in this section should not be considered as the ultimate standard but simply guidelines for your inspiration. Be creative with each idea. If something else pops into your mind while reading, make sure you write it down. It might just be the real deal. Also do enough research on any idea that intrigues you. Be creative and ready to tweak any idea to your own taste. Remember, *Facebook* never started out as the *Facebook* we know today. Hence, just start and perfect things as you go along. Be willing to fumble through it until you get it right. When you find any idea that resonates with you, don't wait. Just start! Some people wait to start big but there is profound power in small beginnings.

You can start out by using social media – it's absolutely free. Let your friends and family know about your new venture. You might be the best thing since sliced bread but if nobody knows about you, then it's useless. Social media is a powerful marketing tool that will cost you nothing.

Some of the ideas I've listed require nothing more than an internet connection, while others require some start-up capital and technical skills. Either way, you have the responsibility to go out there and create your own economy. Without further ado, here we go.

1. Mobile Saloon or Barbershop on wheels

Things are changing and so are ideas around certain business models. Instead of customers coming to you, you can go to them. Create a buzz about a new way to get a haircut or hairdo. Instead of buying a business premises, buy a vehicle that can be converted into a mini saloon. You can even add Wi-Fi and TV inside. You can serve children, busy moms, offices and especially hospitals as sick people don't usually have the luxury of a hair-cut or hairdo.

2. Influencer Marketing

Who doesn't love *Facebook*, *Instagram*, *YouTube* or *Twitter*! Even corporations do. You can build a digital marketing agency if you fancy yourself to be a whiz on social media platforms or the internet. Companies are always looking for influencer marketers. You can build your influence online and partner with corporations to market their products. Influencer marketing identifies the individuals that have influence over potential customers, and orientates marketing activities around such individuals. This trend is here to stay and new platforms are being released, making the possibilities for expansion limitless. As a digital influencer marketer you can partner with companies that are looking for unconventional ways to put their products/services in front of their target audience. A good example of a social influencer to emulate is Kylie Jenner, with a whopping 130 million followers. She is known as the most popular Instagram Influencer in the world today. A recent report found that the makeup mogul's Instagram post is now worth more than $1 million.

3. Start an Incubator Programme or Co-working Space

Great attention is being paid on how to sprinkle the fairy dust of innovation outside Silicon Valley. Are you a tech enthusiast? Are you passionate about building tech start-ups? You can create a co-working space to solve the problem of office-space, electricity, and access to internet for start-ups in your community. You can also design an incubator programme to build a start-up ecosystem where you'd nurture and mentor young tech enthusiasts and champion the development of local technology solutions in your community or country. An innovation hub company can create space for high-tech entrepreneurs, world-class businesses, academics, researchers and venture capitalists to meet, network, learn from each other, make connections and prosper. A business incubator is a company that helps start-ups into full scale businesses. These programmes are catalyst tools for regional or national economic development. Start-ups beget more start-ups, and there'll be a point at which the floodgates will just open. Your start-up ecosystem can extend to universities and even high schools around you. There's talent in schools waiting around to be discovered.

4. Teach Creative Skills

Are you an IT guru? App/web developer? Jewellery maker? Graphic designer? Do you know how to play a certain musical instrument? You can use your skills to teach others for a fee. You can build a business around teaching technical skills you've learned and practised over the years. All you need is adequate knowledge in the subjects you'd like to tutor. As the saying goes, 'money grows on skills, not trees'. There are many people who don't know how to use a computer to improve their lives. You could bring them up to speed on the basics. You can set up your own website, sell e-courses or e-books as well as organise seminars and workshops on different topics you teach.

5. App Developer, Web Developer or Graphic Designer

We live in a digital world where every business needs an online presence. This is an industry that will never die for want of tech savvy entrepreneurs. Web design and mobile apps continue to be a huge and rapidly growing field. New apps are launched on a daily basis and if you have a unique idea, you can create your own apps to sell. You can also offer your services designing websites and apps for businesses. These are skills you can learn online on your own if you have the passion for building apps but don't know how. Companies are constantly searching for a branding process that communicates what they do. For creative entrepreneurs who want to work with other business owners, you can offer design services where you help businesses design basic branding materials like logos, fliers, newsletters, magazines, information sheets, letters, advertisements, etc. You can also teach yourself the skill of graphic design through tutorials available on *YouTube.*

6. Start an Innovative Agriculture Business

Ever wondered what life would be like without farmers? Many young people view agriculture as old fashioned and uncool but Jim Rogers, business mogul and financial commentator, predicts that 'People working with agriculture will be the world's next billionaires! Wealth will come from farms. Farmers will be the owners of Lamborghinis in the future, not the smart guys working in offices.' According to the UN, projections estimate that the Earth's population will exceed nine billion by 2050. To adequately feed all those people will need a 70% increase in food production. This makes agriculture a no brainer. Keep in mind that agriculture doesn't necessarily mean you pick a shovel and go digging. With the aid of technology, there are different innovative ways you can get into this billion dollar industry. Strive Masiyiwa wrote, *Macdonalds* is an Agri-food business. It is worth over $140bn (that's more than 90% of African countries' entire annual budgets). *Nestlé* is an agri-food business, started by a guy who sold milk. It is worth over $300bn (only Nigeria, Egypt, and SA are bigger)! These agri-food businesses, including *Coca-Cola* and *Pepsi,* employ hundreds of thousands of people. They were all started by entrepreneurs, just like you today. It is time to innovate around the agriculture products grown in our countries. It will lift incomes, create jobs, and generate wealth.

7. Start-up Investor

This type of opportunity used to be restricted only to the elite, big investors and venture capitalists with a lot of money, but with the rise in crowd funding there's an opportunity for anyone to be an investor. There are now many options for start-ups where early investors get equity in return. You don't necessarily need to have a lot of money. You just need to know how to spot a good opportunity and you can build a good fortune investing in start-ups. Your $100 investment in a good start-up can yield gigantic returns in the future. Investing in different companies and industries has proven to being a lucrative way to create wealth. However, it is a very high-risk business and requires you to do your homework well before you venture. Warren Buffett is known as the number one richest investor in the world.

8. Become an Inventor

Most engineers sit on their skills and only focus on using their certificates (expertise) to get a job. You can make the shift and start thinking about what you could create with your knowledge. Are you curious about gadgets? There are self-made engineers – people who have never formally studied engineering – who have invented things through sheer passion, curiosity and grit. Inventions are now critical to Africa's transformation. You can use your engineering skills and technical know-how to invent programmes and implements that'll have a direct impact on your communities. You can think and create specialised solutions to the unique challenges that society faces. You can design programmes that will address climate change, education systems, various healthcare challenges, or focus on the use of mobile technology to encourage greater citizen engagement. You can think of ways to innovate already available inventions to improve on their uses. You only need the passion, the ability to stretch your imagination, to create something and make a difference. Steve Jobs and Elon Musk are listed among the top 10 richest inventors of our time.

9. Speech Writer, Resume Writer, Bio Writer or LinkedIn Profile Expert

Are you good with words? Do you have an eye for detail? There are very few people that enjoy writing their own bio, speech or resume. Some don't even know how to write it or where to start. Most CEOs and top politicians are frightened by the idea of writing their speeches. You can build a business around that and brand yourself as an oratory pro. People are willing to pay good money to have their personal opinions, statements and credentials put on paper for them. Speechwriters, remains the best kept secret that few are willing to divulge. Many of us love President Barack Obama but many don't know Jonathan Edward Favreau, his chief speechwriter during his time in office, as well as Jon Cayzer, the brains behind speeches of some of South Africa's business leaders and political heavyweights.

10. Visual Artist or Jewellery Maker

If you are a natural and love painting, you can create original drawings and paintings. You can also design wearable art like necklaces, bracelets, rings and earrings using wire, beads or any other materials to put together unique jewellery and then sell your work on local art fairs, *Instagram* and other social media platforms thereby building a business around selling paintings, or drawings or making customised art. Again, these are skills you can learn free of charge with *YouTube* tutorials. If you are a real dedicated visual artist capable to transform your ideas to canvas, then there is hardly any reason of not becoming successful. Damien Hirst is globally renowned and known as the United Kingdom's richest living artist according to Sunday Times.

11. Become an Uber or Bolt(Taxify) Driver

Taxify recently rebranded and change its name to Bolt. With the rise of ride-sharing apps, many people are choosing to earn a living as an *Uber* or *Bolt* driver. In Part Two of this book I told the success story of a man who quit his job and became an *Uber* driver earning four times more than what his job used to pay him. Flexible hours, an already established brand and being able to be your own boss are just some of the benefits of being an *Uber* or *Bolt* driver. Another perk is that you can still keep your day job while creating a second source of income by registering your car(s) with *Uber* or *Bolt*, then work during night time or employ other people to drive the cars for you on commission. Either way, you can't be too proud to be rich when Uber/*Bolt* drivers make more money than most Uber/*Bolt* employees

12. Photographer

You don't have to be a professional to start but you have to start so that you can become a professional. Do you love taking photos? Photography is creative and fun. Venturing into photography can change your life. All you need is the passion, a camera, maybe a website or an *Instagram* or *Facebook* page and the desire to learn and keep perfecting on your craft. You can take a digital photography course to learn the finer details of becoming a professional photographer. Even though we live in a selfie generation, the demand for photographers remains high as there are plenty of opportunities to be tapped into. Photography is a growing market. Morgan Norman is known as the richest photographer in the world with a unique sense of photography that the fashion industry appreciates. He has shot for several magazines, advertising agencies and record labels.

13. Personal Trainer

Are you a fitness junkie? You can channel that energy into a cause where nutrition, bank balance and the anatomy of the body are also covered. People are willing to pay good money to have a certain body. You really don't need to own a gym yourself, you can train people through your local gym or in the comfort of their own homes, or even from a park in your neighbourhood. Just start and brand yourself accordingly. Tony Little, Jane Fonda, Tracy Anderson and Chuck Norris are all in the top 5 richest personal trainers in the world. According to *The Economist*, Gym companies are making a killing in South Africa, where the industry generates almost $1 billion in revenue every year.

14. Innovative Event Planner

Are you a social butterfly? You can turn that into a business. Instead of being known only as the party queen/king among your peers, you can also make money out of it working with people to create the party of their dreams. There are always annual business events, birthdays, anniversaries, house warmings, baby-showers, special functions, etc.

Event planners are always in demand and you can incorporate both business and private clientele into your calendar as well as study to bring to your fingertips all the innovative ways that can make you stand out from the rest as a high end planner for private functions or otherwise.

15. Innovative Baker

There are plenty of opportunities out there for entrepreneurs to build businesses around baking. Events always happen and people celebrate with cakes. Baking is a lucrative venture that has transformed the lives of ordinary people. You can bake cakes for various occasions such as birthdays, graduations, and weddings, as well as other celebrations. You can't go wrong with a baking business, combine passion with effort and you'll become the best in your niche. For the tech-savvy baker, you could even put together a mobile app that offers baking tips, recipes and other baking-related content for users. Look for innovative trends in baking relating to health, pleasure, and convenience. You can come up with novel ideas around gluten-free baking, vegan baking and organic baking.

16. Mobile Lunch Service or Restaurant

Are you a food lover? Are you a whiz in the kitchen? Can you create mouth-watering dishes? Are you close to offices or a business centre? Then with a cooler box, or a mini food stand, or from the boot of your car, you could be on your way to becoming the next best chef. You can grow into a fully-fledged restaurant if you so desire. Many business people do not have time to make a lunchbox at home and some don't like eating junk food always. You'd be filling a much-needed gap. You can brand yourself anything you like, from 'the car boot restaurant', to 'lunchbox on wheels' to 'mobile healthy food supplier'.

17. Mobile Car Repairs

Everyone's experienced that ugly sensation of rushing out to the car in the morning only to discover that it won't start, or being stuck in the supermarket parking lot or on the side of the highway. Cars always have problems and people are looking for the most convenient way to solve them. You can offer that convenience and be the guy who is just a phone call away. This can be a great business if you have experience in the automotive industry or know how to repair common vehicle problems. If you are curious or have the passion for auto repairs, there's a wealth of information and tutorials on the internet free of charge. Those who already know about auto repairs can still polish their skills by watching videos on *YouTube*. You just need a keen eye for detail and a love for getting your hands dirty. This is a very rewarding business that can become extremely profitable with the right promotional avenues. You can go general on auto repairs or pick only certain prestigious cars, study everything about those specific cars and brand yourself as the artistic celebrity auto guy/lady who gives your car the artistic touch it deserves. Post pictures of you and your craft on social media and watch them go viral. This can be a satisfying, stimulating career that'll offer you time-freedom – and financial freedom, of course. It can also be quite gratifying as people are appreciative when you get their baby back on the road, and doing it on their turf makes you even more of a miracle-worker. Your clients can be anyone with wheels. You can target the average driver on the street as well as corporations and institutions that will be delighted to have you do their auto maintenance on-site. This isn't a business only for men; it's even more powerful when a woman rocks up with her toolbox. Women like Faye Hadley are making a killing in mobile auto repairs. Why should people tow their car to a shop, when you can bring the shop to them? If you are nervous to go solo, you can partner with a reliable platform like *Fixxr*, the *Uber* of car mechanics. *Fixxr* is one of the best automotive repair services in South Africa. A convenient, affordable and transparent online car services platform that matches car owners with awesome mobile mechanics nearby.

18. Innovative Cleaning Services, Landscaping & Gardening

The grass will always grow whether you water it or not. Trees expand wherever they want and so there'll always be a need for someone to keep a tap on nature. There is always a demand for corporate cleaning services. Thus, deliver a professional service at competitive rates, and you will enjoy return business, and reap the benefits of word-of-mouth referrals. You can start your business in your community. People are often too tired to clean after a party, you can step in and save the day by offering after-party cleaning services. You can also expand to commercial cleaning as well as explore construction site clean-ups. The possibilities are endless.

19. Fashion Designer

Do you easily spot trends in fashion? Do you have a creative flare and an eye for colour? Do you have a certain connection with garments? You don't necessarily need a degree in fashion design. Passion, curiosity and a taste in clothes can fast-forward your growth in the industry much more than a certificate. If you are handy with the basics like a sewing machine and know how to make basic alterations to clothing, you could be well on your way to being the next big thing. That's how some of the world's great fashion designers started, with nothing but passion and a sewing machine. This is a business you can launch from your bedroom. Create your own unique styles and put your name on it. Study the industry until you've got it all at your fingertips, watch tutorials on dress-making, watch videos of successful fashion designers you look up to. Have a *Facebook* or *Instagram* page to showcase your designs. You can even start a fashion blog to write about fashion, with a blog you'd become an authority and go-to person in your niche. Put your name on your branded items and slowly work to get your brand featured in big stores and boutiques. Think big, start small. If you can alter a shirt, you can design a shirt. The richest fashion designer in the world is Miuccia Prada, second by Giorgio Armani. Some African fashion designers that are putting the continent on the global fashion map are Duro Oluwo, David Tlale, Thula Sindi, Kofi Ansah, Mataano, Rich Mnisi and much more. They have become icons of hope, inspiration and admiration. You too can become the next big thing.

20. Online Store

The world is going digital and so are businesses. You can take advantage of the opportunity by going into retail and starting your own online store. With no rents to pay and relatively low overheads, you can sell your products directly to customers. There are no restrictions to what you can sell online, except of course illegal stuff. You can sell shoes, makeup, clothes, hair products, skin care, food, groceries, jewellery, children's stuff, stationery or seasonal things like back-to-school items, Christmas gifts, Valentine's Day gifts, etc. You can start on social media, using *WhatsApp*, *Facebook*, *Instagram*, etc., to advertise your products. Build a client base slowly and grow to launching your own fully-fledged e-commerce website. More and more South Africans and many other countries across the continent are accepting e-commerce as a valid retail channel, hence an online business like *Takealot Dot Com* had a turnover of about $3.5 million in its first year.

21. Blogger, Content Writer, Copywriter, Ghost-writer, Freelance Editor or Proof Reader

Are you a wizard with words? Do you have a knack for language? Do you have a passion for creative writing? It is amazing to see how blogging has become so popular these days. Previously associated with the west, blogging is now a growing trend across Africa. Throw yourself in the creative world of writing and you'll never know where it can lead you. When it comes to writing, it's good to write from a place of passion. You can start a blog about food, fashion, makeup, animals, love, teen pregnancy, dating, parenting, marriage, celibacy, personal development, poetry, personal finance, debts, etc. The list is endless. Choose your niche according to what you're passionate about. The demand for freelance writers, editors and proof readers is increasing and blogging can help you hone these skills. Even though it takes time for a blogger to gain momentum, with patience and valuable content, you'll be on your way to becoming an authority and a force to be reckoned with. You can make money on blogging or vlogging by offering advertising space and reviews of products on your platform. Vlogging is a form of blogging for which the medium is videos and that's where *YouTube* comes in. So, grab your video camera, start a *YouTube* channel on any topic you are passionate about, express yourself in a whole new way and be on your way to becoming a millionaire like Jake Paul and Daniel Robert Middleton, known on *Youtube* as DanTDM. Some of the richest bloggers in the world are Syed Balkhi of *WPBeginner*, Pete Cashmore of *Mashable*, Brian Clark of *CopyBlogger* and Michael Arrington of *TechCrunch* all earning over $2 million per month from their blogs. Linda Ikeji is regarded as the highest-paid and richest blogger in Africa. Her net worth is estimated at $40 million

22. Become an Author

Once you step into the world of blogging and start connecting with your passion through writing, a book is usually the brain child of such an engagement. Therefore, take your writing to the next level and become an author. You can either publish your book in print or as an e-book. People take books more seriously than almost any other form of writing. Being a book author gives you a level of credibility like almost nothing else. Let's face it, saying you're a book author has a lot more power than saying you're a blogger. If you want to establish yourself as the 'go-to' person in your industry, you cannot beat the power of a book. James Patterson, J.K. Rowling, John Grisham and Stephen King are some of the world's richest authors.

23. Become a Musician or An Entertainer

For most people, entertainment is just a hobby that brings in zero income. You are a show-stopper. You know the names of every musician/ rapper at your fingertips. Your friends know they'll be in for a long night once you show up. You spend so much money on entertainment every weekend and on Monday you are broke. Well, since you love entertainment so much, why not consider turning your obsession into a business? Music is a business. People working in the entertainment industry are handsomely rewarded for their talent. You can explore different areas and see which sticks the most with you. You can be a DJ, music producer, song writer, singer, musician, dancer, comedy, MC, etc.

24. Personal Stylist and Makeup Artist

You are the face expert. You know every detail. You know skin tone, shape of the face and makeup colours matchings like no one else. You know how to measure the distance between the cheeks, nose and forehead. People drool at the sight of your impeccable makeup skills. Your friends constantly queue for makeup tips from you, yet you are still going around with a CV looking for a job. Why not turn your gift into a business? Lots of people don't have time to shop for makeup; some don't know what or where to buy. In addition to doing makeup, you can step in and fill that gap by mixing the right colours for different skin tones and selling beginners' make-up kit-bags or advanced kits. You also have a great eye for fashion and style. You can add personal stylist to your make-up skills and build a unique business helping high profile people shop, put together outfits and do their make-up. So, get your business cards, social media handles and brand yourself accordingly.

25. Private Chef, Special Diet or Organic Food Specialist

Do you love making a difference? Do you have a knack for special food? Private Chef is a new trend and the super wealthy don't cook their own food. You can leverage on that if you are a foodie. The demand for organic food is on the rise as well as demand for private chefs. There are people on special diets and eating plans. You can take advantage by tapping into this seemingly new market. Source out the best vegan food, best food for diabetics, best food for cancer patients, etc. You can sell speciality food products from your home/website, provide an order and delivery service to make it easier for your customers to maintain their eating habits. If you have the land and the capacity, you can also focus on cultivating your own organic food. You can further appeal to clients by offering them private chef services for intimate events. You can take it a step further by writing a book on 'special diets' as well as offering healthy cooking classes primarily to domestic workers who are caregivers to people on special diets.

Conclusion

A great business idea can only get you so far. You need an entrepreneurial mind-set and skills to match. To succeed in business requires a mental shift from employee to business owner. Even those who have never worked before still need to prepare themselves mentally to transition into the world of business, because we are all programmed from childhood to think like employees. One of the secrets to success in the business world is this: people who work for themselves must also work on themselves. Personal development is a key requirement to personal success and that's why this book *Disrupt Yourself Or Be Disrupted* is critical.

Zig Zigla, a veteran salesman and author, once said: 'You don't have to be great to start but you have to start to become great.' As mentioned before, global conglomerates like *Microsoft*, *Dell*, *Google*,

Hewlett Packard, *Amazon* and many more started in a garage. So, don't get stuck in wanting to start from an upmarket fully furnished office in the heart of the city. You can kick start your idea or whatever dreams you have from anywhere with whatever resources you have available. Your bedroom, garage, sitting room, boot of your car, cell phone, laptop, trolley, street corners, are all resources you can use and leverage on. As Misty Copeland, an American ballet dancer, said, 'Start unknown and finish unforgettable.'

> Instead of waiting to start big, start small so that you can grow big.

There is money out there with your name on it but it won't come and find you. You must go get it yourself. It is my utmost desire that this book will ignite an entrepreneurial revolution across the African continent; that people, especially the youth, will find hope in understanding that success is a DIY job and that 'we are the architects of our own futures'.

Instead of waiting to start big, start small so that you can grow big. Things will fall into place as you fumble through it. The internet is a school on its own. The internet has made it increasingly possible for anyone to brush up on their skills level or learn new ones.

Michael Kerr, an international business speaker, once said, 'Entrepreneurship is a mind-set. It is an attitude and approach to a way of thinking that actively seeks out change, rather than waiting to adapt to change. It's a mind-set that embraces critical questioning, innovation, service and continuous improvement. It's about seeing the big picture and thinking like an owner. It's being agile, taking ownership, never resting on your laurels. It's about shaking off the cloak of complacency and seeking out new opportunities.'

When we take the decision to stand on our own two feet and enter into the world of business or follow our passion, we often do so against a backdrop of inadequate resources, armed with nothing but dreams and hopes of a better reality than the one we were born into. Most people on this treacherous path of entrepreneurship have no blueprint or roadmap of what success ought to look and feel like

– but that's okay. You'll figure things out as you go along. As a dream chaser, you've simply made a stern resolution, that the economic reality your parents and grandparents accepted as normal is not what you are willing to settle for. You are yearning for change and an opportunity to be in control of your own economic destiny, to restore your dignity and to affirm to the hopeless that it's possible to come from nothing and become something.

You'll get burnt and knocked down more often than not. You'll feel like giving up more times than you can imagine. Pain, frustrations, and disappointments are an inevitable part of this journey. You'll incur gigantic debts, gain insane levels of stress, get avoided by friends and family because they know that your calls mean you need money or some type of bail out. But don't give up. Dreams do come true and when they do, that'll be the exciting part when all your neurons are firing.

It's important always to remember the compelling reasons that made you choose this path for your life. Always remember your WHY. As Friedrich Nietzsche said: 'He or she who has a WHY, can endure any HOW.'

As you take your rightful place in the world of business, remember that you are entitled to nothing; not funding, not connections, not access to markets, and not handouts. Anything and everything that you will achieve will be as a direct result of your handiwork, strategic planning and the value you create for your clients. Therefore, your highest aim should be to create value that will improve the standard of living for people. Clients remain loyal to any brand as long as it improves their lives in one way or another.

> Africa's hopeful transformation lies in entrepreneurship and we cannot afford to be reckless about what will transform our continent.

We are like the guinea pigs of this rising wave of new pioneers, innovators, disruptors and entrepreneurship in Africa and other developing frontier markets across the world. We see opportunities where others see obstacles, and we are take risks where others take refuge. Africa's necessary transformation lies in entrepreneurship and the big shift in mind-set that this requires. But the road to growth, transformation, and eventual success is a long one. You need to be patient and persistent. Also, be open-minded, teachable and take each and every word of advice you can get along the way. Read as many books as you can. Open yourself up to the process of personal development, as no business can grow more than the owner.

Aspire to make a difference, not just a living. There are many people out there – including children growing up in rural areas and villages – who believe certain privileges of life are not meant for them. Our mandate is to change that. And the only way we can successfully change such thinking is when we ourselves continue to break the shackles of conformity and thrive against all odds.

There is a huge price to pay for Africa's transformation. There are huge repercussions for opting to pursue a better life than the one you were born into. By virtue of choosing to go off the tarred road and find new paths you will get dirty from all the mud and gravel; the shovels will wrinkle your hands; snakes and scorpions will sting at times; but you will eventually break through those paths and life will have no choice but to be gracious to your cause. No matter what happens, remain hopeful and fight until your talents, calling or business inspires those who will come after you.

According to 2019 IMF report, the continent's population accounts for about half of the world's fastest–growing economies. I am therefore certain that we are more than capable to do even more. We are the new breed of Africans and history is staring at us. We have a continent to build!

References

Artificial Intelligence, Robotics and Digitization:
https://www.forbes.com/sites/forbestechcouncil/2018/02/26/artificial-intelligence-will-take-your-job-what-you-can-do-today-to-protect-it-tomorrow/#16d7cfb64f27
https://businesstech.co.za/news/banking/305404/standard-bank-to-cut-1200-jobs-as-part-of-digital-shift/
https://www.forbes.com/sites/karenhigginbottom/2018/06/14/the-impact-of-ai-on-the-hr-profession/#7bb6127d91ca (Accessed August 20, 2018)
https://www.forbes.com/sites/bernardmarr/2016/04/25/surprisingly-these-10-professional-jobs-are-under-threat-from-big-data/#2864e59e7426 (Accessed July 15, 2017)
https://www.linkedin.com/pulse/i-have-job-future-impact-digitization-vishal-sadar/
http://pwc.blogs.com/press_room/2017/03/up-to-30-of-existing-uk-jobs-could-be-impacted-by-automation-by-early-2030s-but-this-should-be-offse.html (Accessed Sept 10, 2017)
https://www.cio.com/article/3254744/emerging-technology/technologies-that-will-disrupt-business.html
https://www.forbes.com/sites/bernardmarr/2016/04/25/surprisingly-these-10-professional-jobs-are-under-threat-from-big-data/#6eb672327426
https://www.digitaltrends.com/cool-tech/8-example-of-jobs-automated/ (Accessed Oct 18, 2018)
http://www.europe-infos.eu/impacts-of-digitalisation-on-employment-in-europe

General Motors:
http://houseofbots.com/news-detail/2984-1-changing-scenario-of-automation-over-the-years

Automation:
https://businesstech.co.za/news/technology/238193/the-jobs-insouth-africa-most-at-risk-of-total-digital-automation-and-the-skills-you-need-to-learn-to-remain-relevant/
https://www.bbc.com/news/technology-33327659 (Accessed Sept 10, 2017)
http://www.hrinasia.com/hr-tech/when-robots-steal-jobs-7-occupations-most-at-risk-of-being-replaced-by-automation/ (Accessed Feb 2018)

Virtual reality marketing:
https://magazine.startus.cc/how-virtual-reality-and-augmented-reality-are-revolutionizing-digital-marketing/ (Accessed October 19, 2018)

Power of blockchain:
https://www.forbes.com/sites/suparnadutt/2017/12/18/dubai-

sets-sights-on-becoming-the-worlds-first-blockchain-powered-government/#71857dd7454b

Technology in Africa:

https://www.pulse.ng/communities/student/bobai-ephraim-kato-rejected-by-abu-kasu-24-yr-old-nigerian-software-engineer-builds-artificial-intelligence-robot-at-sri-lankan-university-id4191659.html (Accessed July 14, 2018)

https://www.huffingtonpost.co.za/2017/11/23/this-nigerian-guy-is-building-a-flying-car-from-waste_a_23286312/ (Accessed Jan 26, 2018)

https://www.finglobal.com/2016/06/09/out-of-africa-inventions-from-the-african-continent/ (Accessed Feb 24, 2017)

3D Printing in South Africa:

https://www.businessinsider.co.za/lonmin-using-platinum-powder-to-3d-print-platinum-metals-like-jewellery-2018-10 (Accessed Oct 29, 2018)

3D Printing Food:

https://showme.co.za/secunda/news/business-news/sas-first-3d-food-printer-is-here/

South Africa has the world's biggest 3D printer:

https://www.thesouthafrican.com/aeroswift-biggest-3d-printer/ (Accessed Sept 10, 2018)

South Africa Inventions:

https://www.sagoodnews.co.za/top-10-south-african-inventions/

http://venturesafrica.com/10-under-30-african-inventors-set-to-change-the-world/

https://www.theguardian.com/global-development/2019/jan/01/africa-inspired-inventors-royal-academy-of-engineering-prize?CMP=share_btn_tw

https://answersafrica.com/african-inventions.html

Africa's largest 3Dprinter https://news.mandela.ac.za/News/Largest-3D-printer-in-Africa-built-at-NMMU (Accessed Nov 18, 2017)

https://www.orange.com/en/Footer/Thematic-features/2014/digital-Africa-s-dynamic-development/Folder/Togo (Accessed May 17, 2017)

Africa's first smartphone:

https://www.zdnet.com/article/first-african-designed-smartphone-and-tablet-hit-market/ (Accessed Feb 10, 2018)

Drones:

https://3dinsider.com/drone-uses/

https://www.iotforall.com/impact-of-artificial-intelligence-job-losses/amp/

https://www.themuse.com/advice/4-ways-vr-will-impact-the-future-of-tech-careers

https://www.inquisitr.com/4721900/will-blockchain-impact-jobs-three-things-you-need-to-know/

Bicycles Research:
https://blogs.worldbank.org/publicsphere/cycling-everyone-s-business
Lottery winners:
https://www.businessinsider.com/lottery-winners-lost-everything-2017-8?IR=T#michael-carroll-lived-in-the-fast-lane-and-blew-it-all-11
The Story of Iddris Sandu
https://face2faceafrica.com/article/at-just-21-iddris-sandu-is-the-tech-genius-behind-uber-instagram-and-snapchat?fbclid=IwAR37mwqF4ou_Shlv9ICNmBYYe8t1VW50xsTgpd6DPXNXgAz5Lfh5bOvZtU0
(Accessed Sept 10, 2018)
https://infamouspr.com/client/IDDRIS%20SANDU (Accessed Sept 19, 2018)
https://fixxr.co.za/
https://www.atqnews.com/ng/linda-ikeji-africas-richest-blogger-is-worth-40million-plus-more/
https://www.forbes.com/sites/robertadams/2017/03/02/top-income-earning-blogs/#1ef303d12377
https://www.bizcommunity.com/Article/196/430/162153.html
https://answersafrica.com/african-fashion-designers.html
https://www.w24.co.za/SelfCare/Wellness/Body/sa-gym-clubs-making-r125-billion-in-revenue-every-year-20170115

About The Author

After being retrenched from a job she held onto for dear life, Nicky hit rock bottom, literally! However, she dug deep into her shadows to understand why retrenchment is more rampant than ever before. Her quest led her to the discovery of emerging technologies and how they are playing a major role in job displacement and redundancy.

Having no University Degree or background in IT, Nicky Verd armed herself with nothing but curiosity as she embarked on a journey to understand the holistic nature of the Fourth Industrial Revolution and is now dedicated to empowering people to understand how disruptive technologies are impacting the workplace and how they can take control of their own digital up-skilling. Nicky Verd is particularly passionate about unleashing the potential of Africa's youth, impacting them to rise above their circumstances, disrupt the status quo, embrace 4IR and become part of the revolution.

According to Nicky, many people think of disruption only in terms of new business models but disruption also work at a personal level, where people who want to pivot change and move ahead in life can disrupt and reinvent themselves, Personal disruption at its core is the ability to adopt forward thinking and evolve, supplemented by a cycle of learning, unlearning, relearning and repeat.

Nicky Verd is passionate about igniting human potential in the age of Artificial Intelligence. She believes entrepreneurship, innovation and creativity are some of the untapped opportunities in 4IR. She is the founder of SpacezHub™, an online market place connecting companies with extra space to startups and creatives that need flexible workspaces on flexible terms. She is also a contributing blogger for the Huffington Post and a brand ambassador for Southern Africa Startup Awards. Nicky Verd Lives in Johannesburg, South Africa.

For more Info about the Author
Visit her online home @ www.nickyverd.africa

Note to the Reader

Dear Reader,

*Thank you for purchasing my book '***Disrupt Yourself Or Be Disrupted***.'*
I know you could have picked any book out there to read, but you picked this book and for that I am deeply grateful.
I hope that it has added value and quality to your everyday life. If so, it would be really nice to hear from you. If it isn't too much to ask, could you please take some time to post a review on Amazon? Your feedback and support will help me to greatly improve my writing craft for future projects and make this book even better.
And if you don't mind, could you also please share with your friends and family by posting images of this book on social media.
You can always tag Nicky Verd if you wish!

Yours Sincerely,
Nicky

Printed in Poland
by Amazon Fulfillment
Poland Sp. z o.o., Wrocław

60858834R00150